THE PUNJAB IN PEACE AND WAR

THE PUNJAB IN PEACE AND WAR

BY

S. S. THORBURN

GYAN

Published by

Gyan Publishing House
5, Ansari Road
Daryaganj, New Delhi-110002
Phone: 011-47034999, 9811692060
E-mail: books@gyanbooks.com

Distribution Network
gyanbooks.com
India, USA, Canada, UK, Australia

ISBN: 978-93-6208-502-3 (PB)
First Published, 1904

2nd Impression 2024

Printed at: Gyan Press, Delhi.

THE PUNJAB IN PEACE AND WAR
Author: S. S. THORBURN

THE PUNJAB IN PEACE AND WAR

THE PUNJAB IN PEACE AND WAR

BY

S. S. THORBURN

INDIAN CIVIL SERVICE (RETIRED)

LATE FINANCIAL COMMISSIONER, PUNJAB; AUTHOR OF 'ASIATIC NEIGHBOURS,' ETC., ETC.

WILLIAM BLACKWOOD AND SONS
EDINBURGH AND LONDON
MCMIV

CONTENTS.

PLANS AND MAPS.

THE PUNJAB IN PEACE AND WAR.

CHAPTER I.

RUNJIT SINGH AND HIS RELATIONS WITH THE ENGLISH.

Alexander the Great was the first European conqueror who set foot in the Punjāb; the next, after an interval of two thousand years, was Lord Lake, when in 1805 he followed the fleeing Mahrattas under Holkar to the banks of the Beas. Two years previously, at the battle of Delhi, 5000 Sikhs had swelled the Mahratta hosts, but had failed to distinguish themselves. At the time, all that the English general knew about his enemy's allies was, that they were members of a "strange sect" who fought on horseback, hated Muhammadans, and inhabited the country of Porus, whom Alexander had overthrown. Had Lord Lake applied for further information to the Government of India at Calcutta, the archives would have been searched in vain for accounts of the Punjab more recent than those contained in the works of Strabo and Arrian, who, writing respectively about 10 B.C. and 125 A.D., had described the countries between the Indus and the Sutlej as they were when the great Macedonian marched through them.

At the dawn of the nineteenth century the Hon. East India Company, though masters of half of India, still looked upon their possessions in that continent as an estate to be managed on commercial principles alone, and regarded their employees, from the Governor-General down to the last joined writer, as servants whose sole duty was to carry on the business of the firm quietly and economically, with a view to the distribution of handsome dividends amongst the shareholders. Money-making being the object, the Directors held that the collection of information about countries lying outside the spheres of immediately profitable trading was useless, and likely to lead to unnecessary expenditure and entanglements. Accordingly, they impressed upon successive Governors-General the paramount importance of remembering they were traders, not empire-builders, and exacted a promise from each that peace and retrenchment should be the aim of his administration, and each in turn bound himself to observe his instructions—if he could. In 1798 they had sent out Lord Mornington, afterwards Marquis Wellesley, as Governor-General. He, too, undertook to rule peacefully—if he could; but from the date of his arrival in Calcutta to that of his supersession in 1805 he involved his masters in continuous wars. That with the Mahrattas had begun in 1803, and two years later was still in leisurely progress. Finding the treasury empty, dividends nil, and stock depreciated, the Directors held council. Their conclusion was that the desperate state of their affairs was due to their local manager's persistent disregard of the spirit of his orders—a disregard which, whilst gaining him a marquisate, had reduced a flourishing concern to the verge of bankruptcy. They decided to recall the great offender; they wanted no more empire-builders in India, but safe, level-headed men, free from the taint of ambitious aspirations. In their search for a successor to Marquis Wellesley, it occurred to them that his penultimate predecessor, Lord Cornwallis, had shown business qualities of a high order, and they believed that as he was now an old man, full of honours and in declining health, he possessed qualities which eminently fitted him for the *rôle* of peacemaker. So thinking, they asked him to return to India. He consented, landed in Calcutta early in October 1805, and at once initiated the course of policy desired by his masters, but death came to him before he had accomplished half his mission.

Lord Lake, meanwhile, with stately stride, was following the demoralised Mahrattas into the very heart of the country of the trans-Sutlej Sikhs. As the huge camp, more moving city than pursuing army, swept slowly forwards, the cis-Sutlej Sikhs joined the victorious English general. Though for many years they had been fitfully quarrelling and fighting amongst themselves, a common dread was now uniting them. Runjit Singh—"the little boy Raja of Lahore," as they used to call him—was growing fast, and when King of all the Sikhs, where would they be?—they would be ruled, not rulers. They told Lord Lake that Runjit Singh was already master of 50,000 horsemen, a numerous artillery, and thousands of Akāli fanatics, and that if Holkar and he were to join forces, the combination might prove disastrous, both for themselves and the army of the English. To our officers the prospect of a big fight was cheering: they believed that hordes of wild horsemen, dashing against their disciplined infantry, would break like waves beating against rocks. And the men? Well, the white soldiers had faith in themselves and the sepoys in the sahibs and their guns. Lord Lake, cognisant of the financial and political situation in Leadenhall Street and Calcutta, assured his timorous well-wishers that if they performed their duty and furnished sufficient supplies for his army, he would see that the consummation they feared would not occur. Meanwhile he continued to move towards the Beas, making no attempt to force a battle. As pursuers and pursued approached Amritsar, the holy city of the Sikhs, Runjit Singh felt inclined to throw in his lot with Holkar and roll back the white intruders; but before committing himself he secretly visited the English camp, and noted the machine-like drill of the sepoy battalions, the mobility of the Company's artillery, and the solidity of the British regiments, horse and foot. The sight convinced him that peace was more to his advantage than war. Like Lord Lake, he presently had other reasons for avoiding an appeal to force. He learnt or shrewdly suspected that Lord Wellesley's expansion policy would soon be reversed, and that the Jamna would then be fixed as the northern limit of British interests. Having made up his mind that his best policy was to get rid of both Mahrattas and English, Runjit Singh definitely rejected Holkar's overtures, and advised him to come to terms with his opponent. The matter was easily arranged, and soon afterwards the two armies retired within their respective territories in Hindustan. The Raja of Lahore had now a clear field for prosecuting his designs against the independence of the petty rulers holding the country between the Sutlej and the Jamna. For the next two years he made the most of his opportunities, whilst our impatient politicals, sitting idle on their side of the ring-fence ordained by the Directors of the Company in 1805, pretended indifference to all his aggressions.

With India again tranquil, trade active, and stock buoyant, the Court of Directors now congratulated their shareholders upon the success which had followed adherence to the commercial principle of limited liability. Whilst still in that happy frame of mind, a fit of Francophobia, the predecessor of a century of Russophobia, took possession of our leading statesmen. Forgetting their geography, they assumed that, because Napoleon had enslaved continental Europe and talked of marching on India, he could and would repeat in Asia all that Alexander the Great had accomplished there, when the world was young and questions of supply and transport were of small importance. The contagion of alarm spread swiftly. The Directors were infected. Lord Minto, the then Governor-General, caught the disease. In hot haste he arranged to despatch missions to Persia, Afghanistan, and the Punjab, to collect information about those countries, and induce their rulers to co-operate in resisting the impending attack upon their common interests.

Charles Metcalfe, a civilian of twenty-three, at the time first assistant to the Resident at Delhi, was chosen as envoy to the court of Runjit Singh. To that astute ruler the advent of the young diplomatist was unwelcome. In the Raja's opinion the duty of the English was to remain on their own side of the fence, and leave him free to extend his dominions eastwards to the common boundary, the Jamna. He had no delusion about the professed object of the mission. Oppressor of Europe this Napoleon might be; but still he was not God, and could not perform miracles. Were he to attempt to lead an army through the thousands of miles of deserts and mountains which lay between his base and his alleged objective, not a man would survive to reach the Indus. The whole idea appeared to Runjit Singh and his advisers so preposterous that they were convinced it was only put forward as a pretext for a renewal of interference in the regions trans-Jamna. Whether conscious or not of the absurdity of his instructions, Metcalfe urged the Raja—or Mahārājā, as he was now styled in consonance with his risen fortunes—to lose no time in joining a Central Asian coalition against Napoleon.

"The English want my aid to preserve their Empire," the Maharaja observed; "if I agree, I presume they will, in return, help me to consolidate my kingdom."

"In what way?" the envoy inquired.

"By recognising my sovereignty over all the Sikh States on the Hindustan side of the Sutlej," was the prompt reply.

"I have no instructions on the point, but will refer it to my Government," was Metcalfe's answer, delivered without heat or emphasis, as if he were merely repeating a routine formula.

The announcement annoyed Runjit Singh. He knew British methods, and anticipated the result of the reference. However, the reply would be long in coming, and his position as man in possession would be stronger than were he to sit still and remain on his side of the river. He broke off further negotiations, poured his horsemen into the debatable territory, and rioted therein for the next two months, seizing Faridkot and Ambala, exacting tribute from Malerkotla and Thanesar, and exchanging turbans with the Raja of Patiala, a ceremony correctly symbolical of brotherhood, but with Runjit Singh of polite extortion.

Metcalfe remonstrated, but could take no action until the receipt of orders. When they came he informed the Maharaja that his Government had decided to extend its protection to all the cis-Sutlej States, and that to support the decision British troops were marching on Ludhiana. After asking questions about the number and composition of the force, Runjit Singh delivered the caustic comment, that as the Company's declared boundary had been hitherto the Jamna and was now the Sutlej, he presumed that it would soon be pushed to the Beas,—there was no limit to the British appetite.

The envoy endured the taunt in silence, conscious, perhaps, that it was not unreasonable. The Maharaja, still further incensed, his one eye rolling, as it did under excitement, and his pox-pitted face puckering from ill-suppressed rage, seemed about to strike the man sitting there so cool and imperturbable. For some time the two young men—Metcalfe was twenty-three, Runjit Singh twenty-eight—remained facing each other, neither speaking, each expecting the other to say or do something. Presently Runjit Singh ended the tension. Rising abruptly, he ran down from the roof, whereon the interview was being held, and reappearing in the courtyard below, mounted his horse, and bucketed the animal about in full view of the still unruffled but much-wondering Englishman. Having recovered his self-control, the Maharaja returned to a lower room, and intimated through his ministers that he would not oppose the British demands. In the evening, probably emboldened from the effects of brandy, he retracted his too precipitate assent to what to him was an unjustifiable encroachment, but demanded time for deliberation, pointing out with an approximation to theoretical truth, that in a matter involving the dismemberment of the Sikh commonwealth, it was necessary that he should consult the leading men of his nation. A few days later negotiations were resumed at Amritsar. They were protracted for many weeks without a sign of progress when an accident occurred, which not only led to the happiest immediate consequences, but proved the cement which bound the Maharaja to the English until his death thirty years later.

It happened that amongst the envoy's followers were a number of Muhammadans, and that when their sacred month, Muharram, came round, they began the celebration of the martyrdom of their saints, Hasn and Hosain, with the rites and ceremonies customary upon the anniversary in Moslem communities. The passing of the biers to the place of burial, coupled with the wailing and tomtoming of the crowd surrounding them, excited the Akalis of Amritsar to frenzy. They raised the cry that the Moslems were about to defile their temple. The city was soon in uproar. The Akalis seized their arms, ran together, waylaid the procession, and opened a matchlock-fire on the handful of Muhammadans about the biers. A panic ensued, during which the assailants began flourishing their swords and shouting the Sikh war-cry. A rush upon the envoy's camp would have followed, had not his escort—two companies of native infantry and sixteen troopers—turned out and stood to arms. Fixing bayonets, the thin line of disciplined men charged and scattered the rioters, whilst the troopers circled round, cutting down stragglers. Runjit Singh, who must have foreseen a disturbance, came up before it ended, and beheld, according to the official statement, with admiration, but more probably with secret dismay, the routing of his braves by a handful of Hindustanis, a class about whose nerve and courage he had hitherto been doubtful. He hastened to the envoy, made suitable apologies, and complimented him on the conduct of his sepoys.

The impression left upon the Maharaja's mind of the power and effect of discipline was deep and permanent, for he soon after conceded all the British demands,—Napoleon as bogey-man had been dropped,—withdrew his horsemen to the right bank of the Sutlej, and concluded a treaty of "perpetual friendship" with the Company; further, what is more remarkable, though habitually faithless with Indians, he never afterwards broke faith with us. It must be admitted that, though the fracas ended happily, Metcalfe was indiscreet in permitting his people to insult the Sikhs in their religious capital. If to this day the celebration of the Muharram in Delhi, a city of no peculiar sanctity and formerly the Moslem capital of India, in spite of all precautions, frequently leads to bloodshed between Hindus and Musalmans, it is evident that the observance of the festival a hundred years ago in the holy city of the Sikhs was a piece of foolhardy daring, which might have brought about the annihilation of envoy and escort and a war between Sikhs and English. Metcalfe's callousness to the susceptibilities of the Sikhs was in keeping with the lordly scorn which in those days our officers habitually manifested to what they deemed "the superstitions of the heathen Indians." Even thirty-eight years afterwards, when Lahore was first occupied by our troops, "cow-rows," as Englishmen contemptuously called them, — due generally to our Moslem butchers openly slaughtering cattle and hawking beef about,—were of occasional occurrence. In the Punjab we now err, if anything, in the other direction, and by the over-protection of religious prejudices enable cantankerous persons to cause rioting between the followers of the rival creeds. Our policy in this respect is not appreciated, the baser sort assuming that our motive is to keep alive feelings of religious intolerance between Hindus and Muhammadans, and thus bring home to both the necessity of our impartial rule.

To return to Runjit Singh and his doings upon the departure of the Metcalfe mission. He at once proved the sincerity of his new-born belief in discipline by taking in hand the remodelling of his forces. By attracting deserters from our sepoy army into his service, and employing them to drill his foreign mercenaries, he soon obtained the nucleus of a regular army. Hindustanis, Gurkhas, and Afghans enlisted in considerable numbers, the promise of good pay and the certainty of large opportunities drawing them to Lahore. As Runjit Singh's plans developed he exhibited the same cosmopolitanism in the officering of his regular forces. White or brown, Hindu or Moslem, Teuton or Latin, all were employed, provided that they knew their trade. In the latter half of his reign his most competent and least distrusted governors and generals were men of French, Italian, and Dutch extraction — military waifs from war-exhausted Europe. Having accustomed his wild horsemen to the sight of the drill-sergeant, his next step was to extend the new system to them also. They had been chiefly instrumental in raising him from the position of "boy Raja of Lahore" to that of "Maharaja of the Punjab." The Khālsa — the "elect" or "chosen people," as the Sikhs called themselves—did not take kindly to Runjit Singh's innovations. The new restraint was irksome to men accustomed to licence. Moreover, the foreigners, European as well as Indian, according to their numbers, position, and emoluments, *pro tanto* left less for Sikhs and reduced their power in the State. However, as always, Runjit Singh had his way. Probably, except in the case of Metcalfe, he never met the man who thwarted his will. His personal ascendancy was so great, the conviction that he was the only Sikh capable of acquiring and holding an empire for the glory of the Khalsa so general, that no one ever dreamt of opposing his determination to mould his people into soldiers on the English pattern. Thus he gradually fashioned the army, which, after the six years of anarchy following his death, in spite of divided counsels and traitorous leading, all but shattered the fabric of the British dominion in

India. Whilst the reorganisation was in progress, he employed his unscrupulous statecraft and the anti-Moslem fervour of his people in conquering Multan, Kashmir, the Derajat, and Peshawar, all derelicts of the defunct Moghal empire. By 1830 the whilom princelet, one of the many so-called "barons of the Punjab," was the undisputed master of a considerable kingdom. His rise to greatness was more due to adroit statecraft supported by the show of force than to victories on the battlefield.

As an instance of his peculiar methods, the story of his acquisition of the Koh-i-noor is worth recalling.

When in 1811 Shah Shuja, ex-King of Kabul, was wandering about in search of a kingdom, Runjit Singh took little interest in him until informed that the Shah was the possessor of the great historic diamond. Runjit Singh then proposed to recover Kashmir for the Shah, and hinted that the Koh-i-noor would be acceptable as a gift in return for such a disinterested service. As the fish did not rise to the pretty fly, another was tried—the offer of an immediate *jāgīr* or revenue-free estate in the Punjab, and of help at some future time in an attempt upon Kabul. As that fly also failed, resort was had to threats. Letters were forged and read in open durbar which implicated the Shah in a conspiracy against the head of the Khalsa. Pending investigation, the suspect was placed under surveillance, and informed that he would probably be confined in the fortress of Govindgarh. The unfortunate object of the Maharaja's cupidity, being told that the surrender of the diamond would be accepted as proof of his innocence, protested that he had already pawned it. The next step was coercion through starvation. The guard round his house was increased, and ordered to stop all access to it. When the pinch of hunger was felt by the Shah's family, his fortitude gave way. He consented to negotiate, and an arrangement was soon concluded, wholly satisfactory to the jailer and not conspicuously humiliating to the prisoner. Runjit Singh then paid a friendly visit to his victim. After declarations of mutual esteem and amity, the Maharaja proceeded to show his sincerity by exchanging turbans with him. Runjit Singh was a grim humourist in his way, and, holding that exchange was no robbery, expected the Shah to appreciate the delicate consideration with which the transfer of the gem had been effected: diamonds were the adornment of kings, not beggars; the Koh-i-noor might have been taken by force, but instead the Shah had given it to his friend, and received in return a strip of yellow muslin and the promise of a *jagir*. What the Shah felt is not exactly known. How he acted is on record: on the first opportunity he escaped in disguise from Lahore, and soon after found an asylum and pension in British territory at Ludhiana.

As the Koh-i-noor is intrinsically and historically the most valuable diamond in the world, and has since 1851 been the most prized amongst our Sovereign's crown jewels, some encyclopædias give an account of it. Only readers of Bosworth Smith's 'Life of Lord Lawrence' know how nearly it was lost when, after the battle of Gujerat and the annexation of the Punjab in 1849, it was committed to the care of John Lawrence. He thrust it for the moment into his waistcoat-pocket, and some time afterwards happening to feel it there, made it over to his bearer as absent-mindedly as he might his loose rupees. In due course orders were received by the Punjab Board of Administration to transmit the jewel to our Queen.

"Well, send for it," said John Lawrence, supposing it was in the treasury.

"But you have it, John," his brother Henry reminded him.

The whole thing flashed upon John in an instant: he admitted he had it, and was in terrible trouble until he found his bearer, and asked the man if he knew where it was.

"That bit of glass," the old fellow exclaimed. "I put it into some box."

After rummaging about, the bearer discovered it and brought it to his master. "The bit of glass" had been pushed into a discarded tin case with a broken lock in which odds and ends were kept.

The Koh-i-noor case exemplifies Runjit Singh's methods in squeezing others, the progressive steps being artifice, bullying, force, whilst the actual blow was softened by some little device designed to save appearances.

As a hard-hearted man of business the Maharaja should have been superior to all weaknesses, yet at times he was a slave to superstitious feeling. Thus in 1831, just before crossing the Sutlej at Rupar to meet Lord William Bentinck, fearing treachery, his courage failed him. He summoned his priests and ordered them to search the Granth (Sikh Bible), and read therefrom what the issue of his interview with the Governor-General would be. They did as commanded, and announced that all would be well. But Runjit Singh wanted some clearer indication, and ordered his astrologers to read the stars. When they, too, replied as the priests had, he demanded a sign which he himself could see and interpret. The priests and astrologers, having consulted together, said to him, "This shall be the sign. Take two apples, and when you first see the white king and his minister, present one to each, and if they forthwith receive the offerings be assured, otherwise return at once." The Maharaja, apples in hand, crossed the river, and seated on his state elephant advanced at the head of a bodyguard of 4000 horsemen, and when the Governor-General's elephant met his, he held out the apples, and they were smilingly accepted. Not until then did Runjit Singh cast out fear, and step into the howdah of the elephant on which sat Lord William Bentinck. Side by side the two potentates passed in stately procession up the tented street lined by white soldiers, and all happened as had been predicted.

Although little business was transacted during the week of reviews and festivities which followed the first meeting of Runjit Singh and Lord William Bentinck, the consequences were far-reaching. The former returned to Lahore convinced that he had nothing to fear from the English, and confirmed in his belief that their resources and organisation—particularly in the artillery arm—were crushingly superior to his own. Military observers in the British camp scattered to their stations, confident that, should this upstart Maharaja and his swaggering soldiery ever try conclusions with the invincible Anglo-sepoy army, a march on Lahore would be a series of field-day operations. Politically, the immediate result of the Rupar meeting was the Governor-General's decision to forestall the Maharaja in Sindh. That the Indus was a neglected artery of commerce had long been an accepted belief with us, but hitherto we had only meditated commercial aggression in the valley of the Lower Indus. As Runjit Singh had ascertained that the country was defenceless and had hinted his intention of himself giving it a protector, Lord William Bentinck considered that British intervention could no longer be delayed. How to explore Sindh and open negotiations with its Amirs without alarming the Maharaja was solved by the ingenious device of despatching from Bombay by the Indus route, in charge of a political officer, some recently landed English cart-horses, a present sent out for the ruler of the Punjab by our William IV.

The little manœuvre did not deceive Runjit Singh: he foresaw that the English meant to warn him off Sindh and ear-mark the country for themselves. Though illiterate and deriving all his knowledge from his personal experiences in his own little corner of the world, he understood mankind, both brown and white. He knew himself to be a successful adventurer, and he measured others by his own standard. Whether individual or "Company,"—a term conveying to his mind an association of powerful men banded together with the object of exploiting India for their own benefit,—it was his conviction that self-interest was the mainspring of action for both. Moral obligations and high ideals were beyond his comprehension. He remembered how in 1808 the Company's pretended fears of invasion by some French general, whose name he had forgotten, had gained them, and lost him, a province. As to their movements in Sindh, it was obvious to him that the conveyance of his present up the Indus in charge of surveyors and intelligence officers was the preliminary to a commercial treaty and subsequent annexation. The whole proceeding was a piece of statecraft worthy of himself, and extorted his admiration. Not strong enough to oppose, he made the best of the situation, just as a few years later he professed approval of our Afghan policy, and later became a sharer in it.

As the "great game" developed, the ambitious politicals engineering it plunged the Governor-General of the day deeper and deeper into the adventure, until, from the position of friendly backer of the Ludhiana pensioner, he advanced to that of principal actor. Step by step, too, Runjit Singh became involved as an unwilling ally in a war which he foresaw must severely strain English resources and might end in English disaster. He had himself been long nibbling at Afghanistan. In 1823 he had seized and sacked Peshawar, since which time he had maintained a precarious hold upon the valley. If the conquest of a small open country, only separated from the Punjab frontier by a river, was so expensive in men, treasure, and prestige, that of the mountainous districts beyond, with the width of the Punjab and a hundred miles of grim defiles between the Peshawar base and the objective, might cost the British their army, perhaps their empire. So anticipating, the Maharaja calculated that in every eventuality his meddling ally would emerge a sufferer, he a gainer. As the *tertius gaudens* he affixed his saffron-dyed hand to the "tripartite treaty," an instrument under which all the responsibility and expenditure were ours, all the possible advantages his and those of our client.

Just before the campaign opened, Ferozepore was

the scene of a state ceremony, picturesquely splendid yet grotesquely incongruous—the reception by the Governor-General of his friend and ally the Maharaja of the Punjab. The meeting of Lord Auckland, surrounded by the gala-dressed forces of British civilisation in India, with Runjit Singh at the head of what had been called the glittering "horde of barbarians who had overrun the Punjab," and the rejoicings which followed, might have been justified at the end of a victorious war; but as the prelude to the march of an army through unknown deserts into the hostile mountains beyond, it was unseemly.

Lord Auckland, in allowing himself to be committed to the costly enterprise, had assumed that the conditions obtaining at Ferozepore — brilliant sunshine, plentiful supplies, ample transport — would continue until in distant Kabul his irresistible army had unseated the "usurper," restored to the Afghans their "legitimate sovereign," and then withdrawn to Hindustan.

So the army, rejoicing prematurely, set forth on its mission, whilst the Governor - General, already king - maker in anticipation, moved with his large camp to Lahore, was there entertained by the Maharaja, and drank with him success to their alliance.

Now Runjit Singh, like most good Sikhs who could afford it, had been a confirmed toper from his youth upwards, and when not engaged in war, sport, or extracting revenue from the peasantry, enjoyed convivial society. His evening entertainments were lively proceedings, and perhaps the most remarkable characteristic of his court. As the cup circulated, propriety degenerated into debauch, and ended in the indiscriminate bestialisation of king, guests, and nautch-girls. When in the mood the Maharaja would single out a guest for special honour, would press to his lips the royal flagon filled to the brim with his own particular blend—a brandy distilled from raisins and sugared with powdered pearls. Lord Auckland, being a very distinguished personage, received the mark of royal favour. Whether he drained the liquid fire to the dregs, or cleverly spilt it, has not been recorded, but the scene at the parting of host and guest is historical—the Maharaja in a fit from intoxication inarticulate upon a couch, the Governor-General, set and grave, bending over him and uttering conventional words of farewell.

Runjit Singh's excesses during Lord Auckland's visit brought on his death-illness. Until he was fifty his splendid constitution had withstood alternate courses of hardships in the field and orgies in the palace without sign of strain. Then came the first warning—a paralytic seizure. Partially recovered, the strong-willed man reverted to his cups and his nautch-girls. When no longer able to walk unsupported, he still sat his horse like a centaur, and continued to do so to the last. The indignity of being lifted into the saddle was avoided by his first mounting upon the neck of a kneeling attendant, whence on the man's rising the transfer to the back of the horse was easy. At Ferozepore, when attempting to walk unaided, he had stumbled and fallen—ominous sign—over a pile of British shot. Throughout the conferences, though his limbs were then wellnigh powerless, the spell of his bright compelling eye and quick-questioning tongue was felt by all around him. After his second stroke at Lahore articulate speech left him. But to his last gasp he remained absolute master of his people, the sole and only "Lion of the Punjab," as he was often called. During the last month of his life he would ask news of our invading army by a movement of his hand or eye, and give orders by signs. When the advent of fever and dropsy warned him that English and Indian physicians were impotent to further arrest the process of dissolution, he sought to buy from heaven what he had failed to obtain from man. He summoned priests and holy men of all persuasions to his bedside, and lavished his hoarded treasures upon them. He endowed temples and shrines, and sent elephants, favourite horses, golden chairs, and bedsteads as propitiatory offerings to various deities, and all to win a few more days or hours of mental life, for his body was already dead to feeling. On his last day, June 27, 1839, he scattered a million sterling, and even ordered the priceless Koh-i-noor to be sent to the temple of Jaggernath,—an order which, fortunately for the glory of the British crown, was not carried out.

The end came in the evening. Next morning the corpse was washed with Ganges water and conveyed in state to the place of cremation. Behind the bier, surrounded by priests chanting funeral hymns, were conveyed in gorgeous carriages Runjit Singh's four queens in rich clothing sparkling with jewels, and behind the queens walked five slave-girls plainly clad. Arrived, Rānī Kundan, the chief wife, placed the hands of her lord's son, grandson, and prime minister on the breast of the corpse, and caused each to swear to be true to the other two and the Khalsa, otherwise a suttee's curse would bring upon them the torments incurred by the slaughter of a thousand cows. Then mounting the pyre, the brave woman sat down beside the body, and placed the head upon her lap, whilst the other wives and slave-girls—some recent purchases and hardly women yet—grouped themselves around. At the appointed moment the pile was lighted. As the flames shot up, the faces of the devoted women, still calm and transfigured, were visible for the last time : a moment so—then smoke and fire enveloped them. In a little while the sacrifice was consummated ; the great Maharaja, his wives, and his slave-girls were ashes.

So lived, died, and was cremated Runjit Singh, King of the Sikhs. With no advantages of education or person, he had made himself by the unaided force of his genius supreme throughout the Punjab before he was forty, and had ruled autocratically until the last hour of his life. He was fifty-eight when he died, and seventeen when he threw off his mother's authority and stood forth in the political arena determined to fight his way to kingship. Until that birthday he had been in subjection to his mother, a managing woman greatly under the influence of her dīwān or chief steward. As Runjit Singh was wholly illiterate and already addicted to the vices of his time and countrymen, there was nothing to indicate that the short, ugly, one-eyed, pox-pitted boy was the possessor of a master-mind and had the force of character to use it. But seventeen was a critical age in his family. His father had shaken himself free from his mother's thraldom at that age, and had subsequently procured her murder. The son followed his father's example in both respects, for soon after his seventeenth birthday he suddenly assumed the entire charge of his own property, and proved that he intended to be not only master in his own house, but in those of his neighbours as well. His mother was assassinated, her diwan killed in an affray, and Lahore wrested from its slothful rulers, and all this was accomplished by a youth not yet twenty. Almost before the Government of India in distant Calcutta had heard of his existence, he was already the strongest Raja in the Punjab, feared and courted by his brother chiefs, and looked upon by the sturdy commonalty as the coming organiser of victory for the Khalsa. As if to compensate him for his personal disadvantages, nature had endowed him with an iron constitution, an alert intelligence, and an extraordinary memory. More than one of his rivals may have excelled or at least equalled him in tact, cunning, and capacity in the field, but in political sagacity and tenacity of purpose he was a head and shoulders above them all. The want of these qualities amongst the many "barons of the Punjab" gave Runjit Singh a facile victory over all his contemporaries. Friends, enemies, and above all the Khalsa, were not slow in recognising his pre-eminence in statecraft, and soon began to accept his judgment as infallible, even when unable to penetrate his motives or to approve of his policy. In all that he did Runjit Singh was his own adviser; from early manhood until death his *rôle* seemed to be to give orders, that of others to obey. Thus in 1808, perceiving the power of discipline, he began the reorganisation of his army; later, like most tyrants, distrusting his own people, he gave high commands to foreigners, and enlisted whole battalions of Hindustanis, Gurkhas, and other Indians from beyond the Punjab; then, too, throughout his reign he was the friend and ally of the English. His people hated discipline, foreigners, and the English connection, yet, in their blind confidence in the wisdom of their Maharaja, they supported him in all his distasteful innovations. In later life, as the love of hoarding grew upon him, he stripped Sikhs and Moslems alike of their wealth; with millions sterling in the vaults of his treasure-house, Govindgarh, he used to allow the pay of his soldiers to fall into arrears. When they grew mutinous he paid them—in part—not till then. Though grasping and even miserly, he was often generous. His admirers said of him he would conquer a hundred villages in a day, and give them away on the next by a verbal order. He allowed his sirdars and revenue collectors to cheat him and amass wealth, but in the end he balanced the account by plundering their families when they died or fell into disgrace. Whether robbing or worshipping or wallowing in sensualism, he always managed to pose as a good Sikh acting for the glory of the Khalsa. He deserved their gratitude, for he made a people numbering not more than half a million the strongest nation in India. Every Sikh enjoyed all the privileges of Khalsa citizenship—exemption from taxation, liberty to oppress, and opportunity to live like a freebooter. His rule was a tyranny of force. He had no system, no conception of duty to his subjects: he and his people gloried in their ignorance: in his time there were no law courts, no schools, no jails in the Punjab: the only punishments known were fines for the rich, and mutilation—the lopping off of arm or leg—for the poor; until well into the 'sixties maimed specimens of his inhumanity were seen in every town and large village of the Punjab. He never made or repaired a road, bridge, canal, or tank: not a single work of public utility—unless forts be included in the term—was constructed in his reign: those pre-existing were allowed to fall into decay and ruin: the very towns were little better than poverty-stricken collections of huts and tumble-down edifices. The villages, except those of the Sikhs, were generally agglomerations of hovels surrounded by mud walls in disrepair. The cultivators, the dominant Khalsa excepted, were treated like slaves: the country was divided into districts, each containing from ten to four hundred villages, and the right of collecting the revenue—that is, of squeezing as much out of the villagers as could be realised—was sold to the highest bidder or granted to priests or jagirdars: provided that taxes were paid, neither Maharaja, revenue-farmers, nor jagirdars cared whether the peasantry lived, or died of starvation. Up to the last Runjit Singh acted as if for him there could be no death: he made no preparation for the continuance of order, and as a consequence, when he died the fabric, built and held together for forty years by his genius, collapsed from the inherent weakness of its construction.

Judged by the moral standards of to-day, Runjit Singh was a monster; but a century ago good Sikhs had no morals, and those of Anglo-Indians were indifferent. In West and East the age was coarse, and even in straitlaced England to be "drunk as a lord" was no discredit. Thus Runjit Singh's contemporaries from over-sea were lenient to his failings, and as to his own countrymen, with opportunity every one of them would have been his admiring imitator.

In spite of his sins, vices, and crooked ways, Runjit Singh was the greatest Indian of the nineteenth century. He welded his people together into a powerful nation, carved out an empire for himself, held it throughout a long reign, was true to his alliance with us for thirty years, and left behind him an army—his own creation, and all obtained by voluntary enlistment—which after years of anarchy, betrayed and leaderless, was yet strong enough to resist the whole might of our Empire in a series of pitched battles, and just fall short of winning.[1]

[1] As accents over letters are unsightly and rarely necessary, Indian proper names and other words, recurring frequently, will have none, except occasionally when first used. Thus, for instance, Dīwān, *jāgīr*, *kārdār*, Khālsa, Mahārājā, Rānī, Punjāb, &c., will usually be printed without accentuation.

CHAPTER II.

THE WAR ON THE SUTLEJ—MOODKI.

"Oh king, live for ever," the salutation with which the trembling Chaldeans greeted Nebuchadnezzar when he demanded the interpretation of his dream, might well have been the supplication which filled the minds of Runjit Singh's courtiers during the last few years of his life, as they thought of his excesses, his waning powers, and the cataclysm his death would let loose. When that event occurred, even before his ashes had been consigned to the Ganges, the long-restrained waters of suspicion and hate began to find an escape, and sap the foundations of the dam, which he alone had known how to construct and keep in repair.

He died on June 27, 1839, and was succeeded by his legitimate son, an imbecile named Karrak Singh, whose upstart favourite was soon after assassinated in the presence of his terrified master. That was the first of the political murders which, in a few years, removed most of the men holding place in the Punjab at the time of the signing of the tripartite treaty. At first the various competitors for power and wealth observed some decency in compassing each other's destruction. The white intruders from oversea, who, python-like, were successively strangling and swallowing the indigenous states of India, had still their coils round the Punjab—their armies still garrisoned Afghanistan, and encircled Sikh possessions, except towards Kashmir. Until free from their trans-Indus entanglement, self-preservation required them to use all their influence to maintain the Sikh alliance, or at least retard the disintegration of Runjit Singh's kingdom. For more than a year after the great Maharaja's passing, his rough yeomen-soldiery were generally faithful in their allegiance to the throne. But when his legitimate son and grandson had both been removed—the former by poison or his own excesses, the latter by contrived accident—and a reputed son, a nerveless voluptuary, had been installed as Maharaja, the army, impatient for a leader, began to assert itself. The welfare of the Khalsa demanded that the head of the commonwealth should be a capable ruler, not a weakling. Instead, they saw imbecile, sot, voluptuary, each swayed by unworthy favourites, usurping successively the throne of their great master. As guardians of Sikhism pure and undefiled, they felt that, whilst individually looking after their own interests, collectively their duty was to watch and control the executive government at Lahore. Their best men took sides with one or other of the contending factions in the capital, exacting large rewards for themselves and increased pay for the army generally. As patriots the rank and file of the Khalsa were humiliated that their country should be used as a thoroughfare for the passage of Anglo-sepoy troops to and from Peshawar and Multan, and were impatient to end the British connection; they soon began to suspect that the manikins in power at Lahore were in the pay of the English agent at Ludhiana. As the process of disintegration advanced, the men in each regiment formed themselves into political clubs, elected representatives, and sent them to the capital, as occasion demanded, for the purpose of protecting their common interests. The evolution of these military vigilance committees was a simple matter. In matters of rural economy the affairs of each village were always conducted by a panchāyat or elected committee of five or more. The soldiers, being peasants and yeomen when at home and frequently on furlough, were all already familiar with those village parliaments, hence, from their inception, the army was accustomed to the system which the incapacity of Runjit Singh's successors had enabled the Khalsa to adopt. Some years, however, elapsed before the independent committees, occasionally sent to Lahore, began to act in co-operation and form themselves into a sort of Khalsa parliament.

In 1841-42 the British disasters in Afghanistan and withdrawal therefrom cis-Sutlej, with broken prestige, removed the last obstacle to the seizure of power by whomsoever, whether man, party, or soldiery, should prove strongest in the Punjab.

In the struggle the army collectively emerged uppermost, but it was still an army without a head. Its regimental panchayats were true patriots, no doubt, alive to their own interests and those of their comrades, but individually they were jealous and ignorant men, and even when acting together, quite unfit to control their constituents, much more a nation. In their arrogance the soldiery not only set up and pulled down at pleasure the highest place-holders of the State, but drove out of the service the European officers, without whose skill and experience victory in a serious war would be unattainable. By 1845, of all the chiefs of distinction in Runjit Singh's service at the time of his death, Gulab Singh, Raja of Jammu, alone survived—matchlock, sword, poison, or resignation had removed the others.

During the years which had passed since the death of the great Maharaja, Gulab Singh had stood out from amongst his compeers as the one man of capacity in the kingdom. Though a Dogra of humble origin, his good looks, insinuating manners, ability, and undoubted courage had early gained for him the favour of the Maharaja. In 1819 his master had employed him in an enterprise the successful execution of which required considerable finesse—the peaceful acquisition of Kishtwar, a hill principality. The mission was carried out with such tact—the state being seized by artifice and its ruler deported to Lahore and there quietly poisoned—that Gulab Singh's grateful sovereign bestowed Jammu upon him in jagir. The new favourite's experience in Kishtwar was now useful to him; during the next twenty years, by force or fraud, the estates of his neighbours one after another fell into his hands, and so powerful did he become that when his master died he was the greatest man in the Punjab. With the Sikhs themselves he was never popular. As a people they were hearty, boisterous, greedy, and often unscrupulous, but never unnecessarily cruel; and they shrank from a chief who massacred prisoners in cold blood, flayed men alive, stuffed the skins and hung them up like scarecrows, designedly treated his people as peasants do their well-bullocks in a drought year, and was commonly believed to have needlessly put to death over 12,000 persons. In the six years of increasing disorder following Runjit Singh's death, Gulab Singh played his cards with such dexterity that in 1845, by which time the Khalsa army had usurped all authority in the plains, he was ruler in the hills of several principalities, including the valley of Kashmir, and the master of a large army, ill-conditioned levies in reality, but believed by Sikhs and English alike to possess fighting powers of a high order.

Comparatively secure in his mountains, he had acquiesced in the bestowal of the empty title of Maharaja on Dhulip Singh, the child by an unknown father of a nautch-girl named Jindan, who had cleverly affiliated the boy on Runjit Singh. But when the woman, having temporarily bought the support of the military committees, procured the murder of the worthless members of the administration, assumed the office of queen-regent, and appointed her Brahmin paramour, Lal Singh, and another Brahmin admirer of hers, Tej Singh, respectively Vizier and Commander-in-Chief, Gulab Singh began to realise that further aloofness on his part might turn army and Durbar against him. By opportune bribes and promises he obtained for the moment the favour of both. His position was, however, still insecure,—the limits of donatives and increases of pay had been reached, but the appetites of the recipients had only been whetted thereby. He was certain that the army could not stand still. The public treasury was empty, but private coffers were full.

Like the Rani and her lovers, he too had his hoard, and each in succession would be the victim of the greed of the soldiery, unless their energies could be diverted or their power destroyed. He was aware that a war with the English would be popular—even the Hindustanis in the Sikh service were violently anti-English—and began to play with the thought that, by such a war, both he and the Rani would be rescued from the intolerable tyranny of the arrogant Khalsa. They would be defeated and humiliated, he was sure, and then he foresaw would come his opportunity; he would pose as the saviour of his country, and by negotiating terms earn the gratitude of both conquered and conquerors. So calculating, he moved nearer Lahore, and arranged an understanding with the Rani and her supporters, all of whom had equal cause with himself for fearing the military democracy now omnipotent in the Punjab.

The task of the conspirators was easy, because, since our unscrupulous seizure of Sindh, the Khalsa had been convinced that our next aggression would be upon their country.

It is probably true of most of our wars of conquest in India that they were immediately forced upon us by the action of our neighbours, but it is equally true that in almost every case the *causâ causans* was the interfering and even grasping character of our general policy. Though Runjit Singh, when shown a map of India and told that the parts coloured red were British, had remarked, "It will all become red," yet throughout his long reign he was careful that the prophecy should not be fulfilled, in respect of his own dominions at least.

He died, and so narrow had been his despotism that the Punjab did not contain a man—the crooked-minded Gulab Singh excepted—with as much governing capacity as is expected from every English lad who writes C.S. after his name. To this day administration is a weak point with Sikhs. Had they in 1838 possessed the raw material, some statesman might have come to the front before 1845, and, by evolving order and respect for treaties, have saved a grand young people from sacrificing their independence. That, however, is doubtful, for after 1843 an independent Punjab became an impossibility. The Court of Directors and the Governor-General for the time being shut their official eyes to the unavoidable consequences of their Sindh burglary; but neither Sikhs, British officers, nor sepoys were so short-sighted. From that year they all regarded a Punjab war as inevitable.

The conviction was reasonable. Though, from the imperious Marquis Wellesley (1798-1804) onwards, no Governor-General had actively intended a conflict with the Sikhs, yet each in turn had contributed towards it. Lord Wellesley had sanctioned the pursuit of Holkar to within a march of Amritsar (1804-5): Lord Minto had confined Sikh expansion Delhi-wards to the right bank of the Sutlej, and had established a British garrison at Ludhiana, on the left or British bank of that river (1808-9): Lord Auckland, taking advantage of the doctrine of escheat, had made Ferozepore a British cantonment (1838), thus directly threatening Lahore: Lord Ellenborough had used the Punjab as a military highway for Afghanistan (1838-1842), and in 1843 had nefariously seized Sindh, thereby anticipating the Sikhs and extending southwards the British coils about the Punjab from Ferozepore to the Indus.

To our officers and men the prospect of a war with the Sikhs was regarded without misgiving—the Khalsa army was "a military rabble," "an armed mob," "a mutinous soldiery," and so forth; a battle or two of the most approved Anglo-Indian type—a cannonade followed by a general advance and the flight of the enemy—would end the campaign. The Sikh army, without anticipating victory, took a sounder view of their own strength, believing that, if we attacked them, the fighting would be long and severe; their officers realised that in organisation, resources, and trained leaders we were their superiors, but the men considered themselves to be tougher and braver than our soft Hindustani sepoys, and believed that, as our white soldiers were mercenaries and few in number, the comparatively innumerable Khalsa would kill so many that the issue might well be doubtful: as to our artillery, they had the same faith in their own as the sepoys had in ours. In any case the Sikhs were confident that before reaching Lahore we should have to walk over the body of the "Khalsa," as they called their army, and—well—as the Moghals had lost their empire in the attempt, a like result might follow for the cow-killing Feringhees.

When 1843 and 1844 had come and gone and the inevitable had not happened, both the Khalsa and Anglo-sepoy armies began to regard it much as youthful athletes do death. Not until late in 1845, when Rani Jindan and her friends felt it necessary for their own safety to divert the thoughts of the Sikh soldiers from the easy prey within their grasp to the enemy at the gate, did war become actually imminent. The panchayats were told that we had largely augmented our garrison at Ferozepore and Ludhiana, had concentrated a reserve of 10,000 men at Ambala, and were collecting boats and other bridge material on the Sutlej near Ferozepore. On both sides of the river local fire-eaters had been long trailing their coats; but such petty provocatives might have passed almost unnoticed had not the Lahore news-writers sedulously communicated them with embellishments to the now excited soldiery. In Sindh Sir Charles Napier, always an incendiary, perpetrated a foolish after-dinner speech, exaggerated reports of which went the rounds of the English press and were carefully reproduced at Lahore; other officers were equally indiscreet; in Sirhind every act of our political agent, Major Broadfoot, a man of the forward school, already obnoxious to the Sikhs, was represented at Lahore as a deliberate insult to the Khalsa.

The spark which probably fired the magazine was the report that we had actually bridged the Sutlej—we had in fact just brought up from Sindh 56 large boats and a pontoon train—and were about to advance upon Kasūr, a town only two easy marches from Lahore. Whatever it was, the conspirators, backed as they were by the Hindustani element in the Sikh service, succeeded in their object; for on November 17, 1845, the military parliament, now in permanent session at Lahore, suddenly called the nation to arms, and shortly afterwards the army marched to Kasur, and thence to the Sutlej. Instead of forthwith pouring across the river, and attempting to rush Ferozepore, the impatient Khalsa had to wait on their own bank for the next three weeks, whilst their astrologers were pretending to consult the stars. At last in the second week of December an auspicious day was announced, and that evening the invasion of British territory was an accomplished fact. The passage was speedily completed, and by December 16 the army of the Khalsa—some 30,000 regulars, 150 guns, and unnumbered swarms of horsemen and Akalis—were occupying positions a few miles east of our cantonment Ferozepore.

To both Sikhs and English the inevitable had come at last, but in an unexpected form. Two months previously none but the conspiring quartet in Lahore and Jammu could have foreseen that, before the end of the year, the armed might of their nation would be planted on British soil. Now that the Khalsa were there, instead of acting vigorously, they sat still, entrenched, and wrangled. Sirdar Lal Singh was nominally Commander-in-Chief, with Sirdar Tej Singh as Second-in-Command; but in reality the regimental committees were the hydra heads of the army. Some wished to assault Ferozepore forthwith, others to invest it and make a move in strength against Ludhiana, which was only held by four battalions of native infantry. The Sirdars urged that if they stood fast, strengthened their positions, and awaited an onslaught, the English would easily be repulsed, and that afterwards the whole country would rise, and the Khalsa would then march triumphantly upon Delhi. Meanwhile the major-general commanding at Ferozepore, not strong enough to attack, remained inside his cantonment, and watched with amazed satisfaction the growing accumulations of men, guns, and stores on his side of the river. As the invaders were throwing up earthworks and holding together in masses, he hoped that their initiative was already exhausted, and that they would remain where they were until driven into the river by the British army, which was advancing for the purpose by forced marches.

Sir Henry Hardinge, the Governor-General, was probably one of the few Englishmen in India whom the magnificent temerity of the Sikhs did not take wholly by surprise. The expectation had been that when war came, it would begin by an irruption of irregular horsemen into British territory, not by the co-ordinated advance of the whole forces of the Khalsa. With half a century of fighting experience behind him, and full knowledge of the explosive energy of a young democracy trained to arms, the Governor-General on his arrival in Calcutta in 1844 had quickly realised the dangerous isolation of the small garrison at Ferozepore, and acting in harmony with Sir Hugh Gough, the Commander-in-Chief, had taken measures to strengthen it and the military position generally upon his north-west frontier. Thus, before the actual outbreak of hostilities, a gradual convergence of troops towards the Sutlej had been effected, and the work had been done so quietly that neither press nor army had been aware that any special dispositions, outside those of ordinary relief movements, were in progress. In regard to Ferozepore the accomplished fact had to be accepted, as withdrawal to Ludhiana, which was better situated for our most advanced outpost, would have been misinterpreted, and might have precipitated the invasion which it was desirable to prevent or retard. What Sir Henry Hardinge did was to raise the garrison of

Ferozepore to 7000 men, and, setting aside the rule of seniority, to induce the Commander-in-Chief to give the command to a selected officer, Major-General Sir John Littler. In addition, he doubled the force at Ludhiana, and concentrated large reserves at Ambala and Meerut. Having made his preparations, he started for his threatened frontier, and on December 11 was about to attend a ball at Ambala given by the Commander-in-Chief, when information was received that the Sikhs had invaded British territory in force in the neighbourhood of Ferozepore.

The news was a surprise to the camp: no dancing and feasting now, but a hurried advance to meet the bold invader, and thrust him into the river which he had so rashly put behind him. Every vehicle, cart, ekka, buggy, dog-cart, was requisitioned; every animal, fit or lame, impressed with its owner. The rush began next morning. To most the object of haste was not the relief of Littler, but the necessity for catching the Sikhs before they should lose heart and put the river, now like an open grave behind them, in their front again.

From Ambala to Ferozepore the distance was 146 miles over a sandy jungle-covered plain, patched here and there with crops just sprouting. Of the rural population the Sikhs and Hindus generally sided with the invaders, blood being stronger in stirring sentiment than a worn-out gratitude for protection dating back forty years. Muhammadan villages were, however, friendly; but, depressed by generations of Sikh exactions and doubtful as to the issue, afraid to openly show their sympathies. Thus, as our army trudged forwards—and in those days for one fighting man there were several camp-followers and three or four baggage-animals—commissariat difficulties increased. Grain and fodder had everywhere to be taken by force. In spite of all obstacles, the Ambala force, after covering 126 miles in five days, overtook the Ludhiana garrison at Bussean, which had been already converted for the occasion into a supply depot. Men and cattle were now worn out; the last thirty miles of the track were strewn with wreckage and stragglers; haste was no longer thought imperative, as Ferozepore had not been attacked, and the Sikhs had evidently every intention of accepting battle on the British side of the Sutlej.

Next day (December 17) the progress made was only ten miles. On the following morning another short march was ordered, and the army, now 11,000 fighting men, were about to have their breakfasts when the precipitancy of the Commander-in-Chief caused him to commit the first of a series of blunders, which, but for the incapacity, treason, or faint-heartedness of the Sikh leaders, must have resulted in our defeat and withdrawal to a defensive position in the neighbourhood of Delhi. Sir Hugh Gough had ridden on ahead to reconnoitre, when learning that Moodki, a village ten miles nearer Ferozepore than his bivouac, was in the occupation of the enemy, he hurried the troops off at once, hoping to catch the Sikhs in the village. Three miles from it the army was halted and formed in order of battle, the artillery in front supported by the cavalry, the infantry behind in contiguous columns ready for deployment when the attack in line of battle should be made. As the place was approached, the Chief, ever foremost, pushed ahead again, but found no trace of the enemy. The short excitement over, the wearied infantry entered the village about noon. About 3 P.M. the baggage-animals began to straggle in, and the men had just settled down to cook, eat, and rest, when our cavalry pickets, galloping back, announced that the Sikhs were coming on in force, a fact presently confirmed by the appearance of clouds of dust approaching from the west. Though the country immediately round Moodki was open, and the infantry, having already marched twenty-one miles, often ankle-deep in sand, had been ten hours under arms without eating or drinking, Sir Hugh Gough, impatient for a victory, ordered an immediate advance. Once more the army was put in motion, five troops of horse artillery, supported by 1500 cavalry distributed on either flank, leading, the infantry following, thirteen regiments in all, of whom four were British, two of them very weak in numbers, having recently been decimated by cholera.

When two miles had been traversed, sand-hummocks and thick jungle were seen ahead but no enemy, only an overhanging pall of dust. The sun was already setting behind the suspicious-looking country which our troops were now entering. Horse-gunners and cavalry, conscious that the Sikhs were somewhere near them, were intently alert for the revelation of their presence. Suddenly from out of the obscurity into which our men were peering more than twenty guns opened fire, and as the round-shot came lobbing amongst their horses, our gunners quickly unlimbered and replied. For a time both sides pounded away amidst dust and smoke, with nothing but the flashes to guide the aim. Our light 6-pounders, all in the open, made poor practice against the heavier metal from the well-sheltered pieces of the enemy. Meanwhile hordes of Sikh horsemen were creeping round our cavalry and outflanking our infantry, now deployed into line. A charge was ordered. That on our right, led by the 3rd Light Dragoons, supported by a squadron of the 4th Lancers, was vigorously carried out, at such pace and in such order as physical obstacles admitted. A few Sikh troopers stood firm and were overthrown, —many of them to rise and limp away, as our men's sabres could not penetrate their quilted coats,—but the mass, mostly irregulars without cohesion, turned and scattered before the impact, thus uncovering the whole of the Sikh line, down and behind which our men swept from end to end, losing heavily in their rush. All this time our infantry were steadily toiling forwards towards the Sikh guns. Progress was slow and uncertain, and at times amounted to groping in the dark, so thick was the dust raised by the horse artillery and cavalry, who were both in advance of the infantry. Until bayonet met sword and shield the enemy suffered little; after that the Sikh superiority in guns was useless, whilst their immobility—Sikh guns being drawn by oxen —exposed them to capture. In the hand-to-hand struggle which now ensued the confusion was great, and was increased by our lagging sepoy regiments firing again and again wildly into their white comrades. The enemy's staunch infantry and artillerists crowded round their pieces, and, striving to save them, repeatedly met our rushes by counter-rushes. Such determined fighting cowed our sepoys, but only excited the British regiments to greater exertions. Eventually, deserted by their cavalry and borne down by numbers, the Sikh footmen abandoned 17 out of their 22 guns. The remaining five were probably small and safely withdrawn. There was no rout, no pursuit—darkness, physical exhaustion, and the unflinching bravery of the foe made that impossible. Our troops did not get into camp until midnight. So dead-beat were they that whilst they were dragging themselves back to Moodki they did not pause to kill the Sikh marksmen, who, concealed in trees, let sepoys creep along unharmed, but picked off the British officers and privates as they passed beneath.

The force which had won this first battle of the war comprised five troops of horse artillery, making 30 guns, and six British regiments,—four being infantry and two cavalry,—also nine native infantry and three native cavalry regiments. The grand total, British and native, was roundly 11,000 men, of whom rather more than one-third were Europeans. The casualties, which included 51 English and 11 Indian officers, were 872, or 1 in 12. Nearly two-thirds of this loss was contributed by the white troops. The disproportion in British and sepoy casualties, considering the relative numbers engaged, was less due to the cowardice of the Hindustanis than to their inferior stamina: tired out, cold, hungry, and thirsty, Jack Sepoy had no life in him.

Various estimates of the Sikh forces engaged have been made. In so-called cavalry their numbers may have equalled those of our whole army. Their horsemen made a brave show, stirred up much dust, and might have been useful in a pursuit; but as cavalry during actual conflict, both at Moodki and throughout the rest of the campaign, they were of little account. The men who did the fighting were the Sikh regulars, both infantry and gunners. At Moodki there may have been 3000 of the former and 500 of the latter; there were also many irregular footmen, including Akalis, all of whom appear to have behaved well.

In the Anglo-sepoy army that night there was no elation—the capture of 17 guns was small compensation for the heavy list of casualties, particularly in British officers and men. Then, too, the discovery that the Sikh regulars fought a defensive battle better than our sepoys, and that Sikh guns, though wanting in mobility, were well served and out-ranged ours, upset all preconceived estimates of the military value of the Khalsa forces. There was also the uneasy feeling that the Chief expected too much from his troops, and relied too exclusively upon the bayonet. Amongst the Sikhs there was no discouragement. The soldiery in the entrenched camp at Ferozeshah, restrained from attacking Ferozepore, had forced their leaders to permit a reconnaissance in force, which had brought on the engagement, and as in the hand-to-hand fighting round the guns hundreds of Feringhees had been killed, the Khalsa were satisfied—the loss of guns was nothing, they had over 200 more, but to the English the loss of white men was everything, their numbers were few.

During the next day, the 19th, there was no movement on either side; the Chief was reorganising his forces and awaiting the reinforcements for which he should better have halted before advancing to Moodki; the Sikhs at Ferozeshah were completing their arrangements for repelling the attack which they knew would shortly be delivered. About 11 P.M. the additional troops, so anxiously expected,—two regiments of British and two of native infantry, together with some mortars,—were played into camp by the bands of her Majesty's regiments headed by that of the Governor-General, luxuries only possible in the good old days when Indian campaigns were conducted *en prince*, the whole establishment often accompanying the master, whether general or subaltern, upon active service.[1]

[1] In the 'Journal of a Cavalry Officer,' by Captain Humbley, M.A., 9th Queen's Royal Lancers, published in 1854, he states that on January 15, 1846, whilst his regiment was with the cavalry brigade under Colonel Campbell near Sobraon, grain sold at 32 lb. for the rupee,—"a rather dismal prospect for a large army." He then gives the strength of his regiment in fighting men and followers, with a view to show how hard upon both were such high rates during the campaign. He writes, p. 129: "The 9th Lancers had (January 15, 1846) 600 fighting men, and the camp-followers amounted to 3600 men, which gives six to each fighting man. After deducting 1600, the number of followers required for 800 horses, including officers' chargers, and 480 dooly-bearers, there would still remain 1520 followers to be accounted for, and if we again allow the officers, forty in number, say 500 servants,—a very fair portion,—there would then be left 1020, whom we must conclude to have been elephant- and camel-drivers, tent-lascars, bazaar-people, &c."

CHAPTER III.

BATTLE OF FEROZESHAH.

THE 20th was spent in preparations for the battle next day.

Leaving his camp, baggage, sick, and wounded to the protection of two regiments of native infantry, two guns, and weakly details from the various components of his army, the Chief, with the Governor-General acting as his Second-in-Command, began his advance towards Ferozeshah some hours before dawn. As the cold was intense, and the troops, who had been under arms since 2 A.M., had been ordered to discard their greatcoats, the start was cheerless: the sepoys, already numbed and despondent, stumbled along in the darkness over the rough sandy ground, like captives herded to execution; the British soldiers, hardier and better nourished, were in a less unhappy frame of mind—"them Seiks" were going to be wiped out this time.

Making a *détour* to the south-west, in order to facilitate the prearranged junction with the larger part of the Ferozepore garrison under Sir John Littler, the Chief's small army, 11,700 men in all, plodded on without incident until about 10 A.M., when a halt was ordered. Whilst the men were eating scratch breakfasts from their haversacks, Sir Hugh Gough rode forward to see what he could of the enemy's dispositions. As he saw nothing but sand and jungle, with the squalid village of Ferozeshah in the distance, his latest-hour attempt at reconnoitring was hardly a successful reconnaissance, yet it convinced him that the Sikhs were awaiting his onslaught inside their entrenched position, and that his best chance of gaining a complete victory was to attack promptly with his whole force whilst the day was young and his men fresh, leaving Littler with his division to come up as fast as he could and act as a reserve. When he informed his Second-in-Command of his intention, Sir Henry Hardinge, who had been impressed by the stubborn resistance of the Sikhs and the spiritless bearing of our sepoys at Moodki, was of opinion that the plan involved unnecessary risk of disaster, and held that an hour or two of extra daylight and a little additional fatigue for hardy troops were of minor importance compared with the accretion of strength Littler was bringing—5000 men and 21 guns. As the Chief adhered to his view, Sir Henry Hardinge finally ended the discussion by announcing that, as Governor-General, he vetoed the storming of Ferozeshah except in conjunction with the force then on its march from Ferozepore.

The army was then once more put in motion, bearing westwards at a long distance from the Sikh position, until clouds of dust announced the approach of Littler's division. The junction was effected about noon at a point six miles south-west of Ferozeshah. It was two o'clock before the united forces, henceforward known as the army of the Sutlej, had been formed in order of battle and resumed their march.

The direction taken was now north-north-east. The belt of thorny jungle surrounding the hitherto unreconnoitred Sikh position was reached a little before 4 P.M., too late for any new attempt to ascertain the nature of its defences. There was nothing to be done but to go at them and trust to the bayonet—the weapon always most in favour with the Chief.

Thus, in the plan of attack ultimately adopted, not only were the mistakes of Moodki repeated, but a partial success was only possible on the assumption that the army inside Ferozeshah should be driven from their position before the subsidiary Sikh forces, which supposed themselves to be investing Ferozepore, should awake to the fact that the greater part of its garrison had stolen away, or that Ferozeshah was being stormed. That Tej Singh was still supine before the empty cantonment, and that Lal Singh, with the main army, was equally supine inside his entrenchments, showed that, so far, the calculations on which the Chief had acted had been correct. With a little enterprise Tej Singh might have taken Ferozepore and Lal Singh Moodki, and thus captured the whole baggage and stores of the Anglo-sepoy forces. The junction having been effected without the knowledge of the enemy, Sir Hugh Gough was now confident that with 16,700 fighting men, of whom nearly one-third were British, 69 field-guns, the majority 6-, the rest 9-pounders, and six 8-inch howitzers, he would be able to go through with his daring programme—only—only, as at Moodki, no discount had been allowed for the facts that infantry are human beings, and that on December 21 the sun sets about 4 P.M.

When the final arrangements for the assault had

been hastily completed, Littler with his Ferozepore troops—all sepoy infantry except one weak British regiment—was on our extreme left, fronting the centre of the long western face of the Sikh position. On his right was Sir Henry Hardinge's command, Wallace's division, made up of four regiments of infantry and the heavy artillery, and behind them in reserve was Sir Henry Smith's division, one brigade of which was placed on either flank of the artillery. Gilbert's strong division, in which were three regiments of British infantry, was on the right, directly opposite the short southern side of the Sikh position. The dispositions were rough; no plan of attack had been discussed and worked out. "The army," says Sir Harry Smith in his vivid autobiography, "was one unwieldy battalion under one commanding officer, who had not been granted the power of ubiquity." What he meant was that Sir Hugh Gough before Ferozeshah took no one into his confidence, attempted to supervise and direct everything himself, and had no notion of fighting a battle beyond bringing up his troops and ordering them to go straight ahead. Shortly before 4 P.M. the infantry stood deployed in an arc about a mile in length, facing the west and south-west fronts of the oval position held by the Sikhs. The Chief had less than one hour of daylight before him wherein, with foot-sore, famished, and parched troops, to carry a prepared position of unknown strength, defended, it was supposed, by 50,000 men and 100 guns. Should the attack fail, Tej Singh, known to be lying eight or nine miles away between the river, Ferozeshah, and Ferozepore, would be constrained to seize his opportunity and assume a vigorous offensive. The risks of a situation, wholly due to over-daring precipitancy, must have been realised by both Governor-General and Chief as they heard their artillery, standing in the open, answered by the heavier guns of the Sikhs from the shelter of their embrasures.

The assault began by the advance of our artillery and mortars to a line about 1200 yards from that of the entrenchment. As our projectiles fell short, whereas those of the enemy did not, our guns were pushed forward, and continued the harmless bombardment, at progressively diminishing ranges, until the opposing guns were only separated by a space of less than a quarter of a mile. Artillerists and horses were now falling fast, whilst so far no impression had been made upon the enemy's batteries. Littler's division, being comparatively fresh and inexperienced in fighting Sikhs, was more to the front than the others; hence, when the order for the infantry to attack with the bayonet was given, it was the nearest to the Sikh works. Led by the 62nd Queen's, its right brigade advanced steadily amidst a storm of shot and shell to about 150 yards from the smoke-enshrouded batteries, and then the order to charge was given, though probably amidst the din few could have heard it. Instead of plunging forwards, the 62nd wavered, stood still, turned, and stumbled back into shelter,[1]

[1] Major-General Sir John Littler in his despatch, said to have been inadvertently published, described the 62nd Regiment as having been affected by "an immediate panic and hesitation," and got into trouble for using the words. It was afterwards explained that its brigadier (Reid) had ordered the retirement. Whatever the facts, the Duke of Wellington, in a speech on the war in the House of Lords, exonerated the 62nd by pointing out that in the first fifteen minutes the men "were absolutely mowed down by the fire under which they were advancing." In exact numbers the regiment lost 89 killed and 172 wounded, including 17 or one-third of their officers, out of a strength

a movement already begun by the native infantry regiments of the division, most of whom had been hanging back, and even shooting wildly, though their bullets could have hit none but their white comrades. Indeed, as the left brigade, composed of three native infantry regiments under Brigadier Ashburnham, had practically no casualties, it presumably did not move at all except to the rear.

To retrieve the disaster, the whole of the British line not yet engaged was hurriedly hurled at the Sikh works. Wallace's brigades, pushing blindly amidst the dust and confusion through Littler's fleeing men, bore too much to the left and suffered terribly; Smith's division, better in hand, advanced steadily; Gilbert's, after carrying the batteries in its front, was met by a heavy musketry-fire from Sikh infantry lying down from 50 to 100 yards on the inside of the temporarily captured guns. So sudden and continuous was the rain of bullets poured upon Gilbert's men that they were momentarily staggered and began to give way. Happily the penetration of the defences by Smith's reserve on Gilbert's left, and the devoted leading of the British officers generally, restored the fight, and in a few minutes a permanent lodgment had been effected upon the south side of the vast position.

of about 900. One of the other British regiments, the 9th Foot, had 273 casualties and yet carried a battery. Those of the 62nd occurred in a fewer number of minutes than with any other British regiment. There were also other extenuating circumstances: the native infantry regiments of the division were five to only one British, and were hanging back very much; further, the 62nd was practically alone in front of the strongest part of the Sikh entrenchment, and the attack by our centre and right had hardly begun. In justice to one of the native infantry regiments, the 14th, it should be added that a part of it, with the colours, recovered from its panic, and, joining the reserve, subsequently "entered the enemy's batteries."

Smith's men, headed by her Majesty's 50th Foot and joined by stragglers from Gilbert's division, pushed straight onwards right through the crowded village of Ferozeshah and in amongst the tents beyond. They were well supported by some of our cavalry, for, as the British wedge was driven home by Smith, the 3rd Light Dragoons managed to scramble in over the breastworks, and formed up in the clear space beyond the abandoned Sikh guns; then yelling and slashing, they swept through the southern half of the position, carrying consternation amongst the incoherent and undirected crowds whom they encountered in their passage. Whilst our dragoons were raging on, Gilbert's and Smith's divisions also pressed forward.

In the din and obscurity—the twilight deepening into night, a pall of smoke and dust enveloping the combatants, men shouting, mines, tumbrels, and loose powder exploding—formation was lost, sections and even whole companies got separated from their regiments, in some cases from their divisions, and all the time lines and groups of dim figures in British uniforms were following individual officers, bayoneting a way through the dividing and fleeing masses of the enemy, who surged hither and thither in leaderless confusion about them.

Whilst the turmoil was at its height, darkness closed upon the contending crowds, and a night was passed described by the veteran Governor-General as "the most extraordinary in his life"—he might with equal truth have written "in the history of India." He had managed with a portion of his command to join Gilbert's division, with which was the Commander-in-Chief, and it was largely due to the inspiriting example of those two heroes that the greater part of the division was kept together throughout the night, at first inside the partially won entrenchments and, later, in the open ground immediately outside them. From time to time wanderers from one of the other divisions joined Gilbert's men, most of whom, careless of bullets, were already lying dead-beat, asleep or dozing on the frozen ground. Plenty of combustible material, fuel, and broken gun-carriages were lying about, but no fires were allowed, as the enemy's guns commanded the bivouac. About midnight one of the roving bodies of Sikhs brought a big gun to bear, "with," recorded the Chief in his despatch, "deadly effect upon our troops," when Sir Henry Hardinge himself called upon the formed remnants of the 80th Queen's and 1st European Infantry to silence it. The men rose, charged, spiked or upset it, and then returned and lay down again. Neither Governor-General nor Chief knew that night where the rest of their army was. Littler's broken regiments were, in fact, sheltering themselves in the jungle and hamlets directly south-west of the entrenchment which they had failed to penetrate. Some, in their demoralisation, had joined the panic-stricken stream of men treking for Ferozepore.

Smith, with his reserve and various accretions, maintained his position for some hours in the very heart of the Sikh camp. When night had closed, and firing and movement had gradually subsided, uncertain where he was, he had halted and re-formed his men, and, after causing his British infantry to take off the white covers from their caps, had with his whole force lain down. So long as the darkness was complete the prowling collections of the enemy, who were wandering about looting and shooting, did not discover his bivouac; but some time after midnight the moon rose — a thin crescent only — and gradually revealed that those prostrate figures were Englishmen and sepoys. A ring of snipers soon girdled them, and firing was renewed until about 3 A.M., when the general thought it prudent to extricate his force. Guided by a bonfire, he withdrew his remnant to the hamlet of Misriwala, about two miles to the south-west of the Sikh position, and there found some thousands of stragglers already in shelter.

As dawn approached Sir Harry Smith led the remains of his division and all the stragglers he could collect—including some intact portions of Littler's troops—to the position occupied by the Chief, and there heard from the indomitable veterans[1] at the head of the army that, though nearly all the gun ammunition had been expended, they were about to form the troops in line and sweep through the Sikh camp from south to north, so as to emerge on its river side, and thus leave the enemy opportunity for escape.

It was a desperate move, but necessary, as the situation was desperate, should the Sikhs discover the condition of our artillery or Tej Singh become alive to his duty and do it. Happily for the con-

[1] Sir Henry Hardinge was sixty-one, with forty-eight years' service, Sir Hugh Gough was sixty-seven, with fifty-two years' service. A century ago commissions were often given to boys of thirteen or fourteen, and sometimes to children still in frocks. The story will be remembered, of a lady, hearing a row going on in her nursery, calling upstairs to inquire the cause. "Please, mum, it's only the Major crying because the Colonel slapped him," was the reply.

tinuance of the British dominion in India, neither inside nor outside Ferozeshah had the Khalsa any competent leader, nor did their soldiery suspect the harmlessness of our formidable array of guns. Lal Singh and some of his brother sirdars had fled during the night, and the few, who had remained together with the regimental officers, had passed the precious hours in heated discussion and recriminations. Each undirected unit — whether regiment, battery, troop of horsemen, mob of Akalis, or followers—had thus been left to act independently. Some had withdrawn towards the river, some had plundered the treasure-chests and the tents of the sirdars, others had held together, determined to renew the fight in the morning.

As light increased and objects became discernible, Gilbert's men were roused from their cheerless bivouacs and re-formed amongst the captured batteries. Turning their tired eyes northwards towards the interior of the position, they saw with amazement an almost lifeless camp—in the darkness the hosts of the foe had disappeared. The news spread, Smith's men joined Gilbert's, and heard and saw for themselves. The rebound from weary indifference to the exultation of victory was universal; the men moved smartly, the bugles sounded cheerily, the line of battle was arranged, a few guns and rockets were fired,—a mere bluff, yet a notice to quit,—and then our troops advanced, cleared Ferozeshah, changed front, and swept onwards to the north, the horse artillery making a brave show, yet unable to reply to a battery which had opened upon them. Emerging on the river face of the now wholly captured position, and there joined by some of Littler's crestfallen division, the Governor-General and Commander-in-Chief, with what remained of their respective staffs, rode down the huzzaing lines of shivering worn-out troops.

The battle won, the men impatient for food, drink, and rest, were speculating why they were still kept standing, when an ominous rumour ran up and down their ranks that a second Sikh army was approaching, fresh, innumerable, the horse forming the wings overlapping our lines as far as eye could see. The hasty return of some of our cavalry, the levelling of field-glasses by staff officers towards the river, and the galloping about of aides-de-camp were soon confirmatory of the rumour. Clouds of dust were now rising to the north, coming nearer and nearer. Then from amidst the dust guns opened—"playing," wrote the Chief in his despatch, "with great effect, while those of the British were rendered useless from want of ammunition, the whole of which had been expended and could not return a single shot." Our weak cavalry—one of our regiments had "retired" in the night to Ferozepore—was soon driven in, and Tej Singh, by keeping his guns beyond musket-range and pouring grape upon our advancing infantry, might perhaps have won a complete victory, only for some reason he acted like a coward, traitor, or fool. As soon as our infantry began to move forward to attack with the bayonet,—in the situation the only course open,—"supported on the flanks by the cavalry," to again quote from the Chief's despatch, "the Sikhs ceased their firing and abandoned the field." It was a deliverance for which no satisfactory explanation has yet been given.

When our cavalry was driven in, many of the

panic-stricken native troopers galloped to the rear, where the dooly-bearers, water-carriers, grooms, and other camp-followers were collected, and the whole mass, believing that the on-coming hosts of the enemy would overwhelm our thin lines, turned and fled for Ferozepore, strewing the ground with bedding, clothes, horse-gear, and the doolies containing the wounded.

So was fought and so ended the battle known in history as Ferozeshah. Our losses, probably half from grape, were 694 killed and 1712 wounded. The percentage was, as at Moodki, three times as heavy for the British as for the sepoy troops; indeed some of the native infantry regiments could hardly be driven up to the Sikh batteries, and, owing to their hanging back and flurried shooting, they must have disabled more of their white comrades than they did of the enemy. They afterwards excused their spiritless conduct by pointing out that, as they were exhausted from thirst and hunger, they were good for nothing. Excluding guns thrown down wells and not recovered, the Sikhs abandoned 73 inside their entrenchment, many of them large "brass" guns of position — 18- and 24-pounders — excellently cast and exquisitely finished.

As regards the numbers and qualities of the Sikh forces engaged, both inside and outside Ferozeshah, estimates differ. Collating all available information, it would appear that on the evening of the assault there were inside roundly 15,000 regular infantry,— including two regiments of Hindustanis,—88 guns, with perhaps 1000 artillerists, 3000 cavalry of sorts, and from 8000 to 10,000 others, undisciplined yeomen, mounted and unmounted, Akalis, drivers, and miscellaneous followers. Outside, Tej Singh's forces kept at such a respectful distance from our advancing lines that all estimates must be very rough, each reflecting the feelings of the person making it. Thus, the Commander-in-Chief decidedly overstated the numbers of horse in his despatch when he wrote, "Tej Singh brought up fresh battalions and a large park of artillery, supported by 30,000 *ghorcharras* [cavalry], which had been kept as a reserve near the river." What his numbers really were matters little, as evidently neither he nor his horsemen had any stomach for fighting. Upon his retirement he at once withdrew trans-Sutlej, taking all his boats with him, and there awaited our crossing in pursuit. Our losses, the nervous exhaustion of the sepoys, and particularly the want of ammunition and heavy guns, confined Sir Hugh Gough to the vicinity of Ferozeshah for some time. When his army had been reorganised he cautiously advanced nearer the river, and took up a position facing that of the Sikhs on the opposite bank.

CHAPTER IV.

VICTORIES OF ALIWAL AND SOBRAON.

When a week passed and then another, and in our extremity instead of fighting we fell back on the pen and put forth a proclamation—a mere *brutum fulmen*—calling on "all natives of Hindostan" in the Sikh service to desert under pain of being "treated as traitors to their country and enemies of the British Government," the Sikhs began to think that it was time for them to be again stirring. The Commander-in-Chief's paralysis of action after such headlong hurry to close with them and deliver the blows of Moodki and Ferozeshah — a paralysis which continued even after the arrival in his camp of large reinforcements from Meerut—was an unsolved mystery to the Sikhs, until they learnt that he was awaiting the arrival of an immense convoy, including a siege-train, said to be on its way from Delhi under a slender escort of native infantry and cavalry. They then decided to carry the war once more into British territory, and, if possible, to cut our communications and intercept the expected convoy. With these objects they began the construction of a bridge of boats, ten miles up-stream opposite the village of Sobraon, and, being unmolested, proceeded to strongly fortify the bridge-head on the British side of the Sutlej. About the same time, fifty miles farther up the river, a new army, chiefly composed of hill irregulars, stiffened by some companies of regular infantry, with over 50 guns and some thousands of indifferent cavalry, was accumulated, and transferred by boats cis-Sutlej at the Philor crossing opposite Ludhiana.

To meet these movements the Chief, on January 17, 1846, despatched Sir Harry Smith with a considerable force, with orders to clear the country, relieve Ludhiana, and secure the safety of the siege-train, and next day moved with the rest of his troops to a position about five miles from the enemy's bridge-head. Smith, with characteristic concentration of purpose, declined a battle offered him at Badowal by Runjûr Singh, who commanded the Philor army, and on the 21st reached Ludhiana. His running away from a fight with the consequent destruction of his rear-guard—he lost 214 men and most of his baggage—cost him for the moment some prestige and unduly elated the Sikhs, but, considering the stake at issue, was an act of wise self-denial which afterwards received the emphatic approbation of the Duke of Wellington.

Having spent a week in organising his forces, and being strengthened by the Ludhiana garrison, the most serviceable portion of which were two Ghurkha regiments, he moved out of the place, and on the 26th occupied Badowal, from which Runjur Singh, threatened on three sides, had prudently retired towards the river. Further strengthened by additional cavalry and guns and the second brigade of his division under Brigadier Wheeler, Sir Harry Smith at last felt himself strong enough to beat up the enemy, and, in his own expressive phrase, "teach the Sikhs to swim the Sutlej." Meanwhile, Runjur Singh's incoherent force had received from the Sikh main army an important reinforcement—4000 regular infantry, 12 guns, and a large supplement of cavalry. These additions raised his command to roundly 24,000 men and 67 guns; but as more than half his troops were undisciplined and unreliable, and as he himself was known to be inefficient and to possess little personal influence, Smith's confidence in his own ability to achieve a complete victory was reasonable. His compact little army of 11,000 men included three regiments of British infantry, one of British cavalry (16th Lancers), 22 guns, and two howitzers.

Determined not to repeat the blunders of Moodki and Ferozeshah, he rested his men on the 27th and thoroughly reconnoitred the enemy's position, a semicircular entrenchment on the river defended by many guns. Leaving Badowal at dawn next morning, Smith had marched six miles, when, to their mutual surprise, the two armies sighted each other in motion, Runjur Singh's apparently pushing for Jagraon along the left high bank of the river, Smith's for the camp out of which his quarry had just marched. A collision being inevitable, the Sikhs at once took up a defensive position along the crest of a sandy ridge, with the village of Aliwal on their left and the hamlet of Bhundrie, more than a mile distant, on their right. Behind this crest of high ground lay a stretch of nearly two miles of low alluvial land, beyond which were the ferry-head and its defences, the original objective of the English general. By the time that Smith had completed his dispositions for attack, the Sikhs had placed their guns in position and thrown up rough breastworks between the two villages which formed the extreme ends of their line. The regulars held their right, including Bhundrie; but Aliwal, the higher point, was the key of their position. Having eight clear hours for his work,—it was 9 A.M.,—the ground being hard grass-land, the morning sun exhilarating, and the up-stream breeze sufficient to dispel smoke and dust, Smith marshalled his troops with the leisurely precision of a field-day. When all was ready the line advanced, but had to be halted under fire whilst its right was being extended and swung round so as to bring its full weight to bear upon Aliwal. At the same time the cavalry brigade was launched upon the Sikh left. Aliwal was then carried, and the enemy's irregulars driven in flight towards the river.

On Runjur Singh's right the defence by the regular infantry was stubborn. In order to cover the passage of the river, they clung to Bhundrie, and would not have been broken without heavy loss to the assaulting infantry, had not whole companies of the Sikhs, in their excitement, after firing their muskets, thrown them down and rushed at our men sword in hand. During the fighting in this part of the field the 16th Lancers did brilliant service by charging repeatedly through the Sikh regulars, one squadron in particular distinguishing itself by breaking a square. Bhundrie being taken, the horse artillery dashed forward and began firing upon the stream of fugitives. But, even then, a portion of the Sikh regulars held together, and it was not until they had been dislodged from the shelter of a high bank, and pounded for some minutes by the fire of 12 guns placed not 300 yards from where they were standing at bay, that they finally broke and ran. Meanwhile the whole of the British line was converging upon the Sikh camp, and as soon as all our guns had been brought to bear on a common centre—the ford and ferry—the rout was complete. Runjur Singh's army lost everything, including its 67 guns, 56 being captured or destroyed, and 11 sunk in the river. When a few days after his defeat, with the inconsequent buoyancy characteristic of Sikhs in those days, he applied to the Durbar at Lahore for more guns so that he might renew the offensive, he was sarcastically told to recover them from the quicksands of the Sutlej.

Our losses in this the turning battle of the campaign were comparatively insignificant, under 600. The results were immense. The safe passage of the convoy, on which the prosecution of the war depended, was secured; the cis-Sutlej states became loyal to their foreign protectors once more; the Himalayan tribes right up to the borders of Tibet declared for us and rose against their Sikh masters; and finally our sepoys—the Aliwal portion of whom, well fed, well led, and unfatigued, had fought under Smith splendidly—recovered their *morale*, and promised that, as soon as the big guns came, Sobraon would be as decisive a victory as Aliwal.

After Ferozeshah Tej Singh had himself come into the British camp to propose terms and ingratiate himself with the Governor-General. After Aliwal the Lahore Durbar, thinking the power of the soldiers sufficiently crushed, and anxious on their own account, had sent a deputation on a similar errand, but had to be content with the vague announcement that, as soon as the Sikh forces had been disarmed and disbanded and an indemnity paid, the British Government would not object to the concession of a restricted sovereignty to the boy Maharaja, Dhulip Singh. To Gulab Singh, the calculating Raja of Jammu, an assurance had already been conveyed that, in the event of his attitude continuing satisfactory, at the time of settlement his reasonable expectations would be taken into consideration.

Whilst the Governor-General was doing all that was honourably possible to keep the Sikh forces without leaders and Gulab Singh and his overrated Rajput levies neutral, the Commander-in-Chief was drawing the coils closer round the bridge-head at Sobraon. His object was, without provoking an encounter, to detain the enemy in their false position until, with the aid of the whole of the siege-train, he should be in a position to strike the final blow. On February 6 and 7 the convoy arrived—elephants with the big guns, thousands of baggage-animals of sorts, 4000 carts drawn by 24,000 bullocks, and from 7000 to 8000 drivers and carriers. It had taken John Lawrence, Collector and Magistrate of Delhi, a month to collect and organise this enormous transport, and three weeks for the mass to crawl the 200 miles to Sobraon. In movement it covered an extent of ten miles, hence the animals first to start frequently reached the next halting-place before those loaded last had left the previous night's camping-ground. The escort was only one regiment of native infantry and one of cavalry, and the country traversed up to the date of the Aliwal victory was generally hostile, hence an enterprising leader with a handful of active horsemen might have had repeated opportunities for wrecking the whole convoy, but the Sikhs with their 15,000 to 20,000 horsemen did nothing.

When on February 7 Sir Harry Smith, with a large part of his division and the guns and cavalry added to it, rejoined the Chief, the Sikh position was confronted by an army of 20,000 fighting men, all confident that this time the enemy would be crushed. Only three miles of level ground now separated the two armies. That of the Sikhs was somewhat under 30,000 men, of whom perhaps half were good infantry. They were all cooped up inside their horse-shoe entrenchment, which had a frontage of nearly two miles and an extreme depth of about a mile. The two ends rested on the river, and both were to some extent protected by heavy guns placed on the right bank of the main channel. Communication between the two sides was maintained by a strongly constructed bridge of boats. Obviously, though the fact did not appear to have occurred to the defenders, if either end of the horse-shoe could be penetrated and held, not only would the whole of the works be exposed to an enfilading fire, but retreat by the bridge would be compromised. Whether the position was impregnable, as the Sikhs appeared to believe, could only be proved by attacking it. In the British camp the expectation was general that a long bombardment would so shake the defence that entrance would not be very difficult; moreover, as the Sikh troops of all arms, when exercising, were seen to move freely out and in on their own right, there was probably a weak spot in the defences on that side. Thus, though the enemy's field-works were stronger than at Ferozeshah, and only one face was open to assault, the assailants from Chief to sepoy were already discounting difficulties. At Ferozeshah exhausted infantry with inferior artillery had been hurled at sunset upon an unreconnoitred entrenched camp, held in strength by a previously undefeated army supported by 100 powerful guns. At Sobraon a perfectly equipped army, supplemented by a siege-train, after a rest of seven weeks, would at dawn attack an enemy already disheartened by three defeats and the loss of more than half their guns and artillerymen. So sure of the result were the Governor-General and Chief, that the former had already recorded his expectation of full success, and the latter had warned the officer commanding the troops at Ferozepore to be in readiness to move his six battalions of native infantry across the Sutlej by a bridge of boats—already under construction for the purpose —as soon as he should receive news of the expected issue of the battle.

The plan of attack was simple—a bombardment, to be followed by a determined assault on the extreme right of the Sikh defences and feints on the rest of the position, to be pressed home as soon as the left attack had effected an entrance. Sir Robert Dick's division had the post of honour, our extreme left, Gilbert's the centre, and Smith's reduced battalions the right—in all, 13,000 bayonets. Two strong infantry brigades were held in reserve, one on the left, the other in support of the centre and right. Sir Joseph Thackwell commanded the cavalry division, which, with the exception of one brigade on the left, was placed on our extreme right, with the object of preventing retreat by the Harriki ford after the battle, or advance during it by the enemy's horse, which lay along the opposite bank facing the ford.

Our artillery, over 100 pieces, which included 25 howitzers, ranging from 5½ to 8 inches, five 24-pounders, five 18-pounders, and fifteen 9-pounders enlarged into 12's, was arranged—to quote from the Chief's despatch — "in an extended semicircle, embracing within its fire the works of the Sikhs." In spreading his attack, both by guns and infantry, over the whole face of the enemy's position, the Chief followed his usual practice. It is a question whether concentration rather than diffusion would not have been sounder tactics.

Long before dawn on February 10 detachments from her Majesty's 62nd Foot moved silently from camp, and, after passing our outlying post in the Rhodawala hamlet, divided, one creeping under the cover of the night and the heavy river-fog upon a small entrenched look-out of the enemy known as the three-tree picket, and the other upon Chota Sobraon, a fortified hamlet a mile or more to the right, supposed to be held by a strong picket. Arrived, our men sprang into the trenches and swarmed up the banks, to find both places unoccupied. The good news was immediately conveyed back to our cautiously advancing army; the elephants drew the big guns into position; the field artillery was pushed still nearer, but for a time not a shot was fired. Dawn approached, but the mists were still impenetrable. Just before sunrise the bombardment began. Though obscurity continued, the target was large, as it included the whole crowded camp of the enemy. As our guns opened the drums of the Sikhs beat to arms: in their careless trust in their defences the enemy had evidently been taken by surprise, as was proved by the fact that their pickets had withdrawn at nightfall to enjoy the comforts of their camp. In a few minutes the Sikh guns began to reply. As the sun rose higher the fog rolled off, revealing the row of British guns and the long lines of our infantry standing 300 yards behind in readiness for the order to advance. The space between the contending batteries was about 1000 yards. For two hours the artillery duel continued, our heavy pieces sending shot and shell into and beyond the outer defences of the Sikhs, theirs doing little damage to us, the shooting being wild and the shell-fuses badly timed. Soon after 9 A.M. our big-gun ammunition began to give out,—it was said in lame excuse that the elephants with fresh supplies could not be induced to enter the zone of fire. The predicament might have been awkward had not the successive advances of the field artillery, followed by the infantry at regulation distance, reduced the distance between Sir Robert Dick's infantry and the Sikh guns in their front to about 600 yards.

As our cannonade slackened the Chief ordered Dick to attack with the bayonet. His supporting artillery—followed at the double by her Majesty's 10th and 53rd Regiments and the 45th and 59th Native Infantry, most of them hitherto unblooded troops — galloped up to within 300 yards of the enemy's outer defences, unlimbered and fired, and then amidst the smoke and din the assaulting lines charged — the 53rd happily finding ingress through the bed of a dry nullah left open as a passage for the garrison. In a few minutes a lodgment was effected; but the defenders threw themselves upon the breathless intruders, and for twenty minutes bayonet met sword and shield in confused *mêlée*, those outside each other's reach loading and firing their clumsy muskets as opportunity offered. Help came to both sides—to the assaulters in thin streams as Dick's second brigade began to scramble in, to the defenders in a converging flood from the central part of their entrenchment. Our men were staggered—their leader Dick had already fallen—and were giving ground, when, being joined by some of the reserve battalions, equality was restored to the fight. To relieve the pressure on his left the Chief had already ordered Gilbert and Smith to storm the works where they could. The troops of the former, headed by her Majesty's 29th Foot and the 1st Europeans, rushed across a dry nullah, unsupported by artillery-fire, but were brought to a standstill by the unscalable nature of the bank and breastwork on the farther side. As they ran back to partial shelter the Sikhs poured out and decapitated the wounded. On the right Smith's attack—he only had 2400 bayonets—was at first repulsed, but what he called his "bull-dogs of the 31st and old 50th stood up like men, and were well supported by the native regiments." The hand-to-hand conflict went on for twenty-five minutes, after which resistance collapsed. It did so because by then our left attack had penetrated the second line of the right defences of the position, and had thus enabled Sir Joseph Thackwell's cavalry, headed by the 3rd Light Dragoons, to enter, form inside, and charge down in rear of the Sikh batteries.

It was now 10 A.M., the outer ring of the entrenchment had been won, the inner pierced, and the Sikh irregulars and camp-followers were converging in a wild mob on their bridge. Most of the regular infantry were still in formation, fighting stubbornly.

Headed by Sham Singh, an old friend and contemporary of Runjit Singh, they tried to stem the fleeing torrent and delay the moment when defeat would change to rout. But Sham Singh, who had before the assault proclaimed his intention of devoting himself, was at last killed, and some unknown hand cut adrift the centre boat of the bridge. Then all was lost; the staunchest of the infantry were already yielding to panic as our horse artillery galloped forwards and began to fire upon the masses struggling on the broken bridge, and wading, swimming, and drowning in the Sutlej, which had opportunely for us risen some inches that morning, and was consequently nowhere fordable for footmen.

By 10.30 A.M. the forces of the Khalsa had been annihilated as an army. Out of 30,000 men, who three hours before had stood lustily defiant behind their guns, a round third were now lying dead or wounded about their position or in the river, the rest had scattered. The victory cost us 320 killed and 2083 wounded; but the injuries being mostly by sword and musket-ball, and help being near and ready, the suffering was less, and the percentage of recoveries larger, than after any of the previous battles of the campaign. Of the enemy's wounded probably more than half died miserably from want of treatment or the savage humour of our men, who had many acts of barbarity to avenge. Though, as always, the proportion of British to sepoy casualties was excessive, in no other battle of the war had the native infantry fought so well up to the standard of their white comrades. Amongst the British regiments the losses were very unevenly distributed. Thus the Queen's Own (50th), 53rd Foot, and 1st

Europeans lost between them 37 officers and 587 men, nearly a quarter of their effective strength, whilst her Majesty's 9th, 80th, and 62nd Regiments suffered comparatively little.

The Sikhs abandoned all their cannon, 70, thus raising the number taken during the war to 213. In addition more than 200 *zambūraks* or small camel-guns were found left behind in their works.

On the evening of the victory the six regiments of native infantry held in readiness near Ferozepore, twenty-five miles below Sobraon, crossed the Sutlej by the bridge, which had been prepared in anticipation of the result of the battle. By the 14th the whole of our army was encamped at Kasur, thirty-two miles south of the Sikh capital. Next day Gulab Singh, accompanied by two members of the Durbar, arrived in the camp of the Governor-General to sue for terms, of the nature of which the deputation was already aware. A few days afterwards the army of the Sutlej advanced to Lahore, and there under its walls peace was ratified.

The conditions imposed included the cession not only of the Beas Doab, the rich and beautiful country, hill and plain, between the Sutlej and the Beas, but of Jammu and Kashmir as well, both of which latter were at once sold to "Maharaja" Gulab Singh for £750,000.

Before the hot weather had set in the Lahore government had been reconstructed: Gulab Singh had received the reward of his neutrality, and was now "recognised as an independent sovereign over the territories" bought by him; the scheming trio at Lahore,—Rani Jindan, Lal Singh, and Tej Singh,—supported by British bayonets, were ruling in the name of the little Maharaja Dhulip Singh over the shrunken dominions of Runjit Singh; and most of their former masters, the men of the Khalsa army, beaten, disarmed, and disbanded, had scattered, some to their hereditary vocation,—husbandry,—some to re-enlist as soldiers under the new administration, and not a few to discontented idling.

Thus, in the settlement the wicked had been exalted, the brave and simple debased. That a cunning opportunist like Gulab Singh should receive a kingdom, and cowards or traitors like the Rani and her friends the means of domineering over the patriotic Khalsa, was due to the exigencies of the situation. The Company's treasury was empty, the military machine overstrained, the Mahrattas and great feudatories restless and suspicious, the Court of Directors impatient for peace and retrenchment. In any case, as the hot weather was approaching and the number of British soldiers fit for duty was only 3200 out of the 7500 who had taken part in the campaign, further military operations were for the time out of the question; and without a renewal of the war by a hill campaign against Gulab Singh, whose redoubtable army was intact, and protracted sieges of strong places, such as Govindgarh, Attock, Multan, and Peshawar, the Punjab could not be annexed. By selling Kashmir and only retaining the Jallandar Doab for ourselves, a dangerous enemy had been placated, the recuperative power of the Sikhs reduced, and a considerable indemnity secured. If the circumstances and the available information of the moment be weighed, the settlement effected, though much criticised at the time and since, was wise and reasonable.

The same cannot be said of our conduct of the campaign or proceedings anterior to it. The maintenance, after the withdrawal from Afghanistan in 1842, of a weak or indeed of any garrison at Ferozepore, only forty-five miles from Lahore, was a threat and provocation to the Sikhs. The position was isolated, far removed from supports, in the midst of a desert, and liable to be rushed at any time. The barren character of the country should have been its own protection, and Ludhiana should alone have been held in strength, that station being an important town with a good fort, situate in a rich country on the main line of communication between Lahore and Delhi, and sufficiently distant from the Sutlej and Amritsar and adjacent to Ambala to be neither a red rag to the impulsive Khalsa nor, should occasion arise, beyond the reach of timely support. During the two years of Sir Henry Hardinge's rule preceding the outbreak of the war, he had done all that was possible, short of reversing the military dispositions of his two predecessors, to remedy the radical error of the Ferozepore position. By raising its garrison to 7000 men, and giving the command to a capable soldier, he had rendered the cantonment secure against any attack which "the mutinous Sikh army" was supposed to be capable of making. When that army suddenly poured across the Sutlej and, still hugging the river, sat down an inert mass before Ferozepore, the headlong haste with which our troops were pushed westwards to meet the invasion of protected territory was, no doubt, warranted up to the forenoon of December 17, 1845, at which time the Ambala and Ludhiana troops, about 11,000 strong, reached a halting-ground only forty miles from Ferozepore. Both Governor-General and Commander-in-Chief then knew that Sir John Littler's garrison was in no immediate danger, and that the whole strength of the Khalsa, roughly guessed at 60,000 men and 100 guns, intent on fighting, lay somewhere between the relieving force and its objective, Ferozepore. Had Sir Hugh Gough now rested and refreshed his army, awaited the arrival of reinforcements,—two British and two native infantry regiments and some mortars were only a day behind,—and by reconnoitring with his cavalry ascertained the strength and dispositions of the enemy, Sobraon might have been ante-dated by a month, and the useless carnage of Moodki and Ferozeshah, with the prolonged paralysis of action which followed, might all have been avoided. Instead, by hurrying on—on—and fighting at Moodki, and then ramming exhausted men late in the afternoon against a position of unknown strength held by more than twice their numbers, he just missed disaster, lost 3300 men, expended all his gun ammunition, and had to stand still playing a game of bluff for seven weeks, until the arrival of his siege-train, ammunition, and reinforcements enabled him to strike the decisive blow at Sobraon.

For their services Sir Henry Hardinge and Sir Hugh Gough were raised to the peerage and granted pensions for their lives, the former being given a viscountship and £3000 a-year, the latter a barony and £2000. Sir Henry Smith received a baronetcy, but no material reward.

CHAPTER V.

THE REGENCY PERIOD, 1846-1848.

As the hot weather advanced, effect was given to the arrangements made after Sobraon. The Punjab was broken up into three parts: (1) Kashmir and its dependencies sold to Gulab Singh; (2) the remnant of Runjit Singh's kingdom, called "the Lahore State," to which Henry Lawrence was appointed Resident; and (3) the annexed territory between the Sutlej and Beas, to which John Lawrence was posted as Commissioner. The first was to be independently governed by its new sovereign; the second by the Durbar, — practically the Maharaja's mother, Rani Jindan, with her lover Lal Singh as vizier,—propped by British bayonets and tutored by the Resident; the third by its commissioner as a civil division, like any other new conquest when incorporated in the Empire.

Of the work intrusted to the brothers Lawrence, Henry's was the more delicate and onerous—to rule by personal influence through the Durbar, without directly interfering in any way in the internal administration. John's was easier, and thoroughly congenial to the blunt, downright, self-confident character of the man —to rule as despot, backed by physical force. His people—Rajputs in the hills, Jats and Sikhs in the plains—being members or connections of the lately dominant Khalsa, had experienced some consideration from their chiefs and revenue-farmers, hence their villages, every one of which was walled and defensible, were fairly strong self-governing communities, the members of which, having intelligence, common institutions, and property, took kindly to the strange experience of being ordered about by a white master, imbued with the novel idea that law, order, and justice were equally binding on all men. John, therefore, had few difficulties which energy, industry, and a knowledge of detail did not fail to surmount. He literally took off his coat and tucked up his sleeves to his work—a habit retained by him even as Viceroy. With such determination did he thrust the administrative methods of Western civilisation upon his bewildered peasantry, whose institutions were centuries old, that within a period of five months he had substituted throughout his 2000 villages fixed money assessments for fluctuating grain exactions, had established courts of justice, made roads, started schools, introduced a postal system, and even attempted to inaugurate by order uniformity in weights and measures—a reform not yet accomplished in any part of India. So satisfied with his efforts was he that he wrote to the Foreign Secretary that he "could easily manage double the extent of country"—and this though his kingdom was as big as Wales, and his people still burnt widows, killed daughters, buried lepers alive, had generally no respect for human life, and were ready, if opportunity offered, to cut his throat and those of all other cow-killing Feringhees.

The Jallandar Doab was a good land, then as now known as the garden of the Punjab; man alone was vile, particularly the lazy blood-suckers encouraged by Runjit Singh's social system, — rajas, sirdars, jagirdars, and the whole tribe of revenue-farmers. With all such John Lawrence had no sympathy: they were useless drones, and should be made to work, or their perquisites should be cut down for the benefit of the patient toiling multitude, the peasants and their dependents, the village artisans and menials. Towards them he was kindly and considerate, towards their oppressors scornful and intolerant. His feelings, translated into action, when not too sudden or sweeping, suited a conquered province, but not an independent state in leading-strings like that of Lahore.

His brother Henry, the Resident of that state, with a heart as big and tender, a brain bigger and finer, and a foresight more comprehensive and penetrating, was striving for months to carry out his impossible mandate of ruling without reigning. He could do nothing except through the queen-mother and her vizier. He sought to introduce reforms far less sweeping than those already carried out by his brother. To do so required money, and that necessitated the reduction of the army, and of hordes of functionaries; but as the pay of all was in arrears, and the abolition of the most objectionable taxes had first to be taken in hand, most of his projects remained good intentions and nothing more. He could effect no ameliorations in existing conditions without causing loss of income to the Durbar or of perquisites to sirdars and sweaters of sorts. To obtain some honesty in officials predicated a perception of principle in persons hereditarily unprincipled. He found the treasury empty, receipts anticipated, the privileged classes solid against reforms: queen-mother, vizier, sirdars, and the higher functionaries of all kinds were hopelessly depraved and ignorant.

His Sisyphean labours would have unstrung him sooner had not relaxation come to him in the form of interludes of action. Thus, a "cow-row" at Lahore gave him excitement, and a military mission to Kangra an enjoyable holiday from office amidst lovely surroundings. Devoted to duty, he battled against ill-health, lies, intrigues, and obstruction until the following August, when he broke down. His brother John took his place. Chafing at his impotence for good—cis-Beas he had been omnipotent—John bluntly represented to Lord Hardinge that unless the British Resident were empowered to directly govern the country, his presence at Lahore was useless. An opportunity for strengthening his position soon after occurred. Lal Singh, the vizier, who hated Gulab Singh, the purchaser of Kashmir, instigated a rebellion there, and after trial wás found guilty and deported. Lord Hardinge thereupon notified to the queen-mother and her advisers that he could not consent to the retention of the British garrison in Lahore unless he were intrusted with the administration of the country until the Maharaja, then eight years of age, should attain his majority. As that garrison was the sole security against anarchy, the propertied classes amongst the Sikhs agreed to the Governor-General's conditions. A new form of government was then devised—a Council of Regency consisting of eight sirdars, under the "unlimited" control of the British Resident.

The effect of the new arrangement, hardly realised when accepted, soon dawned upon the oppressors of the people: they had imprudently signed away, as they viewed the transaction, the independence of the Khalsa to the English—in other words, had renounced their right to misgovern all classes in their own interests. As reforming Englishmen, ignorant of Punjabis but aware of their own powers, toured throughout the land, redressing abuses and treating as servants men who had been lords of hundreds of villages, the Khalsa, from sirdar to peasant, felt that their *rāj* was over, and that even when the Maharaja came of age and was proclaimed the independent sovereign of the Punjab, he would still be a king in leading-strings. They foresaw that in every case the English would find some plea for perpetuating their straitlaced system, and interdicting a reversion to the methods of the good old days when Runjit Singh was sole lord of the Punjab. That Sikh and Muhammadan, sirdar and peasant, should be treated alike would be a climax to their humiliation which no true member of the Khalsa could tolerate. As self-interest rules actions, and in no state does the dominant party concede equal rights to others except under coercion, Sikh resentment under the new order was natural. Whether, as the malcontents assumed, our conduct was due to the detached and contemptuous indifference with which in those days we habitually regarded the privileges or usurpations of class amongst Indians whilst vigilantly protecting our own, will best be judged by a consideration of the condition of "the Lahore State" at the time we assumed responsibility for its administration, and the ameliorations which we attempted to introduce.

By the annexation of the Jallandar Doab and the transfer of Jammu and Kashmir to Gulab Singh the Sikh kingdom was reduced to the triangle of plain south of the Himalayas between the Sutlej-cum-Beas and the valley of the Indus, which latter it included—in all about 74,000 square miles, five-sixths of it at the time jungle and desert. Of this area the essentially Sikh part was the Mānjha, or upper portion of the Bari Doab, a strip about 200 miles long by 50 broad, lying between the Beas and Ravi rivers. In the heart of this country were Lahore and Amritsar, respectively the political and religious capitals of the Sikhs, and about them clustered the villages and strongholds of the sturdy Jat peasantry, whose youth supplied most of the regular infantry and many of the artillerists of the Khalsa army. In 1847 the total Sikh population of the Mānjha was probably under 250,000, of whom perhaps a sixth part had taken part in the war against us. Had these Manjha Sikhs depended on husbandry alone for their livelihood they would have been very poor, as their country was unirrigated and the rainfall uncertain; but from the rise of Runjit Singh until the collapse of his kingdom at Sobraon, service and the opportunities occurring during it had kept them in comparative affluence. Disbandment, therefore, impoverished many thousands, and filled the villages with discontented idlers.

Westwards of the Ravi, throughout the doabs known as the Rechna, Jetch, and Sindh Sāgar,—words composed from the first letters of the names of the rivers forming the boundaries of each doab,—and the strips of plain or valley between the Indus and mountains beyond, the population was progressively more and more Muhammadan, intensifying from the mild cis-Chenab blends of Jats and Rajputs, whose Moslem sections were lukewarm proselytes of a few generations, to the uncompromising bigots of the Indus regions.

South of those northern and central tracts lay what may be conveniently termed the province of Multan, a country of deserts, jungle, and riverain belts of alluvial soil, in which the rivers of the various doabs successively united their streams. Those wild regions were occupied by groups of rude Muhammadam tribes, most of them breeders and herders of cattle, and all of them thievish as Ishmaelites.

Speaking broadly, Runjit Singh's power was never consolidated beyond a radius of about 100 miles from Amritsar. Certainly west of the Jhelam to the day of his death he was always carrying on a crusade against all Muhammadans, fighting and plundering but not governing them. Wherever his arms penetrated he built forts, located garrisons, and extracted what he could from the peasantry. Immediately upon his death the process of disintegration began, but was not at first quick, as the army was young and vigorous, and everywhere masterful. As power passed from Lahore to local centres, each under some form of democratic militarism, every section of the civil population, other than Sikh and in a varying degree Hindu, was more and more oppressed. From Durbar and provincial governor or revenue-farmer down to common soldier every man had some authority, and exacted service or produce from those immediately controlled by him. The consequences were soon apparent: husbandry, trade, and manufactures—those of muskets, swords, and cannons excepted — became losing occupations, villages and wells were deserted, cultivation dwindled, and the population declined. As the sources of production contracted, collectors were unable to realise taxes and dues except at the sword's point. The pay of the troops being always in arrears, they in turn were compelled to live upon the people. Indeed, even in Runjit Singh's time he often paid his clamorous soldiery as well as civil officials by *tankhwāhs* or orders of assignment on the revenue-farmer of a tract, whereupon the prospective payees were billeted upon a group of villages until arrears had been realised in full, a consummation which only happened when the assignees had eaten, destroyed, or carried off all movables. As the power of the Durbar waned, concessions of increased pay were repeatedly made to the troops, and equilibrium sometimes temporarily obtained by cuttings (*kasarāt*) for parts of equipment and fines, or by debasing the coinage — devices not unknown in more civilised states.

When in January 1847 the government of "the Lahore State," or what may more conveniently be called the Punjab, was put in commission, a number of Englishmen, most of them young military officers, were appointed as assistants to the Resident. The country was divided into inspection circles, and each officer at the end of his tour made a report to the Resident or quasi-Regent, Sir Henry Lawrence. Those reports testify to the general misery of the rural masses, Sikhs excepted, and the demoralisation of all classes of society. The *kārdārs* or district governors and tax-collectors having one and all paid heavily for their appointments, and having only a few precarious years of office wherein to meet the demands of the Durbar and their supporters at Lahore, and amass fortunes for themselves, were what the Resident called "the chief oppressors, being invariably judges and magistrates as well as collectors," and performing no action, good or bad, except for a sufficient fee or gratification.

Looking through the reports made in 1847, we find that the country between Attock and Peshawar was almost a waste from lawlessness, whilst the revenue-collectors and their village agents were "gorged with plunder." It was the same throughout the whole valley of the Indus. In every village were rival chieftains, one or other of whom acted as the kardar's assistant, receiving a share in the collections and military aid when wanted. "Each of such men," so ran the report, "has a body of horsemen, whom he pretends to pay, but who in reality live on the ryots, and are known to be engaged in most of the robberies which take place in a district," the employer either receiving a share of the plunder or restoring it when the bribe was high enough. From the Sutlej to the Indus, Lawrence himself reported to the Governor-General, "no one seems to have thought that the law was intended for any but the rich and powerful. The poor settled their affairs in their own way by village arbitrations, by the sabre, or the cudgel. . . . The only officers exercising judicial powers were those from whom the people required most protection: the kardars, holding jagirs or receiving salaries of from 1000 to 3000 rupees a-year, have had districts yielding from one to ten lakhs made over to them, to the plunder and harrying of which they would devote themselves with indefatigable zeal, leaving all their proper duties to be performed by hungry deputies on ten or twenty rupees a-month. . . . No punishment seems to have been inflicted on kardars except when defaulters to the state; they had, therefore, nothing to do but squeeze out of the ryots all that was to be squeezed above the government revenue. In this manner for years and years the State did not receive from some of the richest tracts in the Punjab a half or a quarter of what they actually yielded. It is true that Runjit Singh balanced the account in the end by plundering the families of his officials after their death; but during the last seven years the country has been much more the property of the kardars than of the Maharaja of the day."

Being a general picture in black tints, its effect is perhaps too sombre; for in Sikh, and in some degree in Hindu, Jat, and Rajput villages, the kardars were afraid to go to extremities with members of the dominant class or their supporters. Moreover, amongst the fifty odd kardars of the kingdom a few were men of considerable intelligence. Thus for twenty years Diwan Sawan Mull had governed the Multan province with such enlightenment that, whilst extracting the government share of the produce, from a half to a third, for himself, he protected the cultivators against further exactions by his subordinates; so great was the confidence felt in him that during his administration thousands of masonry irrigation-wells were sunk in places formerly desert. He died in 1845 and was succeeded by his son, Diwan Mulraj, whom circumstances drove into rebellion three years afterwards. The father had managed his district despotically, yet without overstepping his position as a mere revenue-farmer. The son, weak, vain, and grasping, aspired to rule as a sovereign, but had not the capacity to exact obedience from his own servants, hence during his short *régime* disorders reappeared, and the partially reclaimed pastoral tribes, outside the irrigated tracts in the neighbourhood of Multan, relapsed into their pristine state of barbarism. Reporting upon them, John Nicholson wrote, "The people are universally robbers, graziers, and trackers, or a combination of all, now feeding their flocks, now stealing their neighbours'." That description fairly represented, even for many years after annexation, the character of the rural population throughout the unirrigated jungle tracts of the Punjab. Under a strong executive indulgence in crimes of violence is always repressible, but the instinct remains, and on opportunity asserts itself so long as the pastoral condition continues.

In cleaning his Augean stable the Resident's first aims, under his enhanced powers, were to establish elementary justice, introduce order in the finances, and by paying off the arrears due to the troops and irregulars, gradually reduce the army to the scale prescribed at the time when peace was ratified, 15,000 infantry and 10,000 cavalry. As a first step in those directions rude courts of justice were established, a settlement of outstanding accounts was required from the kardars, and what is called a summary settlement was begun with the village communities—*i.e.*, a fixed cash assessment was offered to the best men of each, and on acceptance an engagement in writing taken for its regular payment.

Henry Lawrence's methods in establishing orderly rule based on justice between man and man differed widely from those followed by his brother John in the Jallandar Doab. John formulated commandments, each beginning "thou shalt" or "thou shalt not," and, like an angry Jove, launched his thunderbolts upon all who disobeyed. Henry, always gentle and considerate, sought to gain his ends by working through his Council of Eight, rewarding the good, showing patience with the obstructive, and shutting his eyes to much that was evil.

The loud-voiced gratitude of the people for the protection accorded to them, and the apparent acquiescence of their oppressors in the transfer of power to the English and the use they made of it, encouraged the Resident and his assistants to tighten their grip. Here and there the kardars were compelled to disgorge plunder and return it to their victims; Diwan Mulraj himself, hitherto left alone, was ordered to submit his accounts. Such proceedings pleased the labouring masses, but fanned the smouldering discontent of their former masters. Possibly Henry Lawrence trusted too much to the effects of a just administration, forgetting that the benefits of good laws certainly administered cannot be felt by those who have never known them: their necessity is only perceived when they have been long enjoyed. If so, the most politic method of winning the lately dominant Khalsa and their sirdars to ways of peace and order would have been by conciliating them, not the people whom they had victimised. Sympathising with both classes, loving justice, yet protecting privileges, Henry Lawrence strove to temper equality of treatment for all men with special consideration for those whom his reforms injured in status or income. For a time the ultimate success of his gentle methods appeared hopeful. In writing to the Governor-General early in the hot weather of 1847, after taking note of the dissatisfied elements in the population, he recorded that his "great wonder had been the good conduct of the Sikh army during the last twelve months, and the almost perfect quiet that had during the past five months pervaded the land."

Kindly and liberal as was the treatment of the beneficiaries under the superseded system, every reform necessarily caused injury to some interest; every reward bestowed, whether title, place, or money, offence to disappointed competitors; every act of justice for the wronged, loss of privilege for the wrong-doers. Of the sufferers from our reluctantly grasped usurpation of power, the greatest was Rani Jindan, the queen-mother. Not only had her chief paramour, Lal Singh, been torn from her arms and deported as a traitor, but she herself, until then supreme in the State, had been deprived of all share in the government and given as a sop an annuity of £15,000. She now hated the Resident as the cause of all her wrongs, hated the members of the Council, or Durbar as they were called, as the creatures of the English; above all she hated Tej Singh, her quondam supporter and admirer, as he was in favour with her enemies, and was about to receive from the hands of her son the title of Raja. That was the climax to her indignities. From brooding over them she now proceeded to action. She sought to enlist Maharaja Gulab Singh of Jammu and Diwan Mulraj, the kardar of Multan, in her cause, or, as she preferred to call it, in the cause of the suffering Khalsa, but both were too cautious to give her encouragement: she started a sort of political *salon* in Lahore, and her receptions were largely attended: she daily fed numbers of Brahmins and washed their feet, owing to which good Hindus and Sikhs praised her piety and forgave her profligacy. The Resident thought differently and gave her a scolding; he wrote to her officially that her conduct "in receiving fifteen or twenty sirdars at a time" and "feeding and washing the feet of fifty Brahmins within the private apartments of the palace" was "without precedent, and a breach of female decorum and royal etiquette"; he admonished her to only admit "her own servants and confidential followers" to her presence, and to dispense her charities "on the first of each month," and ended by advising her when talking with men to "sit behind the screen as do the princesses of other courts." The insulted lady, who was plentifully endowed with woman's wit, replied in a letter of stinging sarcasm, that as the Resident was in Lahore "solely for the sake of punishing the faithless servants of the state, defending the Maharaja and herself [myself], and protecting the people," he had better attend to his own business. Then she went on, "So long as the Maharaja is sovereign of his own kingdom, it is the same as if I was sovereign"—a sentence which the Resident interpreted to the Governor-General as meaning that she claimed the sovereignty for herself. Finally, after satirically traversing all Lawrence's assertions, she concluded, "It is a subject of deep congratulation to me that both the Maharaja and myself are now reaping the benefits of the friendship which Maharaja Runjit

Singh sowed with the Company. Continue, if you please, to give me good advice."

On the surface the quarrel was comical, and the Resident deserved his snubbing. In reality Lawrence penned his curious remonstrance in all earnestness, and the Rani her brilliant reply in bitterness of heart. It was now war to the knife between them. The Resident appealed to Calcutta, the Rani to her child —and others, including her brother, a worthless debauchee.

A few days after the comedy of the letters the Resident arranged that the boy Maharaja should invest a number of Sikh gentlemen with titles of honour, and amongst them Tej Singh, the Rani's particular aversion. The court astrologer having fixed the auspicious day, hour, and minute for the investiture,—8.17 A.M., August 2, 1847,—the ceremonial began. In due course Tej Singh, in resplendent robes, advanced to the throne on which sat the Maharaja, and making obeisance presented his face to his boy sovereign. Instead of dipping a finger into the dish containing the saffron paste, and making the yellow mark of rajaship on the smirking expectant's forehead, the little fellow, tutored previously no doubt by his mother, folded his arms, and curling himself up in his chair, looked defiance at the glittering throng of agitated men surrounding him. In the midst of the general consternation the high priest of the Sikhs was put forward and hurriedly completed the investiture.

Lawrence immediately reported the grave *contretemps* to the Governor-General, insisted that Raja Tej Singh's life was now in danger, called the Rani many hard names, and urged that she should be deported. Having despatched his letter, he prepared for the evening's function, a grand dinner-party, followed by fireworks, given to the English officers in Lahore. The Maharaja was to be present, as well as all the recipients of the morning's titles, and the members of Council, but the boy-king's mother refused to let him change his clothes. Once more the official world was in consternation, as the festivities would be a fiasco unless the Maharaja attended them. After much consultation amongst the high officers of state, the Rani's brother was told he must go and bring his nephew or, failing, he would be deprived of his jagirs. The child was then brought, but sat listless and silent, and would not look at the fireworks.

"Your Highness is out of spirits," uncle whispered to nephew; "shall I fetch a company and show you some sport?"

Happily the words were overheard and understood, and the "company" was not brought, otherwise the rejoicings would have ended in a massacre. The meaner conspirators were at once arrested, tried, and sentenced to various terms of imprisonment, but the chief offender, the queen-mother, was treated more leniently. In her case, though the finding amounted to "not proven," it was ordered that she should be separated from her son "with as little pain as possible" and confined in a fortress outside Lahore, and there looked after by "some respectable old attendants who have passed the age of passion." The question of who was to bell the cat now perturbed the Durbar. The Rani was still powerful, she might throw herself upon the protection of the army, refuse to leave Lahore or give up her child, and, if so, to incur her displeasure would be to risk one's life. The Resident cut the knot by deputing one of his assistants to carry out the orders, in conjunction with some of the less nervous members of the Durbar. The boy-king was inveigled to a picnic and there presented with a new mechanical toy. In his absence the queen-mother was removed, screaming as she entered her carriage she would "appeal to London," and holding tightly on to her jewel-case, in which were valuables worth £60,000. Her abduction accomplished, the little Maharaja was told of his bereavement. "But I have this," said the boy, holding up his toy. His mother was already less to him than a new plaything apparently, and he never mentioned her again. The army, too, received the news with indifference, being at the moment more interested in pension-rules than politics.

Thus the evil woman disappeared from the immediate scene of her triumphs, intrigues, and humiliations.

The Rani having ceased from troubling, Henry Lawrence, whose health had again failed, went on leave, his brother John acting for him. The difference between the two brothers was soon evident in every branch of the administration. Henry's hand, though firm, had been always warm and softly gloved. John's was hard as iron and never gloved. Henry had loved all men great and small, was loved by them in return, did not believe that Indian institutions were wholly bad or English wholly good, and expected to see the Maharaja rule alone in a few years; accordingly, in spite of his increased powers, he still preferred to effect changes gradually through orders emanating from the Durbar rather than from himself. John cared little for the feelings of the great,—most of them in this case discontented men,—sympathised generally with the small, and had no belief in Indian but perfect faith in English methods of rule. Naturally, then, he acted as if convinced that by a few months of rigorous administration upon English lines he could revolutionise a system of fifty years' growth and habits of mind evolved by the environments of centuries.

He at once proceeded to initiate and push root-and-branch reforms; he gave minute instructions to his assistants for carrying out the land-revenue settlement in every part of the Maharaja's kingdom, which he treated as if already conquered and annexed, and in his despatch on the subject to the Governor-General explained that by his "plan, the amount demandable from every village shall be defined with punctual return of the collections." He promised that the work would be completed within a year, and so confident of success was he that he wrote to his assistant at Peshawar, "I consider that you will have no difficulty in assessing the whole province in three months." The hastiness of this opinion may be judged from the fact that subsequently, after fifteen years of British administration, it took a large staff seven years of concentrated labour to effect the first regular settlement of each of the districts in the said "province." Having started his assessments, he next reformed the customs and excise systems, and then turned his attention to methodising the administration of justice by appointing the best men available as judges in different localities, and preparing codes and rules of procedure for their guidance. In other departments he was equally energetic; for instance, he appointed a Postmaster-

General and introduced the penny post, reporting with satisfaction after the scheme had been tried for a few weeks that in six days 150 letters, for each one of which one anna had been prepaid, had been despatched from Lahore to Peshawar. In the delicate field of domestic politics he was not less decided. Thus, he annulled the Sikh law which forbade the *azan* or Muhammadan call for prayers being cried in the hearing of Hindus, and regarding kardars, whose payments were in arrears,—some of them men hitherto quasi-sovereigns within their respective jurisdictions,—as mere revenue defaulters, ordered them to settle their accounts at once, and if they failed imprisoned them like felons. Except for a fortnight in October whilst his brother Henry, still in broken health, was at Lahore, John ruled as autocrat until the end of the year.

His enthusiasm for what he called in his December report to the Governor-General "carrying out the different plans which had been laid down for the amelioration of the condition of the people, and the improvement of the finances of the [Maharaja's] Government," was unbounded. In the same despatch he stated: "The assessment of the land-tax is progressing admirably. The Durbar have resigned all control over it. . . . I am sanguine that in another three months the whole assessment of the Punjab will be determined and recorded; a change to the benefit of the agriculturists, which no one, not conversant with the enormous evils of the former system, can fully appreciate." A little further on, after explaining how he had effected a saving of £6000 a-year by discharging a number of superfluous regimental accountants, he naïvely remarked that his action had created "much sensation," adding, "Nothing in my mind shows more clearly the necessity of full interference and thorough scrutiny into every charge than this reduction." In concluding this despatch he mentioned that Diwan Mulraj was in Lahore and wished to resign, as the new customs and assessment systems had reduced his income. "It will be well to get rid of the Diwan" in a year or so, was John's view, as he had no one to spare for Multan at the time. A few weeks later he reported that "the accounts of the large farmers and great officers of state, which have so long been under scrutiny, have been disposed of, with the exception of Sirdar Ranjore Singh's. Diwan Mulraj is in confinement, and his balances in train of liquidation." Such a sentence shows that the Acting Resident was no respecter of persons. To treat dignitaries, who for years had exercised despotic powers within their principalities, like common defaulters and malefactors may have been justice but was not wisdom. In the sequel Diwan Mulraj led the upheaval at Multan, which ended in the battle of Gujerat. Not only were the "great officers of state" subjected to personal indignities, but the jagirdars or feudal barons, who held half their fiefs on service conditions, were mulcted of most of their perquisites. They could not have expected generosity from the man who, according to his brother, regarded them "as nuisances and enemies," but ordinary prudence demanded that they should not be publicly insulted and driven into rebellion. When they objected that his reforms were impoverishing them, he reminded them that they had already recouped themselves by calling "men in buckram" "retainers in chain armour," and added that they might dismiss their paper contingents if they liked, "the government to have the benefit of half the saving and they of the other." "To this," he informed the Governor-General, "they all demurred, but it had the effect of silencing all complaints." Quite so: they ceased to protest and began to plot. What they had been doing was the practice in feudal times, both in Europe and Asia. Provided that each fief-holder turned out for service with his proper contingent in war-time, the State was wisely oblivious to the number of men-at-arms he kept up in peace-time.

John Lawrence, however, at this period of his career, thought more of measures than of men; he would not or could not perceive the growing impatience of the classes with his hard exactitude in business, and disregard for what they considered their rights or perquisites. To the last day of his retention of the post of Acting Resident his reports show that politically he was blind, seeing things only from the standpoint of the energetic district and settlement officer, posted to a backward tract in a British province, and not as British Resident holding extraordinary powers for a few years in a warlike kingdom, which would shortly be absolutely autonomous, if not independent.

On January 12, 1848, Lord Dalhousie, the new Governor-General, landed in Calcutta, and in the following week Lord Hardinge, accompanied by Henry Lawrence, sailed for England, after assuring his successor that "it would not be necessary to fire a gun in India for seven years to come." The paper outlook justified the too confident assumption of a long period of peace, for up to the day on which the slighted Mulraj unsheathed the sword at Multan the Punjab was continuously reported to be "perfectly tranquil."

From John Lawrence's despatches it is clear that the idea that his sweeping reforms and harsh treatment of some of the leading sirdars might induce a rising never occurred to him. He was so engrossed in revenue details that he wrote and thought of little else. He made over charge of the Residentship to Sir Frederick Currie on March 8, 1848, but remained at Lahore to the end of the month, on the last day of which he sent a lengthy letter to the Government of India, chiefly on revenue matters. He mentioned in it that Multan "by the new arrangement consequent on Mulraj's resignation might yield an increase of four or five lakhs." Exactly a fortnight after that letter was written Mr Vans Agnew and Lieutenant Anderson, sent to receive the Diwan's resignation, were murdered, and the man whom Lawrence had imprisoned as a revenue-defaulter, and, for the settlement of whose affairs, Lawrence had reported that the deputation to Multan of "one of the junior assistants" would suffice, had placed himself at the head of the final struggle of the Sikhs to shake off the English yoke.

Whether John Lawrence's conduct of affairs during the eight months preceding the Multan outbreak goaded the Sikh leaders into rising against us, or merely precipitated a contest which was inevitable, cannot be determined. This much, however, is certain :—he rushed his reforms with indiscreet haste, and treated many of the proud sensitive chiefs of the country with contumely, and thus transgressed his instructions both in spirit and letter. These facts are undeniable, hence on his head rests the chief responsibility for the universal odium in which Sikhs of all classes regarded the English dominion throughout 1848.

Lord Hardinge in July 1847, shortly before John Lawrence had been appointed Acting Resident, had carefully defined the limits of power created by the "unlimited" control agreement of the preceding December. "Our position," his Excellency laid down, "is not that of active agents, but of friendly advisers, with the power, where necessary, of enforcing our advice, and, when justice cannot otherwise be obtained, of directly acting ourselves; but this must be the last resource." From the day on which John Lawrence took over office from his brother he ignored that instruction; he treated the Maharaja's kingdom as British territory, and compressed into a few months a series of revolutionary changes which should have been spread over as many years, and then only after the country had been subdued and annexed. His palliation was that retrenchment was the necessary preliminary to administrative reforms, and that unless the privileged plunderers of the state were summarily restrained, not only would the charges for the maintenance of the British garrison —£240,000 annually—never be paid, but the State itself would become bankrupt.

That Sir F. Currie was soon convinced that his predecessor had exceeded his duty and created a dangerous situation is evident from his first lengthy despatch to the Government of India, written on April 5, a month after his arrival in Lahore. Whilst admitting that "perfect tranquillity prevails, at present, throughout all the territories under the

Lahore Government," and that he had "no reason to think that the apparent contentment of the people is other than real," he wrote: "I could wish that our interference with these details [financial matters] had been less, but it is impossible now to recede. . . . In the judicial department, also, our interference with details has gone further than was at first intended." And a little further on he remarks plaintively: "I do not like to make alterations, where not absolutely necessary, in rules that have so lately been introduced by the Resident; but some of these rules must be modified — for instance, in civil cases, the rule of limitation has been fixed for suits for real property at sixty years! I need hardly remark that the whole property of the country has changed hands and the whole state of society has been altered, in all its elements, two or three times, during the revolutions that have taken place in these parts within the period."

CHAPTER VI.

THE CALL TO ARMS.

CURRIE'S further criticisms on his predecessor's administration were cut short by the outbreak at Multan already referred to, a veritable "bolt from the blue" to our reforming zealots. Mr Vans Agnew, a young civilian of promise, had been selected to rule the province after receiving the resignation of Diwan Mulraj, its much-worried governor. Lieutenant W. A. Anderson was to accompany Vans Agnew as his assistant, whilst, to preserve appearances, a Sikh gentleman was nominated by the Durbar as titular successor to the Diwan. As the weather was warm, the beginning of April, the mission peaceful, and the distance considerable—220 miles—the Englishmen, lazily inclined, dropped down the Sutlej by boat instead of marching with their escort of Durbar troops, which included a regiment of Ghurkhas. By the 18th they were all encamped in the Idgah, a mosque and garden about half a mile from the Multan Fort. The Englishmen occupied the building, their escort the garden surrounding it. Next morning the two Sahibs, with the Diwan and two companies of Ghurkhas, made a cursory inspection of the fort. The Ghurkhas having relieved the

Diwan's guard at one of the gates, the mounted party turned to leave, the local soldiery hanging about them and impeding progress. As they were passing out one of the Diwan's officers demanded of the Diwan what his orders were.

"You are the Sahib's servant now; ask him," Mulraj replied with a shrug.

"When I have had my discharge I shall know," returned the man, scowling at the Englishmen.

"Don't fear; the Diwan's servants shall be as mine," hastily interposed Vans Agnew.

The party then pushed on through the sullen crowd, and had reached the drawbridge when a Muhammadan irregular thrust at Agnew with his spear, knocked him off his horse, and cut at him with his talwar as he lay on the ground. Cries and confusion followed. A dozen swords were drawn; Anderson received many cuts; the Diwan, unnerved and helpless, was surrounded and hustled away by his shouting followers. The two wounded Englishmen, now left alone with some of their own people, were taken to the Idgah. Next day it was bombarded from the fort and from guns dragged into the open. Until nightfall the escort blazed away wildly, and then, further defence being hopeless, under cover of the darkness went over to the stronger side. Out of a round thousand men hardly one remained faithful. Had our officers marched with their guard from Lahore results might have been different; the Ghurkhas, foreign mercenaries with neither wrongs nor slights to avenge, would perhaps have been true to Vans Agnew and Anderson. Unfortunately, they and their escort were strangers to each other. As the defenders slunk away from their posts, the mob outside, soldiery and city ruffians, closed in upon the Idgah, howling and tom-toming all round it. The end came quickly. Vans Agnew dragged himself to his more severely wounded comrade's cot, and the two friends met death quietly, their hands clasped in the grip of farewell. The murderers looted the place and carried their victims' heads as trophies to the Diwan. They found him sitting silent and dejected amongst his men, more prisoner than master. The heads were thrown down at his feet, and the wretched Diwan, in the grip of his fate, roused himself from his brooding, and, in response to the demands for rewards, ordered golden bracelets and money to be given to the murderers. From that hour until the end came he fought a bad cause with skill and determination, and, though eventually he was convicted of aiding and abetting the murders of the two British officers, there is no doubt that he rather let the catastrophe happen than actively contrived it.

That spear-thrust into Agnew's side was the immediate cause of the second Sikh war and the series of great events which followed it. That the last struggle of the Sikhs for independence should have been begun by a Khatri, the first blow struck by a Muhammadan, and the rising officially termed by us a "rebellion" against the Sikh Government, though in reality it was an attempt to throw off our domination, are amongst the curiosities of history.

The Rubicon crossed, the Diwan passed from self-helpless drifting to bold initiative. He sent inflammatory proclamations throughout the Punjab, particularly all up and down the Indus frontier, a tract wholly inhabited by Pathans, Baluches, and other Muhammadan tribes. He prepared his small strong fort for a siege, filled it with food-supplies and military stores, and remedied its deficiency in guns by spade-work on its mud walls, ditches, and underground galleries and chambers. He had few trained soldiers,—no Sikh regulars at all, apparently, other than those who had deserted,—but by the offer of good pay he attracted thousands of lawless swashbucklers and fanatics to his standard.

Some weeks passed, and to all appearance the Sikh army, about 25,000 men in all, most of them drilled, fed, and paid under the direct supervision of English officers, had no sympathy with the Multan rebels, who as yet were mostly Muhammadans. In point of fact the outbreak had taken the Khalsa by surprise. Their regiments were widely scattered, and communication between them was slow and uncertain. More than half of the troops were distributed throughout the Muhammadan districts west of the Jhelam, from 2000 to 5000 men being located in each of the following localities: Hazara, Peshawar, Bannu, and the Derajat. In the two last-named tracts the aggregate was perhaps 7000, half at Bannu, and the balance at different centres farther south. Left to themselves, the men collectively were not discontented. Well and regularly paid, lightly worked, enjoying liberal hot-weather leave rules, and prospective pensions, they might have gradually acquiesced in the passing of power to the disinterested English, had not disturbing influences, culminating in that untoward incident at Multan and the long delay in punishment which followed it, driven them and their ease-loving sirdars, already exasperated under the grip of John Lawrence's iron hand, into making one more effort to preserve the Punjab for themselves. For some time the restless Rani from her easy confinement in the fort of Shekhapura, only a morning's ride from Lahore, had been intriguing with the sirdars, sending emissaries amongst the Sikh soldiers, and even tampering with our Hindustani sepoys in Lahore, and, all unknown to John Lawrence, the yeast had been working. When the conspiracy was discovered the lady was deported to Ferozepore and thence to Benares, whence she was afterwards allowed to escape to Nipal, where she ended her days.

Though the "Jezebel of the Punjab," as she was called, had been removed, it was too late to undo the evil wrought by her and others, and in a sense caused by the Acting Resident's usurpation of all authority in the State. The malcontent Sikhs were as little prepared for the rising in Multan as was the Government of India. It was premature, unpremeditated, and wholly disconcerting to both sides. The components of the Sikh army, isolated as each garrison was in the midst of their hereditary enemies—the Musalmans of the Western Punjab—now watched and suspected by the English, found concerted action impossible; moreover, amongst them the cautious waverers still outnumbered the patriotic enthusiasts.

Two days after the outbreak a note from Vans Agnew, written immediately after the assault on himself and his assistant, reached Lieutenant Edwardes, who was in charge of the frontier from Bannu southwards. Edwardes at once called on the Nawab of Bhawalpore, the only remaining Muhammadan power in the Punjab, to aid him in attacking the Diwan, and at the same time, by freely enlisting the Pathans and Baluches of the Lower Indus and blooding them in some small actions, secured the aid of the Musulman population of the country in the impending struggle with their hereditary foes and oppressors, the Sikhs. Throughout May the gathering of forces continued. By the middle of June the Diwan, Nawab, and Edwardes had each an army of some 10,000 men in the field, none very anxious to fight, and all three waiting for something to happen—the Diwan for a general Sikh rising, his opponents for the support of British troops and guns, which, in spite of arguments and entreaties, were not sent. The Government of India had decided to let the Punjab abscess come to a head, and when ripe to lance it freely in the coming cold weather; meanwhile the hope was expressed that the family physicians—the Durbar—in consultation with the local surgeons—Edwardes and the Nawab—would succeed in localising the trouble: at the right time the big Simla celebrity—Lord Gough—would descend with his assistants from their cool retreat, and by drastic treatment render any recurrence of the disease impossible.

To drop metaphor, the Government of India, having no trust in the good faith of the Durbar and little in the fighting worth of the Muhammadan levies raised by Edwardes and the Nawab, was convinced that the wisest policy was to be done with half measures; if the Sikhs were so blind to their own interests as to side with the rebel Mulraj, they would have full opportunity throughout the hot months, in which case they would be finally crushed at leisure and their country annexed; this could most conveniently be done in the ensuing cold weather, by which time — if the Sikhs meant rising *en masse* — their whole army and nation would be committed. Holding these views, the Resident was notified that no British troops would be moved to Multan until after the rains, when if necessary a British army of 24,000 men with 50 siege-guns, "exclusive of field and horse artillery, would take the field."

Meanwhile the Durbar, pressed by the perplexed Resident to take strong measures, had collected a considerable force, and marched it two-thirds of the way to Multan, where it was halted. "It is composed," Sir Frederick Currie wrote (June 13) to Edwardes, "of all the sirdars in the Punjab almost, the Jaghirdars' horse, Sher Singh's own artillery, and the two regiments supposed to be best affected and most subordinate." He then explained that he was afraid to allow it to advance farther, as "the whole Sikh army is faithless to the Maharaja,"—in other words, hostile to the British,—and then he added the quaint remark, "A strong desire to aid Mulraj pervades all the soldiers, but they are not heroes enough to join a falling standard."

By the end of the month Edwardes and the Nawab, with their Muhammadan levies, had gained two small victories over the Diwan, driven his levies into Multan, and taken up a position about two miles from the fort. Reassured by these successes, the Resident now took the bit between his teeth and ordered General Whish with a division and 60 guns, about 5000 fighting men in all, to proceed to Multan and reduce the fort, at the same time instructing Sher Singh to resume his march and co-operate. In justifying this assumption of responsibility to Lord

Dalhousie and the Chief, Sir F. Currie wrote, "We now have a faithful army in our interest of about 30,000 Muhammadans with 30 guns investing Multan, and merely requiring British skill and British siege *matériel* to enable them to reduce the fort." Thus forced, the Government of India, whilst recording their "adherence to their former determination in abstaining from moving British troops upon Multan at this season of the year," and washing their hands of the consequences, refrained from interfering with the Resident's action, and, anxious for economy, suspended their preparations for a big cold-weather campaign.

The general situation would now have been hopeful for the Maharaja's, or rather British, cause but for the fact that as fast as the Diwan's Muhammadan adherents deserted him, Sikh recruits from all parts of the Punjab joined him, mostly in small parties. So far the Sikh regulars in their distant and isolated cantonments had not committed themselves. Each garrison was waiting for news from Multan; if General Whish captured its fort, they would risk nothing; if he failed, or Sher Singh went over to the Diwan, they would all rise, and crying, "Wah Guru ji ki fatha!" (Hurrah! victory for the Guru!"), kill as many English as they could and fight to the last man in a holy war.

The die was soon cast. It was now September: General Whish and Sher Singh had joined "the 30,000 Muhammadans with 30 guns investing Multan," and for days the English general had been deliberating on the best method for capturing town and fort. The decision arrived at was that the risks attending an assault were too great unless

Sher Singh and his force should first withdraw to such a distance as would render their participation in any form impossible. Whether influenced by our vacillation or distrust of himself, or the news of Sikh disaffection in Hazara, Sher Singh on the morning of September 14 suddenly ordered the *dharm-ka-dhosa* or holy-war-drum to be beaten, went over with his contingent of 5000 men to the Diwan, and issued a proclamation to the Khalsa that he had done so by direction of the Guru, "with a view to extirpate or expel the tyrannical and crafty Feringhees."

His defection ended doubts, and caused General Whish to raise the siege, and retire to a defensible position, some miles from Multan, there to await the arrival of reinforcements. When the news reached Lord Dalhousie at Calcutta he at once ordered the resumption of the suspended preparations for war on a large scale, the increase of the native army by 17,000 men, the despatch of a strong division of the Bombay army up the Indus to Multan, and the relief of the depleted garrisons of Bengal by troops drawn from Madras. Having initiated the movements which were to destroy Sikh independence for ever, and enable him to annex what remained of the Punjab by right of conquest, the Governor-General, thorough and self-reliant in all his measures, announced to his Council his intention of proceeding to the theatre of war to "regulate our proceedings with reference to the Punjab."

Sher Singh's summons to a holy war reached Chattar Singh, his father, who was titular governor of Hazara and commander of the Sikh forces there, at a time when the irascible old gentleman, between twinges of gout and testiness at his treatment by his bear-leader, Captain Abbott, the local political officer, was in an uncommonly bad temper. He was a Sikh of the old school, lord of many villages, and, until curbed by the Lawrences, a consistent despoiler of the weak. Runjit Singh and all his doings were his admiration, the English and all theirs his detestation. He had gone to Hazara intent on harrying the Muhammadans of the country, but had been thwarted in this Sikh-like object by Captain Abbott, who was a real *gharib-parwar* or "protector of the poor," hence the two men who ought to have worked together in friendly accord were antagonistic from the first, the one looking on the peasantry as creatures to be stamped upon, the other as freemen to be elevated. Each made many complaints about the other to Lahore. Soon after the Multan outbreak Abbott, rightly or wrongly, came to the conclusion that Chattar Singh was a traitor, and attempted to isolate him and his troops by occupying the passes leading down to the plains with the Muhammadan tribesmen of the country. For a time the old gentleman sulked, protested, and plotted; at last, early in November, when his plans were mature, he broke into open rebellion, brushed aside Abbott's levies, and marched off towards Attock, whereupon the Sikh garrisons of Peshawar, Bannu, and elsewhere followed his example.

At first they had no common leader. Each body, whether brigade or single battalion, was an independent unit in motion towards some larger body, all influenced by the idea of rendezvousing towards Gujerat and swooping down upon Lahore before Multan should fall or the tardy British be strong enough to bar the way. From the time when Chattar Singh emerged from the mountains of Hazara he became the directing brain of the national movement. His first objects were to effect a junction with the Peshawar troops, wrest the Attock fort from the small Muhammadan garrison which still held it in the interests of the English, and induce the Amir of Kabul to aid him with an Afghan contingent. To promote his ends he agreed to restore Peshawar and Kohat to the Afghans, thus surrendering to the hereditary enemies of his people districts upon the conquest and retention of which Runjit Singh had been spending blood and treasure for the last twenty years of his reign. He also attempted to draw the wily Ulysses of Jammu, Gulab Singh, into the combination against the English. Meanwhile the rival leaders of the rising at Multan, mutually jealous and suspicious, were acting independently, hence Sher Singh readily accepted his father's plan of campaign, and, leaving the Diwan to his fate, marched northwards in the direction of Lahore, looting and burning the Muhammadan villages on his route.

Before the end of November the concentration of forces for what, after one lamentable British blunder, was to prove the Armageddon of Sikh independence, was well advanced. In the north-west angle of the Punjab plain Chattar Singh was in command of 12,000 good troops, supplemented by 30 guns and an unreliable contingent of Afghan horse, whilst his son Sher Singh was holding the line of the Chenab between Ramnagar and Wazirabad with his own command of 5000 men and 15 to 20 guns,—the pick of the Khalsa army,—and recruits by the hundred were daily flocking to his standard from all parts of the country.

Conscious of the Khalsa inferiority to the English, and anxious to obtain honourable terms, or defer the inevitable issue of the war, Sher Singh, in conjunction with all the chiefs of his party, sent on November 24 detailed statements of the national grievances to the Governor-General, Commander-in-Chief, and Resident at Lahore. The complaints were made nominally against the faithlessness of the Durbar—the fiction that its members constituted the governing body being maintained — but really against the English, who, whilst always professing to desire the stability of the Sikh Government, had "never had at heart the welfare of the Maharaja's kingdom," had used Runjit Singh as their tool, had appropriated eighteen lakhs[1] of Sikh revenue in the cis-Sutlej states, had after the Sutlej campaign—nominally undertaken to punish an army in rebellion against the Maharaja—proved the hollowness of their friendship by fining him two and a half crores[1] of rupees, dismembering his kingdom, seizing a crore of treasure, reducing the State receipts from land-revenue and customs, and throwing a charge of twenty-one lakhs a-year on the Sikhs for the maintenance of a British garrison at Lahore. Sher Singh next complained that the Resident had degraded and punished the sirdars most trusted by Runjit Singh, and rewarded and promoted traitors, sycophants, and incompetents like Tej Singh, and that the British politicals, particularly Captain Abbott in Hazara, Major George Lawrence in Peshawar, and later Major Edwardes in Bannu, had so distrusted and

[1] A lakh was then worth rather more than £10,000, a crore rather more than a million sterling.

aggrieved loyal Sikh gentlemen as to have driven them into taking up arms to protect themselves against further indignities.

The document fairly represented the grievances of Sikh conservatives, and demonstrated that the attempt honestly made, in the insolence of superior British virtue, to force an administration of the regulation Anglo-Indian type upon the Punjab, without first conquering the country, was, even if justifiable, too hasty. By 1854, the year fixed as that in which the little Maharaja should attain his majority, Henry Lawrence might have succeeded in creating a well-ordered state, but by that time it would have been bankrupt and indebted to the extent of nearly two millions sterling to the paramount Power. John Lawrence, by trying to accomplish in a few months what his brother would have failed to do in many years, undoubtedly supplied a colour of truth to the complaints formulated in the memorial.

However, the time for discussion was over. The quarrel had now to be fought out to its foregone conclusion. Inspired by Chattar Singh and his son, Sher Singh, the Khalsa, unable to stem the tide of reforms and recover their lost dominion, were grimly determined to die sword and musket in hand. Their bitterness and that of some of the sirdars of the "old Sikh" school was intelligible and even honourable to them, but that of the two leaders just named, unless wholly ascribable to patriotism, cannot be so easily explained. Neither had any personal cause for dissatisfaction with John Lawrence or English methods in general. Chattar Singh had been allowed to retain his large estates, however acquired, his daughter had recently been betrothed to the Maharaja, and Sher

Singh, his son, destined presently to prove himself the one capable general produced by either war, had been the most popular Sikh gentleman in Lahore, his "frank and bold manner," as Henry Lawrence described his bearing, and his skill in field-sports making him a favourite with the Lawrences, the officers of the British garrison, and the Sikh gentry generally.

CHAPTER VII.

OPENING OF THE CAMPAIGN.

When the Sikh manifesto reached Lord Dalhousie (December 2), he was at Ambala on his leisurely way to the scene of operations. He directed the Resident to inform the "memorialists," as he called the nineteen signatories, "that his only answer will be the advance of the British army." In point of fact, what Henry Lawrence sarcastically termed "the grand *shikār* [hunt] in the cold season under the lead of the Governor-General" had already begun and an action had been fought.

From the raising of the siege of Multan (September 14), owing to Sher Singh's defection, until towards the end of November, our Lahore garrison had been, as the Resident complained to the Chief, "menaced and hemmed in by rebels." On one occasion Sher Singh's horsemen had swept round the city and partially burnt the bridge of boats over the Ravi, not two miles from our cantonment. All that time the Government of India were quietly carrying out their set plan of collecting a large and perfectly equipped army at Ferozepore, not a regiment of which was to be moved thence until all was prepared for a grand and overpowering advance.

The Government had assumed that the initiative lay with them, that the "rebels" would await attack until the aged Chief should come down from Simla, set what was officially designated "the army of the Punjab" in motion, and crush the "rebellion" at a blow. Sher Singh's bold activity disconcerted both Governor-General and Chief, and constrained them to strengthen the Lahore garrison. Meanwhile the Sikh general was concentrating upon the Chenab, in the vicinity of which he was joined by the troops from Bannu and Hazara. By the end of October the forces under his immediate command numbered 28,000 men, and only lacked more and better artillery to be really formidable. Sher Singh's opportunity for a dash upon Lahore had now passed, for Brigadier Cureton at the head of 7000 men had crossed the Ravi, and was covering all approaches from the west to the bridge of boats and city. Early in November most of our unwieldy forces, clogged by an attachment of followers many times as numerous as the fighting men, had been drawn together, and were being slowly pushed forward to Lahore. The difficulties of transport, never wholly surmounted, were being gradually overcome; but the general advance was still delayed, as owing to lack of carriage some of the grand army's components, including the siege-train, were still weeks behind.

Movements that autumn were unusually slow, as the rains had ceased early, and the weather throughout September and October was consequently abnormally hot. The dragging march through the sandy and frequently waterless country between Delhi and Ferozepore had been peculiarly trying to men and animals alike. At Ferozepore about ten per cent of the troops, particularly the British infantry, were prostrate from fever, and followers and quadrupeds alike were in worse condition, food-stuffs of all kinds being at famine prices. On the march the expectation that Ferozepore, the immediate base of operations, would prove an oasis of rest and plenty had helped to energise all men; but when they arrived there it was found to be, as the 'Journal of a Subaltern' describes it, "such a hole—a row of dreary bungalows and barracks looking out disconsolately and sourly on the bleak plain: not the faintest suspicion of a tree or a vestige of herbage for ten miles round." From Ludhiana to Ferozepore, and thence to Lahore, the enemy's horsemen and bands of marauding villagers hung round each unit, murdered stragglers, and cut off camels at browse; but through it all the British soldier was cheerful, buoyant at the thought of another fight with "them Seiks," and Jack Sepoy, encouraged by his white comrades' enthusiasm, was hopeful that this time there would be no Ferozeshah.

During the halt at Ferozepore camp rumours, authentic and otherwise, were eagerly canvassed by the troops. When they heard that Sher Singh, having quarrelled with the Diwan, was nearing Lahore intent on sueing for peace, they used hard language: he was a poor creature after all; as a gentleman he had been bound to make a fight of it after causing so much trouble. Their anger was changed to merriment when news came that a large convoy of supplies for General Whish's camp at Multan had been captured by the Diwan, who, lucky man, had drunk all the brandy, and mistaking the tins of preserved provisions for canister-shot, had fired nothing else for three days into the British camp, thus providing the messes with luxuries which would last till Christmas.

Towards the end of October good rain fell, ushering in the cold weather with a rush. The health of the big camp at once improved, and new arrivals began to look like weathered Englishmen instead of the sickly pale-faced nondescripts of a fortnight before. The change from heat to cold invigorated all ranks: preparations for the general advance were now pushed with a will: Brigadier Cureton was sent with most of the cavalry division to cover Lahore, and keep in touch with Sher Singh, who was believed to be concentrating his forces in the neighbourhood of Ramnagar on the Chenab. The army of the Punjab, convinced at last that the Sikhs would fight, and that there would be no waiting for the fall of Multan, as the Bombay column, under orders to reinforce General Whish, could not reach him before Christmas, was in the highest spirits. The Chief was now daily expected, and his arrival meant hard knocks and an end to the firm of Messrs Sher Singh & Co.

Meanwhile Brigadier Cureton had carried out his orders and established himself in the middle of the Rechna Doab, over fifty miles west of Lahore, and only eight from Ramnagar. On November 16 Brigadier Colin Campbell, afterwards Lord Clyde, joined Cureton at the front with a strong force. Sikhs and British were now in position opposite each other, a flat sandy plain between them, each side receiving almost daily accretions of strength. On November 21 Lord Gough arrived in camp—a Commander-in-Chief in leading strings, for behind him was the Governor-General, little more than half his age, directing and controlling his actions. The army knew the fact, and chafed at the restraint imposed upon their veteran leader by the imperious young civilian at the head of the Government of India. Lord Dalhousie, then thirty-seven, had more confidence in himself as war-lord than in all the generals in the field. He had enjoined Lord Gough to confine his operations to the Chenab, intending to await the fall of Multan and the arrival of the laggard siege-train before he should permit the advance into the Chaj Doab, which was to end the war. The old Chief thought differently; he had 15,000 men within striking distance of the enemy, whose numbers did not greatly exceed his own, and he was told that that enemy, in bravado or to practise his inexperienced artillerists, had been for days cannonading space within sight of the British outposts. Lord Gough came, saw, and listened; his fighting instincts were roused; his instructions permitted him at least to clear the line of the Chenab; by a quick secret movement of cavalry and flying artillery he might surprise half of Sher Singh's army, which lay astride of the river about Ramnagar. Ordering infantry and field-guns to follow, he started at 3 A.M. on November 22, a few hours after he had joined his army, at the head of the 3rd and 14th Dragoons, three regiments of native cavalry, and two batteries of horse artillery, and made a dash upon Ramnagar. As he approached he saw the Sikhs streaming away over the sands of the river in apparently hurried retreat to the farther bank, which was high and abrupt, whereas that on his side was low and level. Guns and cavalry galloped forwards right into the treacherous sands: the guns opened upon the Sikhs now nearing the opposite bank; immediately from masked positions along that bank their fire was returned by heavier ordnance: the shot fell amongst our men and horses, ours barely reached the stream of the river 500 yards away. Our guns were limbered up and taken out of range—all but one stuck helplessly in the sand. It was abandoned, whereupon a rush to capture and remove it was made by crowds of Sikh marksmen, who had been lying in ambush about a small green sand-girt oasis close by. A squadron of the 3rd Dragoons, well supported by the 8th Bengal Cavalry, seeing their opportunity, charged several times; but the ground being impracticable, were withdrawn. Realising the position, the Sikhs swarmed towards the abandoned gun. Colonel Havelock at the head of the 14th Dragoons rode towards it: their gallop fell to a trot and then to a walk, so heavy was the sand. The colonel fell; his men were now floundering in the quicksands: their brigadier (Cureton) made a dash to extricate them and succeeded, but was himself shot dead. After that there was nothing to be done but to retire and return to camp. Taken as a whole, the action from inception to closing disaster was unfortunate, one of those impetuous ventures, frequent at the beginning of campaigns, which prove the high courage of the troops engaged and the inexperience or rashness of their leaders. Had the attack taught Lord Gough's brigadiers and colonels to keep their heads cool, there would have been some compensation for our casualties and the loss of the gun.

After his rebuff the Chief sat still for a week, waiting for reinforcements and the now clearly indispensable heavy guns. During the delay much spade-work was done, and cover for batteries was gradually pushed forward right into the broad hot-weather bed of the river, facing the position held by Sher Singh. That general from his own bank watched Lord Gough's preparations for a frontal attack with much satisfaction. As if to assure us he had no intention of moving, he allowed his gunners for the next week to bang away day and night, thereby expending much powder and tons of iron, but doing no damage, as the distance to our most advanced shelter was about 1300 yards, the shooting wild, and the projectiles buried themselves in the sand wherever they fell.

On the 30th the siege-guns arrived, two days over time. The officer commanding had discovered a small fort midway between Lahore and Ramnagar, which was still held by a Sikh garrison, and as it lay close to our line of communications, had stopped to take and demolish it. Why the British army had not done so weeks before was due to the fact that in those days armies moved blindly. Confident that his guns now outranged those of Sher Singh, Lord Gough resolved to turn his position, supporting the flank movement by a frontal attack. To this end he ordered a force of 7000 men to move up the left bank of the Chenab, cross by the nearest practicable ford, supposed to be only eight miles above Ramnagar, and march down the right bank upon the enemy's left flank. As the success of the turning movement depended on the secrecy with which the passage of the river should be effected, the expeditionary force was ordered to march soon after midnight. By 1 A.M. on December 1 the troops were under arms; but the night was dark, the camp-followers noisy, and, for a portion of the infantry, no guide to the rendezvous had been provided. Thus the start was delayed until after 3 A.M., and when, after dawn, the vicinity of the ford was reached, its exact position was only discovered by the presence of a detachment of Sikh troops on the opposite bank. Brigadier Campbell, always cautious, advised a return to camp; but Sir Joseph Thackwell, the major-general in command, decided to trust to his luck and try for a higher ford. Sending on in advance Lieutenant Nicholson —the John Nicholson of subsequent Mutiny fame— with a party of his Pathan horse to Wazirabad, twelve miles farther up the river, Thackwell pushed on to that town, and there found that the Pathans had secured seventeen large boats. Though it was now late, and the troops had marched over twenty miles, some of the infantry with a few guns were at once embarked, whilst the irregular cavalry plunged into the water and tried to hit off the fords of the several streams as best they could. Those in the boats got across, those who waded failed and passed the night on spits of sand in the bed of the river: the general with the bulk of his command remained on the left bank. With the return of daylight the passage was gradually accomplished, and by midday Thackwell and all his men stood trans-Chenab in a strange country, without guides and without knowledge of the movements of the enemy. About 2 P.M. he began his march down the right high bank of the river, and before darkness came on had covered twelve miles. During the night he received an order from Lord Gough to give battle in the morning in support of the pre-arranged frontal attack; but when he had advanced a few miles he was met by a new order to stand fast until reinforced by Brigadier Godby's brigade, which was crossing by a ford said to have been discovered only six miles above Ramnagar. Thackwell at once halted, and, having seen no signs of the enemy, arranged his bivouac on grassy ground in the vicinity of the hamlets of the large village of Sadullapur. Suddenly shells began bursting among his men. Dispositions to meet the impending attack were at once made, the infantry were ordered to lie down, the artillery to push forward. From 11 A.M. to 4 P.M. the guns on both sides played at long bowls, doing little execution, and then the cannonading ceased. As neither force had shown any desire for close fighting, Thackwell's losses were small, 73 men, the enemy's perhaps more.

Next morning the discovery was made that the Sikhs had retreated, — disappeared southwards apparently,—and Thackwell had to decide whether to follow or wait for fresh orders. He took the latter course:—Godby's brigade had failed to join him, the ford had proved a ferry, the pontoon-train a useless encumbrance, the main army was still standing inactive cis-Chenab, and the enemy was still intact somewhere in the jungles, a protection which tended to neutralise the advantages of discipline.

Though the sound of the guns at Sadullapur and the feeble response to the bombardment of the Sikh position opposite Ramnagar indicated that Sher Singh had either evacuated his lines or detailed a large force to meet Thackwell operating on his left flank, Lord Gough had allowed the day to pass without attempting to cross the river.

Such want of initiative in the old Chief, indeed the vacillation which characterised all his proceedings since the unfortunate opening incident of the campaign, presaged ill for the further conduct of the war. That a self-reliant leader, usually bold to rashness, should suddenly become cautious to timidity, and lose all confidence in himself, can only be accounted for on the hypothesis of mental worry due to the constant stream of commands, injunctions, and suggestions which Lord Dalhousie, since his arrival near the theatre of operations, had been showering upon the object of his distrust. Many thought at the time that on December 3 Lord Gough missed a great opportunity, contending that had he ordered Thackwell to press Sher Singh and himself crossed the Chenab, the Sikhs, caught between two forces, would have been decisively defeated. All that can be said is that the Chief appears to have been unaware that the Sikhs had evacuated their position on that date, and that, as the turning movement had succeeded, though two days later than the date originally fixed, the failure to give the fullest effect to the strategy devised on November 30 showed an infirmity of purpose foreign to Lord Gough's nature, but in keeping with the change in his method of campaigning, dating from his first encounter with the enemy thirteen days before. The true explanation may perhaps be found in the paralysing character of Lord Dalhousie's injunction, "on no account to advance into the doab, except for the purpose of attacking Sher Singh, without further communication with me." If he was not to follow up a successful attack by an immediate pursuit into the doab, the victory could not have been complete; at most it might have resulted in the capture of some of the enemy's ox-drawn guns.

Whatever the causes, the artillery action at Sadullapur, followed as it was by Sher Singh's retirement towards the Jhelam, appeared to Lord Gough of such a decisive character as to warrant his crossing the Chenab next day and following Sher Singh into the heart of the Chaj Doab. His sudden return of energy did not last long. When he had penetrated only eleven miles of the doab, doubts that he had exceeded his instructions seem to have assailed him. He halted at the village of Heilah, and on the 5th wrote a grandiloquent despatch to Lord Dalhousie on the occurrences of the preceding week. In his report he magnified the artillery combat of the 2nd into a great victory. "It has pleased God," he announced, "to vouchsafe to the British army the most successful issue to the extensive combinations rendered necessary for the purpose of effecting the passage of the Chenab, the defeat and dispersion of the Sikh force under the insurgent Rajah Sher Singh." He then stated that the vanquished army "amounted to 30,000 to 40,000 men with 28 guns," and after giving his own version of the turning movement and battle, concluded by stating that "during the night of the 3rd the whole of the Sikh force precipitately fled . . . in the greatest disorder. . . . They have subdivided into three divisions, which have become more a flight than a retreat; and I understand a great portion of those not belonging to the revolted Khalsa army have dispersed and returned to their homes, thus I trust effectually frustrating the views of the rebel Sher Singh and his rebel associates."

What really happened was that Sher Singh, unable

to prolong the defence of the line of the Chenab, and anxious to facilitate his junction with the forces, Sikh and Afghan, his father was expected to bring from Attock, had either on the 2nd or early on the 3rd begun his withdrawal to a stronger position on the Jhelam, concealing the movement from Lord Gough by maintaining a screen of guns along the river-front of his camp, and from General Thackwell by holding him in check at Sadullapur. He effected his object so successfully that when early on December 4 the two British generals realised that he, with all his forces, had disappeared, no immediate attempt to follow them was made. If, as Lord Gough believed, Sher Singh had been beaten and his army scattered, he ought to have instituted an immediate and vigorous pursuit. Instead, he leisurely crossed the river and advanced to Heilah, and there on the 5th wrote his extraordinary despatch. On the following day Thackwell wrote his from the same place—a plain unvarnished tale of an artillery engagement and nothing more. Lord Gough at once sent it on to Lord Dalhousie with a short covering letter. By the time letter and enclosure were received, facts and inferences had already been reduced to their true proportions. Thackwell's despatch was not published until after Chillianwala, probably because its earlier production would have tended to discredit Lord Gough, nominally because therein the writer had thanked "Volunteer Mr John Angelo," "my extra A.D.C.," whereas he was a mere civilian, and such a misdescription was "a serious informality."

Only those who have access to the secret archives now in the India Office can tell with certainty what influences prompted Lord Gough to write as he did.

Doubtless he was chafing under the vexatious restrictions to which he was subjected, and desired to give good reasons for his audacity in having advanced into the proscribed doab "without further communication with" his civilian master; even so, that plea does not explain the precipitancy, inflated language, and misleading statements and inferences of the despatch. In his letter to the Secret Committee, dated Ludhiana, December 22, Lord Dalhousie reported that he had at length given the Chief a free hand, and yet, whilst saying so, he had in fact hedged round the concession with conditions which must have convinced Lord Gough that he was still distrusted and condemned by anticipation, should he attack and fall short of delivering a crushing blow, which, as the Governor-General put it, "without a heavy loss" would destroy the enemy, "add honour to the British arms, and avert the prospect of a protracted and costly war."

After writing his despatch from Heilah, his advanced position, Lord Gough, apparently in conformity with instructions from Lord Dalhousie,[1] returned cis-Chenab to Ramnagar, which for the next month was the headquarters of the army of the Punjab. In the interval the enemy had been located at Rasul on the left bank of the Jhelam, about 10 miles west of Heilah. The intervening country was a sandy plain, covered in places with stretches of

[1] The exact relations between Lords Dalhousie and Gough at this period will not be known before 1910, as Lord Dalhousie, who died in 1860, ordered that none of his private papers "shall be made public until at least fifty years shall have passed after my death." As he also recorded in his will that "it has been the practice of my father and myself to keep a full private journal during our lives, and to preserve papers of personal interest," their publication will lift the veil.

dense jungle: it was all practically waterless, and almost uninhabited except by cattle-herds. For our men the monotony of life in a desert was relieved by occasional brushes with the enemy's ubiquitous horsemen, and the hard labour of jungle-clearance. On December 18 the Chief—now in a sense free to act on his own responsibility, yet still treated like a child—crossed the Chenab and joined the troops at Heilah. On the 19th a salute of many guns in the Sikh camp was understood to announce the fall of Attock. The next fortnight was spent in comparative inaction, each army watching the other and occasionally making small outflanking movements. Sher Singh was waiting for his father with reinforcements estimated at from 10,000 to 15,000 men and guns. Lord Gough, handicapped by the Governor-General's conditions, was hesitating to strike until he should hear of the fall of Multan.

When the new year came in and still the British army did not move, our well-wishers throughout Northern India grew querulous, our secret enemies jubilant that now at last, with Sikhs, Afghans, and thousands of our own ex-sepoys, discharged after the Sutlej campaign, united against us, the *ikbāl* (good fortune) of the hated Feringhees was at an end.

On January 6, 1849, the dulness of camp life was broken by good news from Multan: the Bombay troops had at last arrived, and after prolonged bombardment city and suburbs had been taken by assault on New Year's day, the fall of the citadel was now only a question of hours, or at most a day or two, as the Diwan, with the 4000 desperate men still adhering to him, was shut up there, and must soon surrender or be destroyed.

CHAPTER VIII.

CHILLIANWALA AND AFTER.

THE imminence of the capture of the Diwan's stronghold did not lighten the old Chief's anxieties; neither the good news from Multan nor the consciousness that he had recovered in some measure the confidence of the Governor-General helped him much. What he wanted, and should have waited for, was the material aid which General Whish and his troops could alone give, and another month would go by before they could arrive. From Lahore Lord Dalhousie was now daily urging him to fight—if sure of a big success at small cost: and in his own camp his staff, his generals, and the political agent were also pressing him to attack, for Chattar Singh was approaching Rasul with a large Sikh-Afghan army and many guns. Pushed by the Governor-General, yet held back by him, pushed by those about him, yet solely responsible for the consequences of action, Lord Gough was not the man to prolong the waiting game and forbear to strike until the Multan army should join him, or Sher Singh, reduced to starvation in his impenetrable lair, should be compelled to come out and give battle or move to a cultivated and consequently open country.

Harassed and perplexed, the Chief at last made up his mind to risk another Ferozeshah by assailing the more formidable entrenchments of Rasul. On January 11 he reviewed his army; on the following day he advanced eleven miles to Dinghi.

That night both armies prepared for the impending struggle. In a sense both were equally sanguine of victory, the Sikhs because the battle would be fought upon ground of their own choosing, the English because their co-ordination, disciplined courage, and the mobility of their artillery were bound to tell against mere Asiatics, Sikhs though they were. All that was known of the enemy's position was that it extended from Rasul, a hamlet on the crest of a ridge of low hills, broken by ravines, forming there the left high bank of the Jhelam, to the vicinity of Mung, a village about five miles lower down the river. Immediately below Rasul the ground sloped away into a wide tangle of trees and thorny scrub, intersected by the dry channels of small nullahs, and this belt of difficult country extended south-west for several miles. Rasul, with the ridge of cliffs trending upstream from it, was the key of Sher Singh's position, and the lower part of that key the Sikhs, with their usual skill and laboriousness, had during the preceding weeks of inaction elaborately fortified.

The plan of attack, arranged on the night of the 12th, was that the army should advance next morning by the direct and partially cleared track to Rasul, and, circumstances favouring the movement, turn the left of the Sikh line of defences, distant about eight miles. If carried out, the jungle country would be skirted, not penetrated, and the Sikh army rolled back upon its centre and compelled to retire in disorder across the Jhelam or swept into the wilderness southwards, thus losing connection with Chattar Singh. The plan was excellent had Sher Singh allowed it to be executed, but impracticable should he make full use of his cover, throw forward his right, and threaten or attack Lord Gough's left flank and enormous baggage-train. In that case, even should Sher Singh in actual fight handle his troops as badly as Lal Singh and Tej Singh had done at Ferozeshah, Lord Gough's chances of a decisive victory, cheaply bought, were very small. The force available for the attack, deducting those held back for the protection of the baggage and followers, did not exceed 13,000 men, whereas those of his opponent were fully double that number. In guns Sher Singh was inferior, his 60 pieces being mostly small, whereas Lord Gough had 20 heavy guns and howitzers, 17 field-guns, all 9-pounders, and 25 6-pounders.

Next day Lord Gough broke up camp early. Leaving two regiments of native infantry, two of irregular cavalry, and two guns to escort and protect his baggage-train, he began his advance about 7 A.M. Having traversed about three miles, the troops were halted at a point where the track from Chillianwala on the west joined that from Dinghi to Rasul. Drawn up in order of battle Lord Gough's small army covered a front of about a mile and a half: in the centre were his heavy guns, on either side in contiguous columns of brigades the infantry, twelve regiments in all, making a grand total of nearly 10,000 men, and outside them on each flank was a cavalry brigade in the same formation. The leading regiment in each brigade was British, the 3rd Dragoons on the left, the 14th Dragoons, with the 9th Lancers added, on the right. From left to right came her Majesty's 61st, 24th, 29th, and the Company's 2nd Europeans. The horse and field batteries were posted between the intervals of brigades in support of the infantry, as in those days light guns took a very prominent part in an infantry attack, advancing and firing at successively shorter ranges up to about 250 yards from the enemy's line, when the infantry completed the work with the musket and bayonet. Towards noon the baggage-train came up, and was halted until further orders half a mile in rear of the army. By that time Lord Gough had completed a hasty reconnaissance, and was aware that Sher Singh had swung round his right and centre and was occupying the dense belt of jungle between Rasul and the neighbourhood of Chillianwala.

Further direct advance towards Rasul was therefore impracticable, without exposing the left flank and baggage of the British army to attack. To meet the enemy's unexpected dispositions the Chief extended his brigades into line, and slightly changed the direction of the march towards Chillianwala, his intention being to bivouac on the open ground about the village, and give battle in the morning. When his centre had reached the halting-place, and the work of allocating space for each regiment and battery was in progress, some cannon-balls fired from screened positions in the jungle, which extended westwards towards the river as far as the eye could see, came lobbing amongst our advance pickets. To end the annoyance Lord Gough ordered a shot or two to be returned from his heavy guns. Immediately afterwards, first one and then another, up to a total of 30 guns, responded from different points in the jungle in his front, most of them apparently not more than a mile from the mound on which Lord Gough and his staff were scanning the forbidding country held by the enemy. In a few minutes all our heavy ordnance, and some field batteries as well, were engaged. Whilst the mutually ineffective cannonade was in progress—ineffective for the British because their targets could not be accurately located, and for the Sikhs because their shot fell short—Lord Gough, from the mound, saw Sher Singh's army drawing up for battle on some slightly rising ground about a mile in rear of the line to which his field-pieces had now been advanced. Apparently the Sikhs meant to force a battle that afternoon—the fact was unpleasant. To withdraw to more open ground was to court disaster; to sit still and bivouac was to invite a night assault upon the army, its baggage, or both; to attack at once through the thick unknown belt of jungle was to risk the loss of formation, and, as the day was waning, indecisive results. Lord Gough chose the last alternative. Sher Singh had out-manœuvred him, placed his army in an awkward position; but there was still, the Chief hoped, enough of daylight left to win a battle with the bayonet, though not perhaps to inflict a crushing defeat.

It was 3 P.M. when the order was given for the infantry to advance with their batteries and carry the Sikh position in their front. A few minutes afterwards the devoted battalions—four brigades in all, each with the British regiment in the centre and a native infantry regiment on either side—descended into the dark labyrinth which separated them from the Sikh army, and were almost lost to view from the mound. So close was the undergrowth, so numerous the thorny trees and bushes, that not only was touch lost between brigades, but even between the regiments of each brigade the maintenance of connection was hardly possible. By degrees the line of 10,000 infantry, except on our left, where obstacles were fewer, resolved themselves into companies and groups of scrambling soldiers, none able to see clearly twenty yards in any direction, all pressing forward as fast as their weary frames and nervous tension permitted towards the Sikh batteries in their front. Trees and scrub were full of the enemy's sharpshooters, and all the while the farther Sikh batteries—those in position towards which the advanced field-guns were now retiring—were throwing shot and shell promiscuously in the direction of the occasionally visible red-coats approaching them.

For the next hour the fight was a confused struggle of independent regimental units, the fortunes of some of which must be described separately before any general idea of the conflict can be realised.

On receiving the order to attack, General Campbell, commanding the left division, first rode to Brigadier Pennycuik's brigade, and after explaining that his own further supervision was impossible because of the difficulties of the ground to be traversed, he told the brigadier to act for himself, and then turning to her Majesty's 24th Foot, 1000 strong and recently arrived in India, shouted, "There must be no firing; the work has to be done with the bayonet." Campbell then rode away to the left, joined Brigadier Hoggan's brigade, and accompanied it in its advance.

Her Majesty's 24th, equipped as if for a review, officers and men in full uniform, colours flying, muskets unloaded, received their orders with a cheer, and with wild precipitancy immediately plunged into the jungle. In the excitement caused by a first battle, and the general's admonition about the bayonet, no one gave the command to load, and no one noticed that the brigade field-guns were, by some blunder, being trotted off to the left. It was not until the 24th Foot, followed by the 45th and 25th Native Infantry, had disappeared from view, that the mistake about the guns was discovered, too late for rectification. The regiment was now pressing on through the thorny brushwood, more like a crowd of schoolboys let loose from the class-room than a body of disciplined co-ordinated soldiers. When, with companies broken into sections and files, the men had torn their way through the thickets for more than a mile, they suddenly emerged upon open ground, and saw some fifty yards in front a row of Sikh guns, protected by a swamp and strip of water like a wet ditch, belching grape and canister into them. Instinctively the mass surged forwards, many through, a few round, the water. Headed by their surviving officers, they rushed the opposing battery, and then stood still, uncertain what to do. Some began to load and fire, others did nothing from want of leading. That indecision was fatal. The native infantry regiments were not yet up: the Sikhs, who had at first recoiled, rallied, charged, and after a confused *mêlée* hurled back what remained of the 24th over the ground whence they had come. It was too late for the native infantry regiments, even had they tried, to retrieve the disaster. All three staggered back along their line of advance, followed by swarms of shouting Sikh horsemen and swordsmen. Meanwhile Hoggan's brigade, kept well in hand, had penetrated the Sikh line to the left of the battery taken and abandoned by the 24th, and wheeling on its right was pouring volleys of musketry into the elated masses of the enemy, thus relieving the pressure upon our defeated regiments. For some time the contest was waged on equal terms, when a fresh diversion, caused by the appearance of her Majesty's 29th Foot on the left rear of the struggling Sikhs, brought victory almost within the grasp of the hardly pressed British.

Her Majesty's 29th Foot with the 56th and 30th Native Infantry under Brigadier Mountain composed the left brigade of our right (Gilbert's) division. Whilst the three battalions were still entangled in the jungle, the remnants of Pennycuik's broken brigade had swept by them, followed by the exultant Sikhs. Pushing on in good order, the larger part of Mountain's brigade reached the enemy's guns in its front, and had spiked some of them when the 56th Native Infantry gave way. The 29th Foot, with part of the 30th Native Infantry, still held together, and surging forwards, emerged to the rear of the Sikhs, who were engaged in close combat with her Majesty's 61st and the rest of Hoggan's brigade. Their appearance caused Sikh resistance in that part of the field to collapse.

Had our extreme right been equally successful, Chillianwala might yet have been a British victory. There, General Gilbert's right brigade had at first carried all before them. Led by the 2nd Europeans, they had gained the clear space which served as a glacis to the slightly entrenched guns behind it, and all three regiments, working well together, had burst through the Sikh guns, when suddenly about 100 yards beyond, up rose lines of fresh Sikh infantry, who, shouting and firing, quickly overlapped and enveloped our breathless men in a ring of fire. Completely isolated, the men were faced about by companies; loading and firing, they charged through the guns which they had just before rushed. Once more at a standstill, every bit of cover, trees, ditches, breastworks, swarming with matchlock-men, whilst outside the mounted swordsmen were massing for a rush, the Europeans and native infantry, staunchly supported by Captain Dawe's battery, were handled by Brigadier Godby and the regimental officers as coolly as on parade. Every attempt at a charge of the enemy was met by a shower of grape from the guns. Gradually the brigade, in good order, cleared a way for its retrograde advance, and the enemy, losing heart, relaxed their collective efforts to surround it, though again and again groups and individuals, fighting like devils, threw themselves sword in hand upon our bayonets, slashing wildly until shot or transfixed.

It was not until after night had closed, and the Chief had ridden down what remained of Gilbert's division, and thanked officers and men for their splendid services, that they learnt how it was they had been left without support from the cavalry on their right.

Brigadier Pope, commanding the cavalry on Lord Gough's extreme right,—the 14th Dragoons, 14th and 16th Native Cavalry, and 9th Lancers,—after detaching a portion of his force towards Rasul, had advanced with nine squadrons, without supports, to cover the attack by Gilbert's infantry. Their necessarily slow movement, and the line formation adopted, encouraged parties of the enemy, both horse and foot, to harass our troopers almost with impunity. In the absence of capable leading, the 14th Dragoons had borne to their left, the rest of the line conforming to the direction given by them. The dragoons thus got in front of the horse artillery guns attached to Godby's infantry brigade and obstructed their fire. At this moment Brigadier Pope, an invalid unfit at the time for his command and hardly able to sit on horseback, was wounded. As he was being removed the troop nearest him stopped and wavered. The gunners behind shouted at them to get out of the way, whereupon some flustered individual called out, "Threes about!" About went the whole regiment, and once facing the rear, away the men galloped. The Sikh horsemen, seizing their opportunity, dashed after them with jeering cries. In a minute or two the rest of our cavalry, already more or less at a standstill, seeing the 14th Dragoons fleeing, had also turned and were rushing pell-mell to the rear, in their panic upsetting guns, gunners, and horses, and even riding into the hospital tents fully half a mile from the scene of the disaster. The untoward event, immediately due to incompetent leading and to want of supports, besides compromising Godby's brigade, cost us 4 guns and 52 artillery horses carried off, and lost us for the day the services of 6 other guns, which were spiked. Of the troops who took part in the panic the 9th Lancers alone preserved some order and were rallied behind the wrecked battery. On our extreme left the cavalry under Brigadier White, particularly the 3rd Dragoons, the famed "Moodkiwalas" of the former war, were completely successful in checking every attempt—all rather faint-hearted—of the Sikh right to outflank and get behind our attacking lines.

As night closed upon the incoherent fighting of the short afternoon, portions of three of our shattered infantry brigades, perhaps 5000 men in all, were still in possession of the whole centre of the Sikh line of battle, including all the guns therein, and the defenders had retired in considerable disorder, some to the Jhelam, ready to cross if pursued, some into the jungle southwards, and some into the elaborately entrenched position at Rasul. The Sikh right, though somewhat scattered, was still practically intact, as were most of the enemy's cavalry.

Lord Gough, horrified, should he fall back, at the fate which would await his wounded, and anxious to secure the guns abandoned by the Sikhs, at first decided to bivouac on the battlefield; but General Campbell pointed out to him that the enemy were hardly yet beaten, were already removing the guns on the left of their line, and might renew the fighting, with all the advantages which night and the surrounding jungle would give them. For a time the Chief refused to listen to the advice of his cautious subordinate. "What? Leave my wounded to be cut up! Damned if I do;" was his only answer to the entreaties of his staff to give the only order which would certainly save the army from the risk of further disasters. At last he yielded to the argument that, except by withdrawal to Chillianwala, he could not protect his baggage or even obtain water for his soldiers. With a heavy heart he gave the order to concentrate about the mound. Before the movement was completed the clouds, which had been gathering all the afternoon, attracted and precipitated, so it was said, by the prolonged cannonading, broke into drizzling rain. By 9 P.M. the retirement had been effected, and sufficient order re-established to secure the army against successful attack. Throughout the night, which was very wet, stragglers by the hundred found their way back to the village, in and about which the wrecks of the army of the Punjab were lying, foodless, shelterless, almost waterless,—except for the rain and two wells,—the sepoys prostrate in body and mind from the experiences of that terrible afternoon, the British soldiers full of oaths at their bad luck, and still full of fight if only they could get a good meal and some strong drink.

With the return of daylight the wisdom of the withdrawal was revealed, for there at Rasul, not four miles away, were the Sikhs in strength putting finishing touches to their defences, dragging guns into position and occasionally firing them. Their self-satisfaction was soon manifested, for at sunset their batteries broke out into a grand salute in honour of the "victory" of the previous day. Early that morning Brigadier White, who had commanded the cavalry brigade on our left, scoured the jungles to drive out the still prowling bands of the enemy, recover guns, and bring in the wounded. But the Sikhs had been beforehand: they had already removed their larger pieces to Rasul, had stripped the slain, and killed and mutilated such of the wounded as they could find. During the day British fatigue parties with camels were sent to collect and bring in the dead; the bodies of our officers were taken back to camp with some regard to decency, but those of the privates were roped together, two by two, slung on the backs of camels, and carried into our lines by the hundred. The sight of the gashed, naked, and often headless corpses of their comrades, bobbing and jerking about from the backs of the unsavoury brutes transporting them, was so offensive to the living that all further attempt to collect and bury the British dead in one place was abandoned, and they were henceforth interred in trenches where they had fallen. Naturally they lay thickest about the open ground in the immediate front of the batteries rushed by her Majesty's ill-starred 24th.

Whilst we were throwing earth upon our dead—most of them to be soon torn out of their shallow graves and fought over by hyenas, jackals, and village curs—the Sikhs were cremating theirs. Whether they took equal care of their wounded may be doubted. Apparently, except when looked after by relations or friends, they were left to shift for themselves, to lie out in the cold and wet, or crawl away and live or die as best they could. Though a gentleman, Sher Singh was a Sikh, and Sikhs, like most Asiatic peoples, were in those days callous about suffering; besides, he had no hospital arrangements, and during the fighting no quarter was given on either side.

For three days the gruesome work of collecting the wounded and burying the dead went on, amidst continuous rain and depression of spirits. Then the clouds lifted, the sun shone out, and the army, with camp clean and well ordered, shook off its gloom, began to eat, drink, and be merry once more,—supplies were now abundant, and all horrid sights had been put away. A day or two after, the incidents of the battle were being discussed as if it had been a conflict of the previous war. The mishap to the 24th Foot was ascribed to the exuberant greenness of officers and men: they had raced ahead without loading their muskets and without guns, and had arrived breathless in front of the Sikh batteries before any other regiment in their own or companion brigade had emerged from the jungle. Their punishment had been fearful: 21 officers and 497 men killed and wounded, out of an effective of 960 who went into action. As to the stampede of the 14th Dragoons, followed by that of the rest of Pope's brigade, opinions were charitable: the 14th had a great reputation for dash and bravery, and had charged gallantly at Ramnagar, not two months before Chillianwala; their panic was due to the imbecility of their invalid brigadier and to that cowardly order of "Threes about!"

Even conceding that with capable handling Pennycuik's and Pope's brigades would have escaped disaster, the causes of the British failure at Chillianwala appear to have been less due to the shortcomings of individual officers than to the unfortunate generalship of the grand old soldier at the head of the army, who by attacking with an inadequate and tired force a prepared and unreconnoitred position held in strength by a determined enemy, repeated the mistakes which had almost wrecked his army at Ferozeshah. Lord Gough's friends do not accept that view. They attribute the dubious results of the conflict at Chillianwala to other causes—chiefly to Pennycuik's and Pope's failures—and maintain that with more daylight the "victory" would have been complete. As to the officers just named, the former, who was killed, was reputed a good soldier, the latter was notoriously unfit. Lord Gough, however, was intimately acquainted with the military value of his chief officers, and in calculating his chances of success must have allowed a large discount for bad leading, as he was attacking through thick jungle. In those days promotion usually went by seniority, and a man might serve on until he died of senile decay; besides Pope there were dozens of other field-officers better suited for a club window or an easy-chair by the fireside than for responsible commands on the field of battle. Hodson, afterwards famous in the Mutiny, narrates that during the three most critical days in the war he was told off to lead by the bridle a certain brigadier's charger, and that on one occasion when the horse's flanks were almost touching a line of British bayonets, the old gentleman bent forward and said, "Pray, Mr Hodson, can you tell me which way my men are facing?" In regard to the matter of daylight, the contention that but for the lateness of the hour when the blow was delivered more decided results would have been achieved, is true enough; but, considering the conditions at sunset in both armies, it is questionable which side would have gained an advantage through a prolongation of the struggle. No: it was not the advent of darkness, not the deficiencies of individual brigadiers or colonels, which made Chillianwala a slaughter-yard rather than a British victory, but the rank bad generalship of Lord Gough himself and the superior strategy of Sher Singh, who drew the Commander-in-Chief into the jungle, and induced him to attack a difficult position over ground destructive to cohesion and regular formation. That the defeat of two brigades, and the heavy losses and partial disorganisation of two out of the other four, did not result in greater demoralisation than actually occurred, was due to the dogged heroism of the British soldiers and the splendid leading of the company officers. The British casualties in those two hours of desperate fighting were 697 killed, including missing, and 1641 wounded, rather more than one in six of the troops engaged. The percentage of losses was heaviest in the four infantry brigades, those in the general staff, artillery, and cavalry only contributing 189 to the grand total of 2338. Though twelve Sikh guns were captured and secured, their calibre was small, ranging from 3- to 7-pounders; as a set-off the British lost six guns and five colours, but none of the latter were actually captured in fight, all being found by the enemy in dead hands after the battle.

When the weather had cleared, and Lord Gough, anxious about his communications, was considering the question of withdrawing to Dinghi, a salute of many guns fired from the heights of Rasul announced the arrival of Chattar Singh with his reinforcements from Attock. As the Chief listened to the guns he must have thought of his painful despatch on the battle written the day before (December 16); how, urged by Major Mackerson, the Governor-General's political agent with the army of the Punjab, "to strike an effectual blow at the enemy" before Sher Singh's already formidable numbers—"30,000 to 40,000 men with 62 guns"—should be augmented by those under his father, he had yielded, struck, and failed; and how, now that Chattar Singh had come, he turned out to be only a sort of bogey-man, his reinforcements being only 3000 to 5000 and a few guns. Ah, could Lord Gough relive that last week with his present knowledge how differently he would have acted! But was he now to retreat or stand fast?—that was the question. He reflected that the troops brought by Sher Singh's father were few—only so many more mouths, human and bovine—and not a sack of corn or blade of forage for them nearer than Gujerat. The fact stiffened Lord Gough's bulldog nature; he would strengthen his bridge-head opposite Ramnagar, maintain his present position, and, by starving out Sher Singh and all his hosts, compel him to move towards food-supplies, and then, reinforced by General Whish from Multan, he would crush the Sikhs in the open country. The decision was sound—the pity was it had not been made a few days earlier. Forthwith the Chief gave orders that his camp, already concentrated in a confined square about the mound, should be entrenched—the first instance of the kind in India. The work was done by British soldiers alone, the pampered Hindustanis looking on—being high-caste sepoys, they objected to handle spade and pickaxe like "coolies."

CHAPTER IX.

VICTORY OF GUJERAT.

WHEN the long-expected news of the fall of Multan (January 21) reached the opposing camps, the Sikh leader, feeling that the inevitable issue of the war was now only a matter of a few weeks, at once sought to obtain terms, and, failing, tried to tempt Lord Gough to attack him. Prudent from bitter experience, the Chief declined the challenge. Ten days went by, at the end of which Sikhs and English were apparently still looking at each other, separated only by four miles of jungle and broken ground. Straitened for food, his sirdars yearning for the flesh-pots of Gujerat or Lahore and anxious for a settlement, his men suspicious of their sirdars and weary of inaction, Sher Singh at length decided to abandon his strong position and force an engagement, if he could, by threatening Dinghi and Chillianwala simultaneously. Slipping away from Rasul, he appeared in rear of Lord Gough's entrenchment, and advanced as if to storm it. But the Sikh military organisation, not being constituted for attack, was only formidable for defence behind cover, and Sher Singh's showy movement fizzled out in futile demonstration. Desperate, he held a council of war, at which his sirdars clamoured for food, his soldiers for fight. Yielding to his fate, he resolved to give them both, and marched for Gujerat. Next day (February 15) Lord Gough, after sending back to Lahore 8000 camels and masses of superfluous baggage and followers, followed cautiously in the wake of the enemy. With the fords of the Chenab in his hands, and General Whish hurrying up the left bank of the river, all the Chief had to do was to keep in touch with the Sikhs until, joined by the Multan troops, he should administer the final blow.

By the 20th the army of the Punjab was complete, over 20,000 men with 106 guns, of which eighteen were pieces of the heaviest ordnance in use and sixty-six 9-pounders. The Sikh forces were more than twice as numerous, — some official estimates putting them as high as 60,000,—but as they were weak in guns, having only 59, very few of which were 9-pounders and upwards, and the battle would be decided by artillery-fire, their superiority in men could give them no advantage.

Throughout the 20th the two armies lay opposite each other, the Sikhs round the town of Gujerat, the British about three miles to the south, their left resting on the small town of Kunjah, their centre on the large village of Shadiwal, and their right extending to the low alluvial lands on the Gujerat side of the ford at Wazirabad.

The whole country was perfectly flat, open, and cultivated, dotted by populous villages and covered with the young spring crops, chiefly wheat and barley, at that time of year standing a few inches high. Had Lord Gough searched all India for a battlefield better adapted for the overthrow of the Sikhs, he could have found none more suitable. Both armies passed the night in order of battle,—the British with the confident expectation that, with their overwhelming strength in guns, a cheap and complete victory would be theirs, the Sikhs with the consciousness that they were in a trap, and hopelessly inferior in the arm which, rightly used, would decide the long-protracted struggle. Their infantry and artillery lay between two nullahs; but as that on their right was dry, and the course of both was from north to south, neither would impose any real obstacle to the British advance. If rain fell and, filling them, converted the firm surface-soil into mud, that would aid the defence. But the weather had been clear and cloudless for weeks, and nothing but the special intervention of the Guru seemed likely to change it. In their trouble the Sikhs hastily consulted their priests and astronomers, but those cautious gentlemen were more than usual enigmatical: the Guru did not work miracles—in February, his chosen people must fight well, in which case they would prosper; how or when was not vouchsafed.

The morning of February 21 broke gloriously, a perfect day for battle or review. Having eleven clear hours in which to carry out the work in hand, our troops were given an early breakfast, and then drawn up in battle order and inspected. In the right centre were the heavy guns, drawn by elephants, on the largest of which fluttered the standard of St George: outside were the infantry divisions—Campbell's, Gilbert's, and Whish's—with light field-guns in the intervals of brigades, and strong reserves ready to feed the fighting line as required. On either flank, on the left of both nullahs already mentioned, were our cavalry, 4500 strong, and some troops of horse artillery. In short, the formation and mode of attack accorded with the accepted methods of the day, and was the same as that intended to be followed at Chillianwala, but with this difference, the British force was nearly twice as strong. Chief, divisional generals, and brigadiers could see and control every unit in their respective spheres of responsibility, and, above all, the artillery arm, overpowering in weight and numbers, and every gun with a clearly defined target, was to be used for all it was worth, the bayonet being for once held in reserve as a subsidiary weapon.

As the Chief with his brilliant staff rode down the line, the old man was received with cheers. He had suffered cruelly for the mistakes of Chillianwala, but to-day every soldier was sure that his ill luck had turned, and that before evening his reputation as a general would be redeemed by the utter rout of the enemy.

Towards 8 A.M. the British line, covering a front of more than three miles, began its advance. For half an hour or more it had moved slowly with the precision of a field-day—light field artillery leading, elephant batteries and long double lines of infantry some 300 yards behind, 40,000 eyes straining front watching the movements of small bodies of Sikh horsemen, not another sign of life visible on the green plain stretching back to the groves and commanding citadel of Gujerat—when suddenly, from the left front were seen a flash and a puff of smoke, followed by a booming sound, and then, seconds afterwards, the opening roar of an irregular cannonade from over 50 guns about 1200 yards ahead. Every projectile fell short; the leaders of the Sikhs had omitted to mark distances, and their eager half-disciplined and indifferently controlled artillery had fired too soon, thus revealing the position of every gun. The British infantry lines were at once halted out of range, the elephant batteries unlimbered, the field-guns pushed forwards, and then the ineffectual fire of the enemy was returned. For a quarter of an hour a storm of iron fell about the Sikh batteries, until their fire slackened. A second advance was then made, distances being exactly kept, and the pounding process was renewed. By a succession of such short rapid advances the space between the nearest of the contending rows of guns was soon reduced to not more than a quarter of a mile. For fully two hours the devoted Sikhs submitted to the pounding: by degrees, as they were borne back, their guns and infantry became intermixed in one irregular line, the rain of projectiles still pouring upon them. Soon a trailing to the rear was discernible, loose horses galloped about, and the green expanse became blotched with the *débris* of a collapsing army. The morning breeze, which had hitherto blown aside the smoke, was now dying away and the haze of battle settling down upon the scene. About half-past eleven the British infantry, hitherto mere spectators, were ordered, somewhat prematurely, to advance; for as Penny's and Harvey's brigades on the right were passing the mud-built villages of Kālra Kalān and Kālra Khurd ("great" and "small" Kālra), both supposed to have been already evacuated, a heavy musketry-fire was opened from the walls upon them. Both villages were at once rushed, the larger by the 2nd

Europeans, the smaller by the 10th Foot, each regiment being well supported by the native infantry battalions which made up the two brigades. As the troops entered the defenders shut themselves up in the buildings, the doors of which had to be successively forced, and volleys poured in until the last man was killed. The losses on both sides were severe, for no quarter was asked or given. Of the Sikhs not one survived. That was the only fighting at close quarters which took place during the day.

The whole Sikh centre was now giving way, slowly and sullenly. Their right wing, composed of horsemen, amongst whom was a compact body of 1000 Afghans, led by a brother of the Amir, the famous Dost Muhammad Khan, now made a futile attempt to relieve the pressure on their centre by a showy dash towards the British rear, but being charged by the Sindh Horse, immediately broke and fled without impact. The scattering of the Sikh right laid open their whole defence. Seeing that the battle was now irretrievably lost, the Sikh sirdars, never prominent when a fight was in progress, began to leave the field, thinking only of their own safety. By one o'clock all organised resistance had ceased; the whole of Sher Singh's army was in flight, having abandoned their camp, baggage, and most of their guns. They were followed and cut up by our cavalry and horse artillery for twelve to fourteen miles until nightfall, by which time the Khalsa forces, which had almost beaten the army of the Punjab at Chillianwala, were a scattered rabble of fleeing men, all hurrying north-west, with the common object of putting the Jhelam between them and their pursuers.

Towards sunset the twenty-three Anglo-sepoy infantry regiments which had taken part in the battle were halted beyond the Sikh camp north of the town, and whilst here and there in and about the camp, already being plundered by the followers of the army, mines and loose combustibles were exploding, the regimental bands played independently spirit-stirring airs,—"Rule Britannia," it is recorded, though hardly the most appropriate air for the occasion, being that most in favour with the native infantry regiments.

Though the easy victory of Gujerat,[1] which cost us only 96 lives and seven times that number in wounded, was a foregone conclusion, and the battle for most of the conquerors merely a grand spectacular display, it taught a great lesson by emphasising the mistakes of Ferozeshah and Chillianwala, and the power of superior artillery and disciplined co-operation against a more numerous, equally brave, but less coherent enemy compelled to fight on open ground.

[1] In the text a commonly credited incident of the battle is ignored because it is not true. The story goes that Lord Gough's staff cleverly isolated him for a good hour—put him out of action as it were—on the roof of a building, in order to give our artillery time to thoroughly smash the Sikhs before their bayonet-loving Chief could order a general advance of his infantry. In 1866 the writer went over the battlefield, and was shown the identical bungalow and the identical ladder said to have been removed and hidden by one of the staff after Lord Gough had mounted by it. So far the evidence was corroborative, but a glance round broke down the whole case. The building, a Sikh *bāradarri*, was on the *north* side of the town, hence none of our people could have reached it until the battle had been won. Very likely the Chief did ascend to its roof by the ladder, very likely some accident happened to it, which pounded the party for some minutes, very likely too the Chief may have regretted that the general *débacle* of the Sikhs—visible the moment he stood on the roof—prevented him giving them a taste of cold steel; but the only order he could have given was for an immediate pursuit by horse artillery and cavalry.

On the morning after the battle a vigorous pursuit of the remnants of the Sikh forces was organised, pushed, and continued, and within a month the last of the Sikhs had surrendered and Peshawar had been occupied.

On the 30th of March 1849 the annexation of the Punjab was proclaimed.

CHAPTER X.

THE MAKING OF ORDER.

Ichabod!—the glory had departed from the Khalsa but not the energy, not the manly virtues, which had raised obscure and simple Jats to supreme power in the Punjab, and had almost wrested the sceptre of empire from the hands of the English. Acknowledging no authority but superior force, whilst unsubdued they had resented John Lawrence's despotic methods; overwhelmed, they cheerfully accepted the consequences of defeat. Before the war their victors had been advisers with temporary powers of control in an independent kingdom; now they were its absolute masters by right of conquest. Before the war the English had been bound to maintain Sikh rights and privileges acquired under the ægis of the great Maharaja; now, shackled by no obligations to institutions or individuals, they were free to govern as they pleased, to pull down and set up, to grant and resume according to their novel ideas of equal treatment for all men.

It was Henry Lawrence's refusal to recognise that Gujerat had destroyed all old title-deeds, and given us a clean slate whereon to inscribe our own sovereign will and pleasure, which soon afterwards caused the final breach between him and the self-willed autocrat then guiding our destinies in India. First as Resident and later as quasi-Regent Lawrence had striven to elevate the Sikhs into an orderly law-respecting people, who, when their Maharaja should take over the government, would be worthy subjects of a worthy King. Ill-health had broken the continuity of his influence, and had given his brother John opportunities for rushing the regeneration of "the horde of barbarians who had overrun the Punjab": naturally they preferred persuasion to force, guidance to goading, and would not adapt themselves to the cast-iron methods thrust upon them during Henry Lawrence's absence in England.

From Lord Dalhousie's landing in Calcutta in January 1848 until he laid down his high office eight years afterwards, on the eve of the whirlwind he himself had sown, his continuous policy was, in his own words, to seize all "rightful opportunities of acquiring territory or revenue as may from time to time present themselves." Not unwilling to create such a "rightful opportunity," he had encouraged John to treat the Punjab, whilst still an independent kingdom, as if already a British province, had allowed the local disturbance of Multan to grow into a national Sikh rising, and then had crushed the "rebellion," as the struggle was officially called, and in accordance with his settled policy had annexed the country. Whilst the war was still in progress he had frankly notified his intentions to Henry Lawrence, and later had instructed him to draft the proclamation of annexation, which was to issue as soon as the Khalsa had been finally overthrown. Lawrence, swayed by his sympathies and conscious of the causes which had driven the Sikhs to take up arms, prepared a considerate document, which Lord Dalhousie promptly condemned as "objectionable both in matter and manner." With equal promptitude Lawrence sent in his resignation, whereupon his master, like the Jewish Jehovah prone to wrath, yet sometimes repenting of his haste, wrote soft words, and the resignation was withdrawn. Thus a truce was arranged—a lasting peace was impossible between two such incompatibles. Lord Dalhousie, omnipotence and omniscience incarnate, brooked neither opposition nor advice. He required obedient servants, not opinionated vassals. But he knew that Henry Lawrence was for a time indispensable in the Punjab, and until the wounds caused by the war had been healed, dared not remove the good physician, in whom alone the Sikhs had confidence. For that reason the arbitrary master was constrained not only to retain in the province his equally self-willed servant, but to make him the head of its administration. As sole ruler Henry Lawrence was not to be trusted; he would bankrupt the state in five years and stultify his master, who, when annexing the country, had endeavoured to appease the apprehensions of the Court of Directors by assuring them that their new kingdom would soon prove a "profitable possession"; but if Lawrence had his way he would alienate half the revenue in favour of Runjit Singh's beneficiaries, many of them legally traitors, and all of them economically unproductive consumers: "their lives and bare subsistence" was Lord Dalhousie's view of their deserts, "their jagirs in perpetuity" Lawrence's. To counteract his tenderness of heart Lord Dalhousie decided to give Henry Lawrence a coadjutor, his hard-headed brother John, and as, left to themselves, the brothers were sure to disagree on most subjects connected with expenditure, he added as peacemaker between them a third coadjutor, a civilian named Mansel, a dilettante philosopher and critic, whose habit was to raise objections to every proposal but never to come to any conclusion himself. Thus lubricated, Lord Dalhousie anticipated that his novel administrative machine—a triumvirate directed and controlled from without by a master-mind—would work without much friction until, law and order being established, the man who had opposed him, no longer indispensable, could be safely removed. The machine was officially christened a "Board of Administration," but as President and members had each equal powers, and all three joint responsibility, there was no prospect that such a trinity would be one and indivisible: in the absence of union references to the author of their being in Calcutta or Simla would be frequent, a condition of things probably within the purview of his intentions when Lord Dalhousie conceived and gave birth to his instrument of government. As he knew himself to be always in the right and those who differed from him always in the wrong, he naturally desired to shape the growth towards a restricted autonomy of the province, which was the first fruit of his policy of all India for the English.

Henry Lawrence was not the only thorn in the flesh for the divinity then ruling India, for about that time a rival god appeared at Simla, the Indian Olympus, a little lower in power than the other, being only a Commander-in-Chief. The new-comer though inferior in position was greater in prestige; in addition, he not only knew all men, Lord Dalhousie not excepted, to be fools, but was in the habit of telling them so. Clearly there was no room in India, much less at the same council-table, for two infallibles; one must destroy the other, and before long the prediction was general that the greater would extinguish the lesser, the civilian the soldier.

Sir Charles Napier's appointment occurred in this wise. When the news of Lord Gough's misfortune on the Jhelam, and the position of mutual stale-mate which followed it, reached England, public opinion, already captivated by the Napoleonic glamour of Napier's victories in Sindh, his striking personality, and the vagaries of his self-assertive genius, insisted that he should be sent out to supersede the "butcher" of Chillianwala — Ferozeshah bulking large in the background — with orders to smash the Sikhs as he had the Baluches. Napier, then in England, hurried out; but, hasten as he might, he only reached India three months after Gujerat had been fought.

Soured by his bad luck—he was sixty-eight and had missed his last chance of fame, for, after all, he had only beaten mobs of armed barbarians in Sindh —Napier vented his ill-humour by attacking Lord Dalhousie and his scheme of government for the Punjab. If he could not add "Conqueror of the Sikhs" to his other claims to distinction, his experience and success as Governor of Sindh entitled him to take a leading part in organising the administration of the new province. He advised the Governor-General to model it on that of Sindh, to appoint a soldier as chief commissioner, and save the country from being vivisected by regulation civilians and hair-splitting lawyers. As his ideas were treated with indifference, he lost the remains of his temper, and determined, if he could not have his own way, to make civilian government impossible.

Now Napier, when embittered, was a doughty opponent. His pen was powerful, his tongue biting. He knew himself to be the one wise man of the East, and abused those who did not take him at his own valuation. Happily for those who differed from him, and they were legion, the personal element now so dominated his mind that he expressed his views with such captious extravagance that, right or wrong, they were not taken seriously. The fact was unfortunate, for after eliminating the chaff from the wheat, bizarre intemperance from solid sense, his opinions generally showed sagacity and foresight. Thus he forewarned the nation that "a mutiny with the sepoys is the most formidable danger menacing our Indian Empire," and he foresaw and sought to provide against some of the evils of governing the Punjab on rigid British lines. Had he made his representations with sober moderation, eschewing all offensive exaggeration, his warnings and suggestions would have commanded attention; instead, they were pooh-poohed as the emanations of a distempered mind. Amongst the objects of his scorn, the civilian, particularly the military political, was prominent. To him the former was, in his own language, "a man full of curry and bad Hindustani with a fat liver and no brains," and the latter "a gentleman who wore a red coat but was not a soldier."

During Napier's last year in India, Lord Dalhousie, who was half his age and very small in person, and had been dubbed by him "the Laird o' Cockpen," and the brothers Lawrence—types of the classes he detested—incurred his concentrated displeasure: they opposed his views on the form of government best suited for the Punjab, and were, therefore, his enemies. In October 1849 he started from Simla on a tour in the Punjab, nominally to inspect military arrangements, really to collect material for an attack on the civil government of the province, as devised and administered by the men who had shown their wrong-headedness by scorning his advice. In preparing his elaborate indictment he not only neglected his military duties and wasted his own time, but caused those whom he arraigned to waste theirs also, in drawing up lengthy replies and rejoinders. Nor was the war between them confined only to official writings, for at a later period Henry Lawrence, with the approval of Lord Dalhousie, carried it into the public press, and endeavoured to expose the fallacy of the Chief's facts and arguments in 'The Calcutta Review.'

Nowadays Indian officials are often ridiculed for their *cacoethes scribendi*, but to judge from the outpourings of the brothers Lawrence in 1849-54, it would seem that, although the science of official report-writing and figure-making was at that period in its infancy, indulgence in avoidable scribbling was as much practised then as fifty years later, when a vigorous attempt was made to abate the nuisance. John Lawrence, who rarely wrote a redundant word, literally wore his eyes to blindness by constant pen-driving. In his statue on the Mall in Lahore he stands with a pen in one hand and a sword in the other and asks the Punjabis, "By which will you be governed?" Though the symbolism intended is evident, the effect is unfortunate, as giving too high a place in administration to the power of the pen. It is a fact that in the days of the Lawrences, and even later, Government servants who had the gift were openly press correspondents or leader-writers, and in their literary efforts not only criticised the proceedings of individual officers, but even of departments and the Government itself. In some cases they edited newspapers, and owed their advancement in the service to the freedom and ability with which they used their pens. But *tempora mutantur.* What was then an approved avenue to official success is now a certain road to official failure. Whether the large-minded toleration of criticism which characterised the attitude of the Government until towards the end of the 'seventies, or the muzzling regulations of the present time, are better in the public interest is a matter on which opinions may differ. There can, however, be no doubt that the system now enforced, though convenient for a despotic form of government, is prejudicial to independence of character and the cause of truth.

The smallness of even great minds, when their possessors are officials, is now rarely revealed; hence, when the truth would be inconvenient to highly placed office-holders, it is withheld from the public, or has to be guessed from the edited representations of facts available in Blue-books or published proceedings. But in the 'fifties there was no law of *lése majesté* in India, and in the prosecution of his feud against civilians and soldier-politicals all Sir Charles Napier's dirty linen was washed in public. In the sequel his attack upon Lord Dalhousie and the Lawrences recoiled upon himself. Lord Dalhousie, on the watch for his opportunity, found occasion to severely censure the troubler of his equanimity, whereupon Sir Charles Napier, already marked for death, resigned, to die soon after in England, a mad, sad old man, who thought himself a thwarted Napoleon.

Though fighting the common enemy and sparring with each other pretty hotly at times, the Lawrences, the working members of the Board,—for Mansel only vapoured,—devoted most of their energies to building up a solid structure of good government, which for many years gained for the Punjab its deserved distinction as the "model province" of India.

Of the brothers, Henry, feeble in body, toured and inspected, inspiring all men to do the best that was in them, whilst John, robust and business-minded, sat at his desk fourteen hours a-day, organising and working out details. Some of it was drudgery, no doubt, but he had done much the same work whilst in charge of Jallandar. There, in two years he had converted a lawless doab[1] into a law-abiding commissionership. Though no egoist he had, at the end of his first year, surveyed what he had accomplished, and finding it good, had reported to the Governor-General that he "could easily manage double the extent of country." It was no idle boast, for in the same period of time the two brothers—John taking most of the burden on his own broad shoulders—changed a ruined kingdom into a prosperous British province. Jallandar contained 7000 square miles and a fairly homogeneous population of two and a half millions, all accustomed to obedience. The rest of the Punjab—what had been "the Lahore state"—covered 74,000 square miles, with a mixed population of about ten millions, of whom roundly two-thirds

[1] *Doāb*=two waters=the delta or tongue of land lying between every two of the converging rivers of the Punjab.

were Muhammadans, most of them up to the Indus dull and tractable as buffaloes, but beyond it wild and untamable as wolves. To carry out the orders of the Board in this hitherto misgoverned country, it, including Jallandar, was divided into seven divisions, each composed of three to five districts, and amongst them was distributed a staff of about one hundred British civil officers, half of them picked civilians from the North-West Provinces, the others military men selected from the crowd who preferred the pay and power of administrative work to continuous soldiering.

As the Sikhs were at heart "a nation of shopkeepers," in the sense that they always had a keen eye to business, and as since 1846, whether fighting or farming, they had been receiving more knocks than rupees, when they found that under the new *régime* husbandry—their hereditary occupation—promised them an easy and prosperous life at their homes, they readily went back to the plough. Of the Muhammadans the settled population welcomed the change of rulers as a relief from the yoke of hated oppressors, whilst the rude pastoral nomads, inhabiting the central jungly tracts of the various doabs and the unreclaimed alluvial lands of the Sutlej and Indus, were at first indifferent; to them Sikhs and English were both infidels, and as such would equally harry their flocks and herds, should they fail to pay the poll-tax levied on their cattle. When, however, they found that contractors came amongst them, bags of rupees in hand, to buy sheep and cattle, grass and wood, and hire, not seize, their camels and bullocks, they made up their minds that, if they must have a master, the Feringhee was preferable to the Sikh. As, then, the people of the Punjab either welcomed or acquiesced in the new order of things and were willing to give the English a fair trial, the Board had no serious difficulties before it, provided that its officers tempered zeal with respect for customs and local and tribal sentiment.

The work of pacification, which included the paying off and disbandment of many thousands of Sikh regulars, had to precede that of civil organisation. The frontier districts were poor and troublesome, for the present military rule was good enough for them; but those cis-Indus were rich, and yielded most of the revenue, hence there a finer administration was necessary. Annexation having been proclaimed, and the 55,000 troops retained to garrison the Punjab and hold the Afghans in check having been distributed, the edict went forth that all cis-Indus Punjabis—those of Hazara excepted—should surrender their arms, and that all forts and strong buildings not wanted for military or police purposes should be demolished. The submissive attitude of the people was at once proved by their giving up 120,000 arms, chiefly swords and matchlocks, and by the evident satisfaction which the labouring masses manifested in the dismantling of the castles of their sirdars. When issuing the disarmament proclamation the Board had expected willing and immediate compliance by tribes other than Sikhs, but delays and difficulties with the lately dominant Khalsa. For generations every Sikh had carried arms and lorded it over the rest of the creation, and every sirdar of any pretension had lived in feudal state in some sort of stronghold, whilst not a few had possessed therein arsenals, cannon-foundries, or small-arms factories. If, then, the breaking in of such men, like that of high-spirited colts freshly caught from a run, should require care and patience, what wonder? Instead, one and all bent their heads and submitted, as well-trained carriage-horses do to the collar. Though the Administration had the credit, the higher praise was owed to the political sagacity of the Sikhs, gentle and simple, who appeared to have made up their minds to accept their beating as final, and rise to wealth and honour under a race whose power and worth they had already learnt to appreciate.

Thus within six months of Gujerat, the peoples of the province east of the Indus—Sikhs, Jats, Rajputs, and the various tribes loosely congregated under the term "Punjabi Muhammadans"—were in a state of tranquillity, if not contentment, unknown even by tradition. For the next two years, the harvests being continuously good, remunerative labour abundant, and the demand for products sustained, those happy conditions continued. True, to the warped imagination of Sir Charles Napier, now dying in England, the Punjab was still seething with disaffection, Gulab Singh was plotting treason, and our Hindustani sepoys, aggrieved at their prolonged exile and loss of *batta*—extra pay on active service or when located in a foreign country—and inflated with their (?) victories, were on the brink of mutiny. Napier, however, whether accusing or vaticinating in India or England, was now a modern Cassandra, and his prophecies and warnings were unheeded.

To our young administrators the Punjab, with its thirsty plains, unutilised rivers, and willing, manly population, was like a newly discovered country with great natural resources awaiting the development

L

which English brains, integrity, and organising power alone could give. Every deputy commissioner of a district, every settlement officer, thought himself indispensable to his people, and buckled to his task with the enthusiasm of youth and high resolve, as if the evolution of order and prosperity out of the *débris* of past confusion and misery depended on his individual exertions and governing ability.

Guided by the Lawrences, the business of administration, the foundations of which had been laid during the later period of the regency, went on apace. In the domain of public works the impress of the directing minds and hands naturally began to show results more rapidly than in that called officially "moral progress." Roads, the most certain dissolvent of barbarism, were laid out, bridged, and policed between all important centres, and the continuation of the Grand Trunk Road, already indifferently made from Calcutta to Delhi,—a distance of 1000 miles,—was planned, and construction begun in sections for the remaining 520 miles to Peshawar. The new work—wider, smoother, harder, straighter for longer distances, and better and more durably bridged than any Roman road—was the greatest undertaking of the kind heretofore attempted in Asia. Lord Dalhousie was essentially the great road-maker of India. Before him the East India Company had cared little for roads—in the rainy season "the roads that run," as the navigable rivers are called in Russia, were thought good enough for trading purposes, and at other times the whole country was a highway, for bullock-carts were not much used and pack-carrying animals could take a bee-line in any direction. Even the Grand Trunk Road from Calcutta to Delhi, though aligned in 1795, was until 1849 rough and unsatisfactory, without a single masonry bridge throughout its whole length. During Lord Dalhousie's eight years of office (1848-1856) crores of rupees were spent on the neglected arteries of commerce; probably his most useful achievement was his completion of Asia's greatest highway to and beyond Delhi, and the planning, cutting, and opening of some of the sections of its extension to Peshawar.

If roads were necessary for military, trading, and civilising purposes, irrigation was equally so for the development of the resources of the country. The Board lost no time in preparing plans and estimates for diverting the rivers of the Punjab from their beds in the lowest levels between the doabs to the watersheds thereof, and within a year of Gujerat the Bari Doab Canal was begun. It was designed to irrigate the Mānjha or "middle country" of the Sikhs, which contained Lahore and Amritsar, with Multan 230 miles south-west towards the apex of the triangle. In the matters of barracks, court-houses, jails, dispensaries, and the other material requirements of a settled government, construction also proceeded as fast as money was available: the confusing varieties of coins in circulation, most numerous of which was the multiform Sikh rupee, called *nānak shāhi*, were gradually called in and replaced by Company's rupees.

In the domain of morals real progress was necessarily slow, though the veneer of improvement was everywhere in evidence; indeed by the last day of March 1852, the date on which the official year ends in India, the baneful effects of the long reign of brute force had been wholly obliterated, and the country, except in cantonments, where of course the "mailed fist" was conspicuous, presented the appearance of a young, thriving, law-abiding community, each district obedient to the will of one resident Englishman, whom not a score in a thousand of his subjects had ever seen. These seeming despots, twenty-nine in number, were called deputy commissioners, and in their hands, under the easy control of distant commissioners, who again were under that of the still more distant Board, were concentrated, in the belief of their subjects, all the powers of an earthly providence. To enable them to preserve public order a formidable police force was raised, aggregating 24,000 men, horse and foot — exclusive of 30,000 village watchmen, paid for by rates levied on all classes of residents in each village. Of the provincial police 13,000 were organised as a quasi-military body, one-third of them being stationed in battalions and troops in the frontier districts, two-thirds being distributed in small bodies amongst the cis-Indus districts and employed to patrol roads, furnish guards for jails and treasuries, escorts for civil officers and treasure in transit, and the like. The remaining 11,000 were used as a purely civil constabulary for the detection and prevention of crime. By means of this newly recruited force—the *personnel* of which were mostly Sikhs and Muhammadans—and the hearty co-operation of the villages and towns, the Board was soon able to report, with pardonable exaggeration, to Lord Dalhousie that "all violent crimes have been repressed, all gangs of murderers and robbers have been broken up, and the ringleaders brought to justice. In no part of India is there now more perfect peace than in the territories lately annexed" —and all this within three years of Gujerat.

CHAPTER XI.

PATERNAL GOVERNMENT.

THE country pacified, violent crime suppressed, revenue flowing in, the Administration — Board, Commissioners, Deputy Commissioners, each within their respective spheres—turned their attention to the building up of a system of civil justice suitable to a simple agricultural people. Whilst the Board was maturing civil, criminal, and revenue rules of general application, each district officer, a little king within his own domain, subject to loosely defined limitations, had a free hand in shaping customs as to land tenures. Hitherto the strong man armed, whether community or individual, had acted as he listed, hence practices were in such a fluid state that, it is no exaggeration to say that, in most districts the customary law, as now crystallised by many judicial decisions, was shaped and fixed in its present form in accordance with the views of right and expediency of their earliest deputy commissioners and settlement officers. In the making of the laws generally, for which the Board was responsible, the province was fortunate in the fact that no professional lawyers had a share.

The legislators were merely a few sensible English

gentlemen of Indian and local experience, such as the two Lawrences and several of the commissioners, and they were advised by men of weight from amongst the people. For a working basis the rules framed by John Lawrence when in charge of the Jallandar Doab, and the regulations in force in the North-West Provinces, were used, simplified and adapted to the circumstances of a rough illiterate population. To facilitate the decision of civil disputes popular representatives, drawn from all classes in the country, were assembled in Lahore, and through their instrumentality statements of tribal customs in respect to inheritance, rights of females, adoption, and wills were drawn up, and after revision by the Board confirmed; but those relating to betrothal, marriage, and divorce, where degrading to the weaker sex, were modified in accordance with British ideas of propriety, and when finally passed by the Board were issued as guides to all judges, who were given a wide latitude, being enjoined to decide cases "according to justice, equity, and good conscience." In civil cases the judges, as far as possible, disposed of their work locally and in public, and only made use of their powers when arbitration failed.

From ancient times village panchāyats, or boards of arbitrators, had been the accepted exponents and enforcers of public opinion, hence the Board wisely decided to preserve an institution which had the sanction of prescription, and had always given satisfaction to the people. Judges were instructed to encourage litigants to refer the issues between them to arbitrators chosen for the purpose, the power of giving effect or varying the award being retained by the court. Until some years after the Mutiny the system served its purpose admirably. Afterwards, as the grip of the law became firmer, first village panchayats — in other words, the voice of public opinion—ceased to have authority, and next references to arbitration in lawsuits fell into disrepute. The fact is melancholy that, throughout India, the consolidation of British rule has invariably been the death-warrant for indigenous institutions dependent on the power of popular opinion, and that consequently individualism supported by the law courts has everywhere killed village communities and the panchayat system. The civil court, which made most use of arbitration, was the tahsildar or native subdivisional officer. Each district was broken up into four to seven tahsils or subdivisions, under the immediate management of a tahsildar, who within his jurisdiction was a sort of limited deputy commissioner. This tahsildar was everywhere the local court of first instance for petty civil, criminal, and revenue work. The qualifications and functions of a civil judge are thus described in the Punjab Administrative Report, issued in 1854: "In the opinion of natives, the first and best qualification of a judge is not legal lore or logical acumen, but a knowledge of the position and insight into the character of the persons who come before him. This quality will be possessed by the tahsildars, from their local knowledge, acquired in the course of fiscal business, to a greater degree than by any other class of officers. In this respect no other description of judges can at all approach them. Moreover, on *their* cases alone can local opinion be brought effectually to bear. The judge associates with the people, lives, moves, and has his being among them, not only by social intercourse but in the transaction of business, and this not of one kind but of many. He must therefore observe rustic society in its every phase. The same influences affect the parties as well as the judges. Every suitor and witness acts under the eye of his neighbour, in the presence of many of his acquaintances, who have constantly business to transact at the tahsil."

In the next Report (1856) the system of law and procedure in force was noticed. "We have," it was stated, "the most open and liberal provisions for the admission of evidence. We have complete arrangements for reference to arbitration and for the ascertainment of local custom. We have a procedure without any pretension to exactitude; but a procedure which provides for the litigants and their respective witnesses being confronted in open court, for a decision being arrived at immediately, . . . and for judgment being delivered to the parties then and there."

In a later chapter we shall see how every one of those conditions, emphasised by John Lawrence in 1854 and in 1856 as essential for the just adjudication of rural disputes, was gradually thrown over as the province was increasingly subjected to law, lawyers, and money-lenders.

In the treatment of criminal offences custom and sentiment were respected, but with many limitations, due to the wide difference in moral standards between governors and governed. To the Board cattle-stealing was a serious crime, to the Punjabis a creditable calling — indeed to this day in jungly tracts a youth's claim to manhood is hardly conceded until he has successfully lifted a few camels or bullocks. Again, to the Board, seduction and adultery were wrongs expiable by a few months in jail, civil damages, or both; to the people, they were crimes more heinous than murder, which gave the injured guardian or husband the right to kill or mutilate the transgressors, both men and women. Effect being given to the Board's lenient views, prolonged and relentless vendettas resulted, each act of revenge inducing others. So ramified did these feuds become throughout the frontier districts that, to keep crime within limits, the Government was afterwards constrained, throughout the Indus valley, not only to punish offences against women with extraordinary severity, but to accept as proof hearsay—the mere belief of the country-side that the accused was guilty. On the other hand, the Board, with the concurrence of the community, punished some crimes more severely than later humanitarians hold justifiable; thus for gang-robbery with lethal weapons the sentence was death by hanging.

The general object kept in view by the Board, when introducing their judicial system, was explained by them in 1851 to be "that substantial justice should be plainly dealt out to a simple people, unused to the intricacies of legal proceedings. Their aim is to avoid all technicality, circumlocution, and obscurity, to simplify and abridge every rule, procedure, and process. They would endeavour to form tribunals which shall not be hedged in with forms unintelligible to the vulgar, and only to be interpreted by professional lawyers, but which shall be open and accessible courts of justice, where every man may plead his own cause, be confronted face to face with his opponents, may prosecute his own claim or conduct his own defence."

That wise and broad-minded declaration was probably drawn up by Sir Henry Lawrence, for he had already in 'The Calcutta Review' lamented the prevalence in the regulation provinces of Bengal of the very evils from which the Board were attempting to save the Punjab. Had the principles of justice enunciated in 1851, and further explained in 1854 and 1856, been observed, the progress of the masses towards prosperity would have been promoted, but a time was to come when, to the advanced Administration of the day, the wisdom of the Board was as foolishness, and the strait-waistcoat equipment of the regulation provinces, wisdom. From that period collapse began, and now, as will later be shown, in spite of the repeatedly proclaimed blessings of British rule, fully a third of the agriculturists of the province have lost their birthright, and are the sweated dependents of the small and politically impotent class whom the hard commercial system introduced in the 'sixties chiefly benefits.

The members of the Board, however, and their immediate successors were neither lawyers nor doctrinaires imbued with the conviction that English institutions were the best possible for Punjabis. They were merely practical men, and as such only considered the welfare of the people and the obligation of balancing provincial income and expenditure, exclusive of the larger part of the military charges which concerned India generally.

As the number of regular troops located in the Punjab was large, 55,000, and the maintenance of a considerable garrison would always be necessary for the protection of the Empire from external aggression, the Punjab was only required to raise, equip, and maintain a small army of irregulars for the defence of its frontiers against petty incursions by the independent tribesmen, whose mountains walled in the province from the confines of Kashmir to Sindh. It was further expected to contribute about a quarter of its revenues towards the expenses of the Government of India, which included the upkeep of the regular troops stationed within Punjab limits. For local purposes, in addition to the military police, the Board raised a handy mobile force of 12,000 men, and distributed it in cantonments formed at the headquarter stations of the frontier districts, with detachments in the forts built or under construction at intervals along the border near the mouths of the more important passes between the independent hills and the valley of the Indus.

For the Peshawar district alone the arrangement was different. In that valley were located 10,000 regular troops—raised in 1853 to 12,500—all under the Commander-in-Chief, a constant reminder to the Afghans that, although we had evacuated Kabul, we could always return there, whilst for them the road to Peshawar, the land-door of India, was barred. In addition to this standing garrison a local corps, the famous "Guides" of later years, was raised, or rather expanded from a nucleus formed in 1846 into a very strong regiment of horse and foot combined, stationed at Hoti Mardan near Peshawar, and placed at the disposal of the Board.

The annual cost of all the localised or provincial forces—the "Piffers," the abbreviated name of the Punjab Irregular Frontier Force, and the military police—was estimated at considerably under half a million sterling, and of the civil administration, including political charges and public works, at about a million. On the receipt side the Board expected to be able to realise a revenue of over two millions sterling, three-fourths from "land-tax," as land revenue was at first termed, and the balance from salt, excise on spirits and drugs, stamps, and miscellaneous.

Though dry subjects, some of these items require elucidation, from the consequences for the people, good and evil, which the action taken during the first three years of British rule in the Punjab has since produced.

As regards the "land-tax," the Sikh system—the exaction each harvest from the cultivator of half and sometimes more of his gross produce—was noticed in the first chapter. As a well-regulated government conducted on exact business principles, the Board could not continue a method which was clumsy, inquisitorial, and uncertain in action. On budget considerations alone receipts from taxation had to be as regular as disbursements. But the Board had a higher object as well: as civilised Westerns ruling Asiatics it was their duty to inculcate habits of thrift and foresight, and how could the lesson be better learnt than by taxing agriculture lightly and exacting payment on fixed dates? True, the harvests varied with the amount and opportuneness of the rainfall; but the irregularity of the heavens could be adjusted to the regularity of a fixed demand and low assessments: fixity with moderation would enable the peasants to save in good years and meet the deficiencies of nature in bad years from the surpluses of previous harvests. So theorising, the Board decided to substitute everywhere for the Sikh system that initiated by John Lawrence during the regency period, and already in force in the North-West Provinces. Accordingly, settlement officers were instructed to estimate the average annual yield in all villages, convert the totals into their rupee equivalents, and assess from a quarter to a sixth of the product as the land-tax to be paid by each village-community on certain dates, corresponding with the time of harvest, but irrespective of the character of the out-turn. The change was at first welcomed by the peasantry as emancipation, and, so long as the harvests were normal to bumper and markets were steady, the new departure worked admirably. Those happy conditions lasted for two years, and then prices began to fall owing to over-production and the immense disbursements of the Government. The drop continued until grain sold at 50 per cent below its commutation valuation, then soon afterwards the rains failed, and for a harvest or two there was no production at all. The peasantry, however, had already converted their previous yields into rupees, and had spent the money on their domestic requirements, in which in many families marriage expenses were a considerable item. Having nothing in hand wherefrom to pay the tax-gatherer the cry of over-assessment was raised, and the Government, perceiving the general distress and having no exact data wherefrom to base conclusions, accepted the popular view and lowered the assessments. With reductions and the return of normal seasons the clamour subsided, and the busy Administration congratulated itself that the root-cause of present and future agrarian difficulties had been reached and removed. Any other conclusion would at the time have been rank heresy. The civilians in the Punjab commission had been recruited from the North-West Provinces—a country with usually a regular and heavy monsoon, a blessing not vouchsafed west of Ambala—and in those provinces the creed of fixity with moderation was a cardinal article of faith. In that hurrying period the day's work absorbed all energies; no one had time for thought or investigation; antecedently the gospel according to Thomason was accepted by every revenue Punjab officer; as a consequence, no Government servant questioned it, or even suspected that the inability of the peasantry to pay their revenue instalments after a bad harvest was due not so much to over-assessment, as to fixity of demand in spite of yields varying from nil to a hundred-fold. Thus, by 1852 the change from elastic extortion in kind to moderate fixity in cash was riveted on the Punjab. Some of the consequences will be shown in a later chapter.

The half a million sterling required over and above the land-revenue receipts were, as stated two pages back, obtained from sources all, except stamps, already tapped by the Sikhs. They not only treated all natural products, such as salt, gold, potash, as the property of the State, leasing the monopoly of each to the highest bidder or the court favourites of the day; but they also imposed duties under various names on all goods in transit, and in the course of their conveyance from, say, Amritsar to Peshawar, levied payments not once but a dozen times at as many stations. As they were killing the goose that laid the golden egg, Henry Lawrence, whilst Resident, had induced the Durbar to put all articles on a free list except the twenty yielding most income. The Board, free-traders to a man, decided, with the sanction of Lord Dalhousie, to abolish all transit and excise duties on every species of merchandise—small tolls at ferries excepted—and to recoup the loss to the state by directly working the salt monopoly, and selling the product in convenient blocks at the mine or quarry at a profit of 1600 per cent over the cost of extraction. The tax was so excessive that at first it slightly enhanced the price of salt to the consumer; but, on the other hand, it gave the state £200,000 a-year and quintupled commercial enterprise. Under the Sikhs the gross consumption in the province had only been half, and the profits to the State a quarter, of what they severally reached by 1855. The annual income to the state was in 1900, after allowing for the fall in silver, nearly half a million sterling.

Economically the salt-tax was—and is—indefensible, being drawn from a necessary of life and falling with most severity upon the already heavily burdened rural masses, who being owners of cattle and living on bulky salt-requiring foods, were and always must be, man for man, larger consumers of salt than the comparatively rich and untaxed urban classes. The sole plea for the tax was fifty years ago what it is to-day, convenience and prescription.

There is no occasion to particularise the other taxes imposed, aggregating £300,000, as their individual yields were at first very small. It is, however, worthy of note that the whole revenues of the Punjab from the largest item—land revenue—to the smallest—stamps, £10,000—were practically drawn from the producing masses, whilst the literate and commercial classes, whom the new *régime* was to benefit at the expense of those masses, escaped almost untaxed, and that to this day those relative conditions have little changed.

In 1850 the inequality of incidence, or rather the exemption of the industrial and professional classes from sharing the burden, was unavoidable: with no reliable data to work upon, with nothing in evidence but tangible produce, the Board had no option but to continue, purged of its most objectionable features, the pre-existing system.

CHAPTER XII.

JOHN LAWRENCE AS CHIEF COMMISSIONER, 1853-1858.

HAD the energies of the Lawrences during the four years of their partnership as joint-rulers of the Punjab been confined to the business of pacification, adjustment of taxation, and the initiation of the great public works, which in a few years converted a barren and backward country into a productive and well-managed estate, their comparatively leisured successors might well have marvelled at the extent and success of the Board's achievements, all conceived and carried out at a time when records, experienced advisers, and clerical establishments had as yet either no existence or were still embryonic. But the initiating and controlling activities of the brothers—particularly of John—extended to all the other branches of their expanding administration, to education, jails, dispensaries, post-office, forests, and punitive expeditions on the frontier. No detail was too particular for John's practical mind, no project possibly beneficial to his province too crude or visionary for the consideration of the sympathetic Henry. Whilst John, desk-chained at Lahore, tired his eyes and wearied his brain in plodding through dull and often badly written reports and letters, and, like a caged lion, chafed in his stuffy office-den that all the drudgeries were his, all the pleasures of governing his brother's, Henry, hating office-work, accounts, and details, and loving locomotion, spent the cold weather in camp and the worst of the hot in the Himalayas. During his wanderings he no doubt proved himself a beneficent providence to many a complaining Punjabi; no doubt, too, his officers loved him—indeed, his heart was so easily moved, that no man in difficulty ever appealed to him without receiving help or at least a kindly hearing. During his tours he would, as the spirit moved him, work through his official papers, write his mind as freely to Lord Dalhousie as to his brother, or spend days over a political article, for he belonged to those who "wrote to the newspapers," by preference to 'The Calcutta Review.' All this was not fair to John, who bore it patiently enough, growling, remonstrating, exploding at times, but always working his best and forbearing much, as he knew his brother's great qualities and the feeble state of his health.

When one of a carriage pair always does the greater part of the draught-work he sooner or later breaks down, so it was with John. He pulled and he pulled until he collapsed from fever and overstrain, and then the differences always present between the two brothers—each impervious to arguments against his own views—became acute. By degrees the tension between them became such that the efficiency of the administration began to suffer. Lord Dalhousie, whose special child the Punjab was, and whose correspondence with the Lawrences, particularly Henry, was constant, attempted to ease the situation by appointing Robert Montgomery, the life-friend of both brothers, junior member of the Board *vice* Mansel, late sleeping partner, removed to a snug Residency in Central India. The brothers now made their new coadjutor a sort of umpire between them, and he, being of a practical turn of mind, more often sided with John than with Henry. The patched-up machine of state might have rumbled on for a year or two more, had not decision on a question, upon which the brothers had always been at variance, become imperative. They had often discussed the treatment of the beneficiaries under the Sikh system. Hitherto principles had alone been considered, now the preliminary inquiries having been completed, orders on them had to be passed. There were some 20,000 cases for disposal, and the claimants ranged from the jagirdars or fief-holders of many villages to petty endowed institutions such as almshouses and religious infant-schools in villages. To the former the land revenue of thousands, sometimes tens of thousands, of acres had been alienated; to the latter only an acre or two in each case.

John regarded most of the big grantees either as ex-rebels or drones, and as such undeserving; Henry held that, in the mass, they were worthy patriots fallen on evil days, and politically and morally entitled to liberal treatment. Talk and reason as Montgomery might, he could not shake their conflicting convictions. As their mutual opposition only hardened each against compromise, and the official *impasse* was serious,—dozens of registers on the office-table dumbly awaiting orders, thousands of anxious expectants vociferating outside the office-room,—the disputants agreed to refer their differences to Lord Dalhousie, and each prayed that, as they could no longer work together amicably, he should be transferred elsewhere. Naturally the Governor-General decided in favour of the man of business, not of the man of heart. Naturally, too, he took the opportunity to abolish the triumvirate, and give the now tranquil law-abiding province a one-man government.

Early in 1853 Henry Lawrence was relegated to Rajputana, and John, his brother, was left at Lahore to reign alone as Chief Commissioner of the Punjab. In the opinion of the sirdars and natives generally, the elder brother had been sacrificed because, by the greatness of his love for them, he had offended the Calcutta Lord Sahib; in that of the officers of the local administration, his demission was due to the loftiness of his independence, which had roused the resentment of Lord Dalhousie, and, as some thought, the jealous ambition of the younger brother.

In reality the Governor-General had no choice. Henry Lawrence had neither the expert knowledge nor the business habit now required for the further development and governance of the Punjab, and those qualities were pre-eminently possessed by his brother.

So Henry Lawrence departed, literally amidst a people's lamentations. He had filled his sheet, the writing all in letters of gold, and now, as he thought, his night had come—in reality it was but the short gloom of a transient eclipse, for his sun was soon to shine once more, and then to set in glory, and the whole English-speaking world was to acknowledge that the man who had "tried to do his duty" was the noblest Englishman who had ever set foot in India.

The change in the constitution of the Government—a chief with two subordinate heads of departments, one financial, the other judicial, replacing a co-equal triumvirate—took place in the middle of the period between Gujerat and the Mutiny. The concentration of power in the hands of one man facilitated the rapid disposal of business. John Lawrence's habit was to have no arrears, to daily clear his daily official basket, and this he did until on May 12, 1857, the fateful telegram from Delhi, announcing the seizure of the city by the Meerut mutineers, diverted his energies from the routine of peaceful administration to the stern necessities of a struggle for life and empire. During the preceding four years the history of the province was comprised in two words—successful development. Whatever the Board had begun the Chief Commissioner had vigorously continued.

Reviewing in 1856 each branch of his administration, he recorded with satisfaction "the attachment of the people to their own rude jury system is unabated"; crime is "mild and rare, and on its occurrence is rigorously prosecuted and condignly punished"; "a considerable number of Thugs"—a robber fraternity of highway poisoners and stranglers—"perhaps 400, are still at large; but their devices are utterly confounded, and they find themselves so tracked that they cannot follow their dark profession"; the convict population had risen to 12,000, but "the interior of the jail now resembles an industrial institution"; besides seven Government schools "of a superior kind," and eight "good missionary schools," there were in all 3372 "indigenous or village schools, as yet of the rudest description. . . . The style of education is of course most primitive.

The teachers derive a precarious subsistence from fees. Heretofore there have been no funds available for popular education";—in reality, no children were receiving education at all, the schools referred to being merely infant rote-schools, sort of religious kindergartens, in which the prattlers repeated in Gurmachi, Hindi, Arabic, or Persian sentences from their several scriptures. "As a leaven to operate upon this mass of ignorance" Lawrence wrote that he had arranged to open 30 schools at district headquarters, 100 village schools in rural tracts, four normal schools and a central college at Lahore, the whole to be supervised by one director and two inspectors, and the annual cost to be £30,000, plus £1500 as grants-in-aid to missionary and other private schools. His declared object was that "the mass of the people be taught the plain elements of our knowledge in their own language." The funds for the purpose were to be obtained from the people themselves by a one per cent "education cess" on the land revenue. Had John Lawrence foreseen that the peasantry would not send their sons to school, but that the village money-lenders and traders would, we may be sure that he would not have taxed the former for the benefit of the latter, yet such has been the case throughout 75 per cent of the villages of the Punjab during the half century that has elapsed since popular education was inaugurated.

In his review the Chief Commissioner naturally dwelt at length on his favourite subjects, the "land-tax" and the condition and prospects of the agriculturists. "When it is remembered," he wrote, "that this tax [land revenue] furnishes three-quarters of the state resources, that it is paid by agriculturists comprising three-quarters of the population, that their contentment and happiness is more vitally affected by the manner in which this tax is levied and administered than by any circumstances whatsoever, the extreme importance of the subject is manifest." Discussing his share in the surrender of revenue in the first summary settlement made after annexation, he asserted that "on the whole the reduction of taxation allowed by the British Government on its first occupation of the country was not less than fifty lakhs or £500,000 sterling at the lowest," and that since then—exclusive of "casual remissions," aggregating £305,647—under the operation of regular settlements, further permanent reductions amounting to £234,000 annually had been conceded. To prove the lightness of his assessments, he said he had "ascertained that the Government demand does not exceed one-fifth of the gross value of the produce in rich tracts and one-sixth to one-eighth or even less in poor tracts, and that taking £10 a-year as the standard income of a peasant-proprietor "from his little patrimony," and deducting £2 for his land-tax and £2 more for cost of production, he had a balance of £6 "worth of produce, with which he may maintain his household and save a small surplus as capital." In the calculation, be it noted, Lawrence allowed nothing for bad seasons, cattle disease, deductions from the threshing-floor heap for village services, interest on debts, and the like. Answering the charge made by Sikh sirdars and others, that, in his desire to benefit the cultivators, he had sacrificed income to which landlords and jagirdars were entitled, he said that the allegation was true, and that extreme moderation in assessments had been necessary to ensure peasant prosperity. He then demonstrated by figures that by lapses of fiefs and resumption of jagirs—the point on which he and his brother had differed, and which Lord Dalhousie had decided in his favour—he had recouped to the state all that he had given up for the good of the people. He further explained that his policy "to tax lightly the agriculturists" had been partly due to the more or less permanent fall in prices of "50 per cent nearly" since annexation; but a simple sum in proportion shows that, if, when cash assessments were first imposed, the commutation prices were 50 per cent higher than they subsequently ruled, the reductions made between 1852-56 were incommensurate with the fall in prices.

Discussing prospects, he expected agriculture to remain the sole occupation of Punjabis, and that without facilities for export "there must always be some anxiety regarding our land revenue. Let means of export, the grand desideratum, be once supplied, everything will follow." To supply the peasantry with an outlet for their surplus produce, estimated by him at 777,481 tons annually, he pushed on road-making in all the doabs, and, convinced that "the valley of the Indus must become the great highway for the export trade of the Punjab, and that upon this trade more than upon any other circumstance the entire future of the province will depend," he promoted the extension of that costly failure "the Indus Steam Flotilla" to Makkhad, north of Kalabagh. That non-agriculturist capitalists, after reducing a large part of the peasant proprietary to the condition of villeins, might some day be the only class to share with the Government all the profits of the grain trade, was a contingency which never occurred to him. Whilst admitting that the British system of administration was beneficial to village money-lenders, and "enhanced facilities for recovering their loans from the landholders," he maintained that "on the other hand the proprietary bodies are becoming less and less dependent on them [the money-lenders], as frugality, prudence, and good management increase under the influence of the money-payment system." Their condition to-day shows that John Lawrence's faith in his peasantry and "money-payment system" was misplaced, and that he wholly misapprehended the effects of fixed cash assessments, uncertain harvests, and the possession of credit, plus freedom of contract and an up-to-date legal system.

Of new achievements between 1853 and the Mutiny three require mention—church construction, the first census, and telegraph extension.

State churches in the Punjab date from 1854. Their origin is said to have been owing to a doubt expressed by a wild Afghan trooper whether the English had any religion. In 1852-53 Henry Lawrence had made one of his frequent tours of inspection, and his escort had been furnished by a troop of "Guide" cavalry. The men had seen mosques, temples, and *dharmsālas* by the score, but Christian places of worship not one, and had begun to suspect that their rulers were not even good infidels.

"Lord Sahib," said a bold inquirer to Henry Lawrence, "we have seen that Moslems, Hindus, and Sikhs have each a religion,—have you Feringhees none?"

"We are Christians," was the reply.

"You are Christians, and you alone have no places for prayer!" exclaimed the sceptic.

The reproach struck home: forthwith arrangements were made, and soon in every station of the Punjab a handsome Gothic church was built, evidence to Indians of all creeds that Christians also worshipped God.

Now passing to the second subject—the census—it was taken during the night of December 31, 1854, with the acquiescence and even ready help of the people themselves, a fact proving the confidence and good understanding existing between the governed and the Government. The population of British possessions in the Punjab was found to be nearly thirteen millions, about three millions in excess of the rough guesses of 1849, and its density ranged from 334 a square mile in the richest districts in the Mānjha, about Lahore, Amritsar, and Jallandar, to 62 in the Muhammadan tracts west and south of Lahore. The number of villages was returned as 26,000; the cities with populations exceeding 50,000 were four—Amritsar, 122,000; Lahore, 94,000; Multan, 56,000; Peshawar, 53,000. Of the population seven and a half millions were Muhammadans and five and a half Hindus. The Sikhs were everywhere classed as Hindus, except in the Lahore division, in which they were most numerous and separately counted. In that division they were returned as 200,000 only, out of a population of three millions. The smallness of the total was accounted for by the supposition that, as the Sikhs as a militant commonwealth had been destroyed, their children were no longer initiated, and were consequently regarded as Hindus.

The third subject, the extension of the telegraph system to the Punjab, is specially noteworthy, as through its agency the authorities were forewarned of the seizure of Delhi by the Meerut mutineers, and enabled to take timely measures to disarm sepoy regiments before their plans were ripe for execution. To Lord Dalhousie belongs the credit of introducing and energetically pushing telegraphy in India. By 1857 he had given the country 4000 miles of instantaneous communications, including an excellently equipped line from Calcutta to Peshawar. At that time Indians still believed the sending of messages by wire to be devilish witchcraft, and preferred runners to trained lightning. Thus the Government was everywhere in a position to carry out its plans for self-preservation days before our enemies knew that the time had come for giving effect to theirs for our destruction. Happily for us, on May 12, 1857, what later a doomed sepoy called "the string that strangles us," delivered its message at Lahore, Rawalpindi, and Peshawar, and saved the Punjab from much bloodshed and confusion, perhaps even the British dominion in Bengal from temporary extinction.

CHAPTER XIII.

THE MUTINY—PUNJAB LOYALTY.

ON that particular May morning John Lawrence, weary in mind and body from overwork and a succession of hot weathers in the plains, was at Rawalpindi on his way to recess at Murree in the Himalayas. Hitherto throughout his service he had only thought and talked "shop"—the happenings in his own parish, whether district, division, or province. He knew, of course, that trouble had arisen Calcutta-wards, with some of the sepoy regiments there; but, regarding it as a Bengal affair, had never considered the contingency of serious developments Punjab-wards. When the telegram from Delhi was put into his hands, announcing that "the sepoys from Meerut have come in and are burning everything," his practical mind at once grasped the extent of the peril—the imminent mutiny of the Bengal army[1]—and the means by which it should be overcome. His parochialism had been that of the devoted local officer, not of the cramped understanding: on the instant it overleapt its provincial walls and included all India.

[1] Following unofficial Mutiny literature, the term "Bengal army" in this and the next chapter only refers to the Indian portion of that army recruited inside the Bengal Presidency but outside the Punjab.

That the English in India generally should be caught unprepared by the outbreak of the Mutiny was not surprising,—their habit was to sleep until an emergency roused their latent energies,—but that men of depth and penetration like the two Lawrences should not have anticipated and, by timely warnings, averted or restricted the catastrophe, is not to be explained by reasons applicable to ordinary British officials, both civil and military—ignorance, pre-occupation, remoteness from the centres of disaffection, the discipline or etiquette of the services—none of these pleas were good against the two brothers. The expedience of reorganising the Bengal army had long been recognised; but to smash a working system and conquer the *vis inertiæ* of climate and seniority products in high places demanded a leisured Napier, Dalhousie, or Kitchener, with the powers of a dictator plus the support of proven necessity, and neither postulate was possible without an antecedent compulsion of some sort. The official mind is always conservative: familiarity with routine practices induces blindness to faults or at least dislike for reforms; hence drastic changes in any department of an administration, whether military, revenue, or judicial, are rarely introduced—in India at least—except under the coercion of fear or some great calamity.

Half a century before "greased cartridges" turned the discontent of the Upper Provinces into the caste-panic which was the immediate cause of the mutiny of the Bengal army, two regiments of docile Madrasis had suddenly run amuck at Vellore, unreasonably frenzied by an order altering the shape of their turbans and cut of their beards. Happily, the madness was localised; but for a long period the dread of similar outbreaks on a larger scale was an ever-present nightmare to Indian administrators. With the passing of the years and the distractions of growing empire and successive wars, the lesson of the Vellore incident was crowded out of the mind, and when the Oude sepoys had stood the ordeals of the Kabul and Sikh wars almost without an insubordinate word or act, faith in their faithfulness became implicit. True, when the Punjab became a British province and foreign service allowances were suddenly discontinued, some of the Purbia regiments serving there showed signs of mutiny, and Sir Charles Napier forthwith urged the employment of low-caste men or, better, of casteless Ghurkas, who "mess together and make few inquiries as to the sex of a beef-steak, and are, therefore, the men with which to meet the Brahmins of Bengal and their bristling prejudices of high caste." Though, fortunately, he had his way about the Ghurkas, his warnings of dangers ahead from the "immense influence" of caste in the Bengal army were unheeded, and so absolute continued confidence in that army, that, up to May 1857, the whole of Bengal east of the Punjab was entrusted to their care.

The fact is that until Lord Dalhousie roused the Company's sleepy style of civil administration into one of up-to-date English efficiency—witness his insistence on good government by native states, his annexations, roads, bridges, telegraph-lines, railways, education policy, and striking reforms in the Punjab—most Governors-General had ruled as Great Moghals, and their local representatives, from heads of provinces to district despots, had exercised their respective functions as if each were a petty Great Moghal himself. Civilly, Lord Dalhousie's activities had revolutionised the old *régime;* but they had not extended to the regular army, which until destroyed by the Mutiny, continued to be rather an unwieldy close corporation of pipeclay men than an efficient war-machine. Sir Charles Napier had been an army reformer, but idiosyncrasies of temper had sterilised his efforts; and having acted flagrantly *ultra vires*, he had been forced to resign, after accomplishing little but the opening of military service under the Company to Ghurkas, and the first steps towards transport organisation. The discovery that both the peace administration of an army, and the conduct of a war, required expert knowledge and brains of a high order was not made until the mutiny of the Hindustanis of the regular Bengal army revealed the rottenness of the system on which it had been built up, and brought young officers of capacity and energy to the front. Until then seniority, tempered by interest, had decided all appointments; and the large majority of our officers, from general to subaltern, satisfied that they and their men were a happy family of good soldiers, mutually necessary to each other, drank, sported, and jollified without a care or a thought higher than those of a drill-sergeant.

On the civil side, the minds of those administering the country were too engrossed with questions of ways and means, and the everyday routine of executive work, to bestow much attention upon the consequences of the changes in distribution and relative strength of the components of military force resulting from the wars and annexations of the first twenty years of Queen Victoria's reign. Between 1838 and 1849, the period extending from just before the first Afghan war to the battle of Gujerat, the native army had been augmented from 154,000 to 260,000 men, whilst the number of British troops serving in Bengal had remained almost stationary. After Gujerat the strength of the native army was rapidly reduced, until in 1856 its grand total stood at 230,000 men, of whom 40,000 were recruited from Oude, the majority being Brahmins, whose influence was paramount with all castes.

Though annexations had now ended, the consequences remained: each new province or territory added to the empire had involved a permanent increase in the numbers of our sepoys, and at the same time a diminution in that of their best English officers, who were drawn away from their regiments to fill civil appointments. The drain had been considerable before the annexation of the Punjab, but between that event and the Mutiny it had so increased—irregulars, police, public works, and district administration absorbing scores of our best Hindustani scholars and most reliable officers in the Company's Indian forces—that many Bengal regiments were left to the charge of a few officers of doubtful efficiency; and not only did the sepoys lose the officers who possessed their confidence, but of the British regiments serving in Bengal, the great majority were located in the new province. In 1856, out of the whole British garrison then in India—only 45,000 men—16,000 were quartered west of Delhi, and thence to Calcutta, a densely populated stretch of country 1000 miles in extent, the number of British bayonets was under 3000. In that year, of the Bengal army alone, 803 officers were on duty in various capacities away from their regiments. Thus, throughout the districts in which the Mutiny afterwards raged most virulently, the English dominion was almost wholly represented by a few civilians and a large number of sepoy regiments, each indifferently supervised by an old *qui hai* or two, an adjutant, and a few English boys, many of them still learning their drill and the rudiments of Hindustani.

In concentrating the great bulk of the British troops allocated to Bengal in the Punjab, and transferring thither the flower of the British officers of the Bengal army, Lord Dalhousie unwittingly supplied that army with a potent provocation to mutiny. In all his annexations, and latterly in entrusting forts, magazines, arsenals, and treasuries to the uncontrolled guardianship of Hindustani troops, he, like most pre-Mutiny Englishmen in authority, seems to have taken it for granted that British rule and institutions were the one thing needful to give Hindus and Muhammadans of all classes and conditions contentment and prosperity. His closing act, the absorption of Oude, the recruiting-ground of a large part of the regulars in the Bengal army, was prompted by the mistaken conviction that thereby he was earning the lasting goodwill, not only of the Oude peasantry, but of our sepoys as well, by securing for their families the full enjoyment of their home rights and privileges, hitherto denied them under the misrule of their vicious indigenous rulers.

Whilst we were empire-building, the collapse of our rapidly rising fabric might have occurred at any moment; we were handling explosives in half a dozen places at the same time, but, trusting to the effect of our prestige and impartial justice, never gave much thought to the danger: pushful and self-confident, we emerged unscathed from each crisis.

Whilst pressing forward to the Indus and beyond, our sepoy mercenaries had little time for plots and combinations: after Gujerat came a period of rest, and with idleness Satan, in the form of suggested suspicions and obvious opportunities for mischief, entered into our sepoys. Outside the army we had many enemies—dispossessed princes, childless rulers fearing extinction, their friends and dependents—and everywhere the interests of caste and privilege were being threatened and undermined by the Westernising processes at work throughout the length and breadth of the land. Thus, beneath an unruffled surface, the Gangetic valley—the home of caste and prejudice, brotherhoods and families, both Hindu and to some extent Muhammadan, each jealous, exclusive, and dissatisfied with present conditions—was restive, suspicious, and expectant. Our Brahmin sepoys, deprived of their trusted friends, the English officers who best understood them, their faith in the limitless power of the Company Bahadar weakened by the disappearance of the *gora logue* (white people = British soldiers), their credulity imposed upon by tales of disaster to our arms in the Crimea and afterwards in Persia, began to think that they were the real masters. Poisonous tongues around them flattered their vanity, and whispered the suspicion that their employers, fearing them, were rapidly forming a formidable army of irregulars in the Punjab, intending to get rid of all Hindustanis or, worse, break their caste, a step towards which had already been taken by the issue of the order that new enlistments should be for general service by land or over-sea. When, then, taunted that, if they bit the cartridges issued with the new Enfield rifle, their brethren in Oude would refuse to eat with them, new terrors assailed them—the grease with which the cartridges were lubricated contained the fat of cows, "and of pigs," added the incendiaries, with a view to inflame the minds of Muhammadans.

The "greased-cartridges" scare was first started in the musketry-school at Dum-Dum near Calcutta in December 1856, and spread rapidly, until on February 26, 1857, the 19th Native Infantry at Barhampur committed an act of insubordination, were threatened and abused by their excited colonel, and, losing their heads, ran to their lines and loaded their muskets, but soon after became submissive again. A month afterwards they were disbanded; but the contagion had already spread throughout the Bengal army. Reason and argument were powerless against the madness of terror for caste and religion which possessed all minds. The epidemic, seemingly suppressed for three months in Lower Bengal, broke out with violence almost simultaneously at Lucknow and Meerut. At the former station Sir Henry Lawrence, by discriminating tact and firmness, checked its progress for a time, at the latter the tremendous sentence of ten years' imprisonment with hard labour on all the 85 troopers—many of them young recruits—who had refused to bite the cartridge, frenzied the whole of the native garrison. On the night of May 10 the comrades of the sentenced troopers rose, broke open the jail, released the 1200 prisoners therein, shot down defenceless Europeans, plundered and burnt half the station, and then, joined by the two native infantry regiments, marched off for Delhi unpursued, although the British portion of the garrison, 1800 in number, including a regiment of cavalry and several troops of horse artillery, was strong enough to have scattered or annihilated them, and thus saved Delhi. General Hewitt, one of the seniority dotards of the time, only "cleared the cantonment," a euphemism for pottering and doing nothing. He had for years been notoriously unfit for employment, and had been removed from Peshawar, because, whilst there he never visited his outposts and was in the habit of inspecting his troops in a buggy, yet under the seniority system he had been afterwards given the most important command outside the Punjab.

Thus, without premeditation or antecedent conspiracy, the mutiny of the Bengal army was successfully begun in the very heart and centre of the Indian Empire. Just as the disregard of sanitary precautions converts sporadic cholera or plague into an epidemic, so our pre-Mutiny neglect of the most ordinary safeguards against the growth of discontent had perverted the minds of the sepoys from their allegiance, and, coupled with the ineptitude shown by the military authorities at Simla and Meerut, changed what John Lawrence afterwards called "the cartridge affair" into a general revolt.

Until, on May 12, the Meerut mutineers streamed into Delhi, and the recently completed wires flashed news of the catastrophe to Ambala and thence to Lahore, Lawrence had only shown himself a shrewd revenue-officer and provincial administrator, and was hardly known outside his province, six months later he was recognised by the whole civilised world as the statesman who had saved the British possessions in India. His sudden rise from successful mediocrity to real greatness was not due to extraordinary talents of any kind, but to his possession of that rare yet unattractive quality, admirable common-sense.

Luck, too, befriended him: the Punjab had just been blessed for the third time in succession with a bumper harvest, and the people were consequently in a very happy frame of mind; its interior cantonments held the bulk of the British troops serving in Bengal, most of them armed with the new Enfield rifle, a weapon crushingly superior to the "gas-pipe" Brown Bess of the mutineers; in addition, the Punjab's Indus frontier was garrisoned by the lately raised provincial army, men heartily loyal and keen for active service in any part of the world. Further, as we had just been coercing Persia to surrender Herat to the aged Amir of Kabul, and were allowing him a subsidy of £120,000 a-year, he and his Afghan subjects were, for the first time in Anglo-Indian history, friendly towards us, and might be expected to remain benevolently neutral, so long at all events as the subsidy was continued, Dost Muhammad Khan lived, and the Punjab was true to its allegiance. Thus the mutiny of the Bengal army could not have occurred at a more opportune time for the effective demonstration of Punjab loyalty, nor could the mutineers have made a move more likely to unite the people of the province, especially Sikhs and frontier tribesmen, against them than by seizing the city, the looting of which had been the object of Muhammadan invasions for centuries, and later of Khalsa ambition. In addition to the prospect of sacking Delhi, the Sikhs had recent scores to pay off: their narrow defeats by the English, good straightforward fighters, had been honourable to the vanquished, but that black effeminate Purbias, who had run away in battle, should form two-thirds of the garrison of the Punjab and boast that they, not the Feringhees, had humbled the pride of the Khalsa and were holding them down, was bitterness to a domineering people, who but for those Feringhees would have long before placed their Maharaja on the peacock throne of the effete Moghal.

Then, too, the Sikhs remembered with bitterness that they had lost their independence through listening to the evil counsels of the Hindustanis in their service—a fact borne out by Sir Henry Lawrence himself, who, writing in 1856 of the causes of our Sikh wars, had said: "Proportionably few of the instigators of opposition at Lahore in the Sikh army were Sikhs. They were mostly British subjects, many of them British deserters. The general feeling of the Sikhs was hardly hostile; many of the Sikhs were friendly, decidedly so, compared with the Hindoostanees in the Punjab service," and, since those wars, not only was the Sikh fatherland garrisoned by those intruders, but every civil post of emolument was held by them. Sikhs, and indeed all Punjabis, had therefore in 1857 good cause for hating Hindustanis.

During the first forty-eight hours after the receipt of the bad news from Delhi, Lawrence at Rawalpindi, and Robert Montgomery, Financial Commissioner, at Lahore, thinking and acting independently, — for telegraphic communication between the two stations was interrupted,—decided to forestall a local mutiny by inducing the military authorities to disarm Bengal regiments, wherever possible, before the secret of the fall of Delhi should ooze out and become bazaar property. At the time there were 36,000 regular Hindustani troops in the province, 8000 of them in the Peshawar valley, between 2000 and 3500 at each of the following cantonments, Rawalpindi, Lahore, Mianmir, Jallandar, Multan, Ferozepore, and Sialkot, and smaller numbers at Jhelam, Amritsar, Ludhiana, Philor, and other secondary stations. Thus, exclusive of Multan, which lay isolated in the far south-west of the province, and was of great importance as the connecting-link between the Punjab and the sea at Karrachi, the great bulk of the sepoy army was massed along the Grand Trunk Road, and a successful rising in any central cantonment, Lahore in particular, would have been the signal for similar movements up and down the line, just as the seizure of Delhi was proving for the Purbia garrisons throughout the valley of the Ganges.

Montgomery lost no time in vain deliberation: that wired warning gave its possessors several days' advantage over their undeclared enemies: telegram in hand he rode to Mianmir and easily converted Brigadier Corbett to his views. A ball was being given that night to the officers of her Majesty's 81st Foot, the only British regiment in the station, and for the following morning a general parade had already been ordered. To lull suspicion no change of programme was made, except that just before moving to the parade-ground the guns of the two batteries of horse artillery in garrison were loaded with grape, balled ammunition was served out to the 81st, and three of its companies were marched off to Lahore. When the parade began, the three native infantry regiments and one irregular cavalry regiment, still unconscious that anything unusual was about to take place, were brought up face to face with the remaining five companies of the 81st, who at once opened out, disclosing twelve guns with port-fires held lighted, in readiness for immediate action. Before the astonished sepoys and troopers had grasped the full meaning of the manœuvre, the words of command, "81st, load!" rang out. Amazed and cowed, all four regiments, as soon as ordered to pile arms, did so after a momentary hesitation: thus in a few minutes over 3000 probable mutineers were weaponless, and impotent for mischief.

Whilst this scene was being enacted at Mianmir, five miles away, the 300 men of her Majesty's 81st who had been sent to Lahore were quietly entering its fort and relieving and disarming its sepoy garrison. Lahore and Mianmir secured, the brigadier put a company of his English infantry into country gigs called ekkas, and ran them through to Amritsar during the night. By breakfast-time on the following morning (May 14) the fort there, called Govindgarh, had also a British garrison. Although the political and commercial capitals of the province were now safe for the moment, the security of the central position on the Punjab chess-board in the game now opening between "white" and "black" required the immediate substitution of British soldiers for sepoys in the two chief arsenals of the province, Ferozepore and Philor.

Unfortunately, the brigadier at the former cantonment, Innes by name, was one of the many incompetents whom the seniority system had raised to responsible positions. Had he followed the advice wired to him from Lahore, arsenal and cantonment would have been by the morning of the 13th as securely British as were Mianmir and Lahore fort. Instead of acting vigorously—he had her Majesty's 61st Foot and some guns—he pottered and harangued.

He sent a company of the 61st to garrison the arsenal, but he neither disarmed nor turned out the wing of the 45th Native Infantry, who had been in sole charge of the place. He paraded the regiment and spoke like a father to the sepoys, and forthwith, helped by their comrades inside the arsenal, they attempted to rush the British guard, and not until another company of the 61st was hurried up did the scrimmage cease. Had the mutineers been at once followed and annihilated, the matter would have ended. Instead, the brigadier adopted a defensive attitude, and that night the compromised regiment burnt and plundered most of the station, and then set out for Delhi. In the morning a feeble pursuit was ordered, after which the second native infantry regiment was disarmed; for the time being the native cavalry were trusted.

The change of garrison at Philor—the largest arsenal in the Punjab—was better managed. In the fortunate absence of Brigadier Johnstone at Simla the command in the Jallandar cantonment, twenty-four miles from Philor, was held by Colonel Hartley of the 8th Queen's, who, as soon as he heard the bad news from Delhi, put a company of his men into conveyances and wheeled them down to the Philor fort, whereupon Thomas Atkins marched in and Jack Sepoy walked out. As far as the game had advanced white's novel opening had been successful—the strong central position had been fully secured; but before the attack could be driven home and the black king, already castled at Delhi, could be mated, several of white's pieces, which from careless handling were scattered and isolated, had to be first extricated from false positions.

By May 16, in spite of the closure of all ferries,

the arrest of wandering mendicants, the interception of sepoys' letters, the fall of Delhi and general revolt of the Bengal army were publicly known or suspected. White now ceased to have the initial advantage of prior information; but his central security gave him such vantage that, should black fail to bring off some surprise combination in the Peshawar valley or at Multan, his chances of winning or even drawing the game were now small.

In the Peshawar valley, exclusive of the corps of Guides at Hoti Mardan and some military police, there were three batteries of field and one of horse artillery and about 11,000 regulars,—horse and foot,—of whom two-thirds were Hindustanis of the Bengal army, none trustworthy, but unlikely to attempt collective mischief, so long as the general population of the country and the neighbouring hill tribes were hostile to them, or at least neutral. There was perfect peace inside the valley, a happy condition, in part due to the curious fact that every hill tribe outside it was what was called "under a blockade"—*i.e.*, penally excluded from British territory. Thus the elements of danger were considerable. Luckily the outbreak at Meerut was known to the Commissioner on the night of the 11th, with the further strange addition on the following morning that "the European troops are defending barracks." The two most suspected native infantry regiments, the 64th and 55th,—those with the largest preponderance of Brahmins in their ranks,—were at once crippled for intrigue, the former being distributed in detachments amongst the outposts, each a purgatory for Hindustanis, and the latter transferred to Hoti Mardan to take the place of "that notable corps of *shikāris* of all nations," the "Guides," who, unlike our regulars, were "neither strapped down nor braced up nor button-strangled, but wore their own loose dusky shirts and wide pahjāmahs and sun-proof, sword-proof turbans, and as few accoutrements as possible."

The Guides had crossed the Indus at Attock on their since famous march to Delhi, and the two most tainted native infantry regiments had been segregated amidst a fanatically hostile Muhammadan population, before bazaar, cantonment, and country-side knew for certain that Delhi was in the hands of the Meerut mutineers, and British rule thence to Calcutta in process of extinction. The discovery found none of the hitherto subject or restrained forces of the valley and neighbourhood—8000 Hindustani troops, city rabble, peasantry all armed, and the hill tribes—prepared for action. The local authorities, Brigadier Cotton, Herbert Edwardes (Commissioner), and John Nicholson (Deputy Commissioner), acted promptly, and on May 21 disarmed four of the five Bengal regiments of regulars still in the Peshawar cantonment. The work, which had to be done against the protestations of the British officers of the suspected regiments, was carried out with even greater ease and precision than had been the case eight days before at Mianmir, for not only was the overawing force of British troops much larger, but a body of cut-throat Afridis from the Khyber Pass stood ready to act butcher if wanted. Next day a mixed force was despatched to Hoti Mardan to disarm the 55th Native Infantry there. As the British infantry approached the sepoys became panic-struck and stampeded for the hills. They were pursued, cut up, and captured by the hundred, whilst the 500 who escaped into the mountains were hunted down by the Swatis and other tribesmen and killed to the last man. Their unfortunate colonel, unable to bear the disgrace and destruction of the corps he had loved and trusted to the last, and convinced that his men had been terrorised into flight, committed suicide. The facile disarming of four regiments, annihilation of the fifth, and segregation of another—for the time the native cavalry, all irregulars, and some of the infantry were allowed to retain their arms and treated as loyalists—convinced the population, hill and plain, that the Sahibs were masters still, and going to win at Delhi. Edwardes was quick to take advantage of this trend of public opinion by offering service to every able-bodied dare-devil in and outside the valley, a move which conduced more to the peace and contentment of the country than the presence of an additional brigade.

On one occasion Edwardes demurred to the enlistment of a whole troop of outlaws, most of them proclaimed murderers, but accepted them when their leader, with a twinkle in his eye, pointed out "whether they kill the Purbias or the Purbias them, it will be an equal service to the State"—the fact was undeniable. In all 5667 men were thus enlisted, half in the Derajat, and the others in Peshawar and Kohat. Of the number 1807 served before Delhi and in Oude, and gained a high repute as skirmishers.

Whilst Edwardes is raising, organising, and despatching his levies to Delhi and helping the brigadier to hold stern watch over the Purbia regulars, armed and disarmed, in the valley, a glance at the progress of the game in other parts of the chess-board will show that the ultimate victory of white was long deferred owing to some stupid moves on his part, and to his initial mistake of allowing black to play the match with a double set of pawns: black's pieces throughout were poorly handled, his men did most of the fighting.

From the Beas westwards the more important cantonments along the Grand Trunk Road had by now been partially cleared of armed Hindustanis, but from Jallandar eastwards to Delhi the military authorities had shared the amiable credulity which to the last affected most of the old *qui hai* officers of the army, and the more Lawrence urged the disarmament of their sepoys, the more obstinately did their local colonels and brigadiers cling to the belief that their own particular "children" were good and well behaved. At Jallandar, as we saw, Colonel Hartley of the 8th Queen's, in the lucky absence of Brigadier Johnstone at Simla, had promptly substituted Thomas Atkins for Jack Sepoy as guardian over fort and arsenal at Philor, and had further at Lawrence's suggestion made a similar change in respect of the custody of the civil treasure in Jallandar city. Presently down tumbled—more correctly, was carried—the brigadier from Simla. Like so many others in pre-Mutiny days, he was fitter for a nurse and bath-chair than a command in a crisis. Sick in body, unnerved in mind, he tried to coax his slighted sepoys into good behaviour by restoring the treasure to their charge, and giving them much paternal advice, pointing out that though he had sufficient force at hand—in addition to his British garrison a Sikh regiment was passing through at the time—to disarm or destroy them, he did neither, he trusted them.

The three Bengal regiments repaid his confidence by marching off for Philor (June 7); arrived there, they easily persuaded the recently ejected native infantry regiment, camped outside the fort, to fraternise with them, and then all four regiments began leisurely to cross the Sutlej by boat. As at Meerut and Ferozepore, there was no pursuit; but on the river's left bank the mutineers, 3000 strong, encountered Mr Ricketts, the civilian deputy commissioner of Ludhiana, and a handful of Sikhs, who blazed away at the cowardly sepoys until, ammunition being exhausted, the little force withdrew into the protection of the Ludhiana fort. The mutineers followed, and joined by the town rabble, Kashmiris, Gujars, Afghans, and others, plundered and burnt the station, and then continued their march to Delhi. As soon as they had disappeared, Ricketts exacted heavy compensation from the turbulent townsmen and outside Gujars, tried and executed the ringleaders, and, with a small body of police and a liberal use of the lash, maintained order until, Delhi taken, the reign of law was re-established.

In contrast with the fiasco at Jallandar was the success of the procedure carried out at Multan. As the only British troops in the station were 48 artillerymen in the fort, whilst outside there were two native infantry regiments, the risk of drawing their teeth with no backing of force other than the irregulars, amongst whom were numerous Hindustanis, was so great that Lawrence had long considered that the attempt should be deferred until some of the troops on their way up from Sindh should reach Multan, and that, when made, the Bengal infantry alone should be disarmed. However, when the outbreak at

Jallandar had occurred, he wired to Multan advising immediate action before the news should circulate in the sepoy lines. Accordingly, next morning Colonel Crawford-Chamberlain carried out the bold measure, supported by the handful of British gunners and his own regiment, the 1st Irregular Cavalry, a large proportion of whom were Hindustanis. The work was done quickly and smoothly, as if the piling of arms were a mere parade movement. In surrendering their muskets without the coercion of guns and Enfields in British hands, the Multan sepoys showed a power of calculation unusual amidst the general madness of their countrymen. Isolated in a Muhammadan corner of the Punjab and 600 miles from Delhi, they must have realised that they could hardly hope to reach that city as an organised military body: probably, too, owing to their distance from the centres of the epidemic, they had absorbed less of its poison than had they been stationed nearer their homes.

The Punjab's only means of communication with the outer world being secured, Lawrence's mind was relieved from further immediate anxiety in respect of danger from possible sepoy risings in his province. True, the Bengal regiments in and about Ambala and at most of the secondary stations, aggregating some 20,000 men, still retained their arms; but their powers of combination were circumscribed, and a local outbreak, if not immediately locally crushed, would only be followed by a night of confusion and a hurried march to Delhi. In the case of Ambala the Commander-in-Chief's misguided tenderness for his Bengal regiments would, at the worst, merely increase the number of our armed foes inside Delhi,—what later occurred,—and, elsewhere, as soon as the flying column, in process of formation at Jhelam, was equipped and in motion, the further purging of the province would soon be carried out.

General Anson, the Chief, was at Simla when he heard of the Meerut and Delhi outbreaks. He knew nothing about India and Indian sepoys, but something about regulation campaigns and much about whist, and his headquarters' staff appreciated the necessity and possibility of prompt action as little as he did. They all came comfortably down from their pleasant retreat, and on arrival at Ambala were beginning, with the deliberation traditional in Indian wars, to consider measures for opening the campaign, when letters from Lawrence arrived which must have ruffled their well-regulated minds. He assumed that Brigadier Hewitt at Meerut had already been peremptorily ordered to move on Delhi, urged the immediate disarming of all Hindustani regulars, and insisted on a rapid advance; and further he announced that the Guides and other Punjab irregulars were already on their march to Delhi. Instead of overcoming difficulties the Chief raised them, and even talked of entrenching himself where he was—what practically Hewitt had already done; whereupon Lawrence, quoting a maxim from the Chief's own guide to whist, wired, "When in doubt take the trick: clubs not spades are trumps." After much pressure the advance was begun on May 25, but, a day or two afterwards, General Anson died of cholera at Karnal. Sir Henry Barnard, then at Ambala, succeeded him. Though new to India and wanting experience, he was energetic, and pushed on. Joined by a weak brigade from Meerut, he brushed aside a faint-hearted attempt by the mutineers to bar his progress, and by June 9, reinforced by the invaluable Guides from Hoti Mardan, who had covered 580 miles in twenty-two days, planted himself and his little army of 4000 men, 20 field-guns, and a few pieces of heavy ordnance received from Philor, on the since historic "ridge" about a mile from the north-west corner of the city, and directly facing its Kashmir and Mori gates. There the force lay entrenched—besieged rather than besiegers—for the next three months, until, when Lawrence had sent down his last available man and gun, the desperate venture of assault gave final triumph to the heroes of fifty fruitless victories, and the flag of England waved once more over the blood-stained capital of the Moghals.

Having got the nucleus of an Anglo-Punjab army before Delhi, Lawrence's next business was to maintain it there—to feed it with men, munitions, and supplies — until such time as it should be in a position to strike effectually. The issue depended on the constancy of the Punjabis to the English cause. They were heartily pro-English in the policy of disarming and expelling all Hindustanis, intruding foreigners whose presence deprived Punjabis of service and emoluments rightfully theirs: as to loyalty, or rather far-seeing selfishness, the country recognised that English rule was preferable to a return to its only alternative, a period of topsy-turvydom, ending with the oppressive but precarious supremacy of one rival race over the others. On the whole, then, Punjabis were agreed that so long as English *ikbāl* (prestige) suffered no great disaster, they would be true to their white masters—otherwise they could take care of themselves. For the present, therefore, the fighting manhood of the province responded in thousands to Lawrence's call to arms; but he chose his recruits wisely, so balancing antagonistic nationalities and creeds as to give dangerous preponderance to none. Between the middle of May and end of August he enlisted in all 34,000 men,—almost the exact equivalent to Hindustanis sooner or later disarmed,—and this new army, added to the slightly augmented Frontier Irregular Force (14,000) and Military Police (12,000), made the aggregate number of Punjabis and hillmen put into the field roundly 60.000, of whom nearly half were Muhammadans, a third Sikhs, and the balance miscellaneous Hindus, Mazbis (sweepers turned Sikhs), and even non-Brahmin Hindustanis. Of this considerable army not more than 35,000 saw active service beyond the then limits of the province, the rest, consisting mostly of police and the levies of the cis-Sutlej feudatories and cis- and trans-Indus Muhammadan chiefs of various degrees, being retained in the province to replace the better organised irregulars, "Piffers" and Military Police, sent to the front.

Though fully half of the emergency forces, Sikhs and frontier tribesmen excepted, saw little or no fighting, they protected our one vital line of communication with Delhi, the Grand Trunk Road, escorted supplies, patrolled roads, put down attempts at insurrection, helped to hold the frontier, guarded disarmed Hindustani regiments, and performed most of the duties ordinarily falling on the military garrison and police in time of peace.

CHAPTER XIV.

THE MUTINY—TRIUMPH OF THE PUNJAB.

But recruiting, movements of troops and levies, and the warlike activities of that crisis only affected a small percentage of the general population. Evidence that the Government of the country was fighting for existence was confined to the larger cantonments and the Grand Trunk Road. To the great bulk of the rural communities of the province echoes of the life-and-death struggle going on before Delhi were as void of personal interest as is the roar of breakers to the inmates of snug quarters some distance from the sea. In the absence of agitators, what cared Punjabi villagers for news from places outside their world—bounded usually by the limits of their own group of villages—when in their homes there was abundance, and in their fields promise of more from timely rainfall, when the revenue demand had been paid without borrowing, and remunerative labour on public works was to be had for the asking?

Thank God, those craven shaven Purbias, who monopolised all the well-paid appointments not wanted by the Sahibs for themselves, with now and again a sleek fat-legged Baboo, were being escorted in batches out of their land—a curse upon them all, the Punjab and *sarkāri noukari* (Government service) were for Punjabis, not for the "blacks" from beyond the Ganges. So the volume of rural life flowed on placidly as it usually did, except in lean years, undisturbed by the storm raging east of Ambala.

Here and there, it is true, the most ignorant of the more idle and thriftless amongst the Muhammadan tribes—already under British institutions beginning to lose status and means of easy subsistence—were growing restive as the weeks lengthened and rumours of British disasters circulated. The first to break out into blind, clumsy rebellion against order were branches of that numerous and barbarous people, the Gujars, once supreme in Kashmir, but for centuries scattered as graziers and slovenly cultivators from the Kāghān glen in Hazara to Delhi. About Ludhiana and southwards bands of them collected, and began plundering, but having neither cohesion, intelligence, nor firearms, were easily suppressed.

From time to time other tribes in the same neighbourhood, such as the incorrigibly lazy and improvident Rangarhs and the gipsy fraternities, known as "the criminal tribes," whom neither kindness nor severity has yet tamed to honest labour, also attempted risings, but were at once hunted down by police and levies, and terrorised into their normal condition of inoffensive uselessness. Later, the Kharrals and Dhunds of the hills between Hazara and Rawalpindi made a combined movement against the hill sanitorium, Murree, but their insurrection fizzled out at the sight of a few policemen. Then, towards the end of the long tension in the third month of the struggle before Delhi, an insurrection on a large scale broke out amongst the pastoral Muhammadan tribes, Kharrals and others, inhabiting the jungly tracts between Lahore and Multan. Though their largest gang took, sacked, and for some days occupied a small town, Kot Kamalia, their rebellion was never formidable. They were merely roaming mobs of boors and cattle-stealers, rudely armed, aggregating 7000 or 8000 men and boys. Once only did they venture on a combat with a small troop of horse. Wild and cunning as jackals in shifting from lair to lair, their suppression gave occupation for three months to several flying columns, and not until trackers followed up their spoor, and their flocks and herds were captured, did the troublesome business end.

With those insignificant exceptions—ripples here and there on the glassy surface of a tranquil ocean—the Punjab was as quiet and law-abiding throughout 1857 as during any year before or since. Towards the last, when all the world wondered as, day after day, news of the long-expected assault on Delhi did not arrive, there was impatience rather than wavering. Had Lawrence died, or the attack miscarried and withdrawal cis-Indus from Peshawar been ordered—a contingency already considered and threshed out between the Chief Commissioner and his advisers—the strain might have overcome the loyal endurance of one or more of the stronger nationalities of the Punjab. Even so, the probabilities are that the grand common-sense of the mass of the people, particularly of the Sikhs, would have kept them to their allegiance, for the conviction lay deep in most minds that no force in India could ultimately prevail against English organisation and resources.

However, even throughout June, when our anxieties were greatest and fortunes lowest, the Punjab was unmoved, though the armed Hindustani troops still in it were a source of anxiety. Happy in past rainfall, and occupied in preparing their fields for autumn sowings, the peasantry took little heed of the movements of troops and levies on the Grand Trunk Road, and as for the "row" (*hangāma*), as they called the struggle going on at Delhi, they were sure the Sahibs would win, for were not the Punjab *jawāns* (young men) fighting for the Feringhees? When they heard that their own "Jān Lārans" was extracting a "voluntary" loan "by order" from the money-lenders,—not one of whom subscribed except under compulsion,—and that the rajas and sirdars of the land were also contributors, they chuckled gleefully and remarked, "Just what our great Maharaja would have done." Could rustic approbation rise higher? Whilst outwardly the administration was going on as if the war were in China and not at the very threshold, Lawrence was trying to stave off further mutinies in the cantonments now drained of their British protection. From the middle of May onwards he had been continuously despatching a stream of reinforcements to the front. A pause had occurred whilst recruits were being drilled, and a flying column organised, whose business was to finish the purging of the province and then sweep on to the "ridge."

The nucleus of this column, marching down the Grand Trunk Road, reached Lahore early in June, and quietly took over the horses of the disarmed but not yet dismounted native cavalry regiment there. Whilst still completing its numbers and equipment, its brigadier, Neville Chamberlain, was called away to serve as Adjutant-General of the Field Force before Delhi, and the vacant command was given to John Nicholson—tremendous promotion for a regimental captain, one, moreover, who for years had been in civil employ. He joined his command on June 21 at Jallandar, and forthwith by bold and clever management peaceably disembarrassed himself of suspects by disarming the two native infantry regiments with his column, who, until then, had fondly imagined that the confiding Sahibs were taking them on to Delhi. Rid of 1500 undeclared mutineers, instead of continuing his march Delhi-wards, Nicholson doubled back to Amritsar and disarmed another native infantry regiment there. So far the only British troops with him were her Majesty's 52nd Foot, received from Sialkot, and 100 artillerymen with 9 guns. Before the withdrawal of the 52nd, Lawrence had urged Brigadier Brind, commanding at Sialkot, to disarm his Hindustanis, the 25th and 46th Native Infantry, and three troops of the 9th Light Cavalry; but the brigadier preferred to trust his men, and but for the mutiny of the cavalry, his confidence might not have been misplaced. The object with which Nicholson's flying column had been formed was now widely known, and apprehension was general amongst all sepoy regiments within striking distance. At Lawrence's instance the military authorities at Rawalpindi had just disarmed two regiments there with the aid of five companies of her Majesty's 24th Foot, and had then sent a mixed force to Jhelam to overawe the 14th Native Infantry into surrendering their arms. Upon its approach (July 6) the disaffected regiment fled to their lines, and fought desperately all day, but escaped into the open country during the night. Though eventually all were killed or captured, the news of the outbreak, coupled with the dread of Nicholson's arrival to draw their teeth, drove the troopers of the 9th Light Cavalry at Sialkot into immediate mutiny. They rose, ran amuck, burning and looting part of the station and killing several Englishmen, including among them their credulous brigadier, and, by the force of their bad example and common brotherhood, drew away from their allegiance their hitherto orderly comrades of the 46th Native Infantry. Before morning the whole body, over 1000 strong, had set off for Delhi.

Nicholson, who was still at Amritsar, received news of the Jhelam and Sialkot incidents on July 10. He calculated that if he could reach the Trimmu ford and ferry over the Ravi near Gurdaspur by the 13th, he should be in time to intercept the mutineers. The distance was fifty-four miles, and it had to be covered in forty-eight hours, at a season when the thermometer in the shade ranged from 90° to 130° in the day. Seizing all the carriage within reach,—gigs, light carts, and ponies,—and allowing neither man nor beast any rest, he caught up his prey at the crossing. The mutinous cavalry easily dispersed the mounted Punjabi levies with Nicholson; but the British infantry, though utterly exhausted, formed line and advanced firing towards the ferry. The Brown Bess of the 46th Native Infantry was useless against the Enfields of our men, hence the enemy were quickly driven into the river, and, wading and swimming, took shelter with their women on an island, beyond which was the deep unfordable main stream. Seeing that the quarry was hopelessly trapped, the pursuers were rested for three days, whilst boats were being procured, after which on the 16th a leisurely crossing to the island was effected, and in another hour not a sepoy or trooper remained alive—bullet, sword, and water had given them all their quietus. What happened to the women is not recorded. It was butchery, no doubt, and the 46th Native Infantry, who had protected their officers, hardly deserved annihilation, but the holocaust was necessary. That the 52nd Foot should have executed sentence on their former comrades at Sialkot was a curious Nemesis.

At Lahore the news seems to have worked the 26th Native Infantry, one of the four disarmed regiments there and at Mianmir, into a frenzy of apprehension. After brooding over their wrongs and fears for some days, they made up their minds to escape, and quietly disposed of their property. The start was arranged for July 30, and the men were cooking their last meal when the major and several sergeants, all Englishmen, hearing of their intentions, went down to their lines to expostulate. Whilst the major was speaking, he and the sergeants were felled and murdered, whereupon the whole regiment made for the open country. They were at once pursued and slaughtered wholesale, making no attempt at resistance; over 200 were captured in an exhausted state and confined all night in a sort of "black hole," in which twenty-five died. In the morning the survivors were brought out in batches of ten and shot, a repulsively executed butchery. The other three disarmed regiments, who were at Mianmir, kept their heads, and remained quiet to the end.

Two weeks later, a rising of the same kind occurred at Ferozepore: the previously disarmed but not dismounted 10th Light Cavalry, on being ordered to give up their horses, refused, made a dash to carry off some guns, and, failing, rode away. What was more, they were not followed. Whilst the confusion was at its height, Brigadier Innes turned his guns on his own horses, tethered near the arsenal, and killed a hundred of them. "He will probably be knighted for this exploit," was John Lawrence's sarcastic comment when he heard of the affair; but he was wrong, for the unfortunate man was superseded.

Soon after the blotting out of the Sialkot mutineers, Lawrence thought his province sufficiently cleared of armed Hindustanis to warrant his making a supreme effort to reinforce the wasting force on the "ridge." Within a short time of each other, the Maharaja of Kashmir's contingent of 2000 Dogras from Jammu, a full siege-train from Philor and Ferozepore, and Nicholson's column, augmented to 2500 men, were all on the march for Delhi. Nicholson's force had the start of the others. On the way, in defiance of his civil chief and without asking the permission of the local brigadier, he showed his indifference for constituted authorities by sweeping into his column Colonel Dawes' battery,—presumably the Dawes of Chillianwala fame,—and when called on for an explanation, apologised curtly on paper, but immediately afterwards showed the shallowness of his repentance by carrying off all the artillerymen he found in the fort at Philor!

When he had passed eastwards of Ludhiana, the British infantry retained in the Punjab did not exceed 6000 men, whilst, except at Peshawar and Mianmir, there was not a field or horse battery in the province. The "ridge" had absorbed all the others, and cis-Indus the Punjab was almost as denuded of British troops as the valley of the Ganges had been just before the Meerut outbreak. Even so the daily cry from before Delhi was for more men, more guns, more ammunition; and the capture of the city appeared farther off than it had done nearly two months previously, and this, although since the early days of June the fighting of the mutineers had become contemptible. They were, however, now so strong in numbers that our foothold on the "ridge" was often surrounded by their sharpshooters, and their tenacity behind cover was considerable. When attacked, they gave way, but returned as soon as we had retired. Every little action weakened us materially, without bringing the capture of the city any nearer. The prolonged deadlock and the exasperation caused by knowledge of the details of atrocities at Cawnpore and elsewhere inflamed British and Punjabis alike with a murderous hatred of all Hindustanis. Conscious of the execration in which they were held, and fearful for their lives, the disarmed thousands in the various cantonments of the province suffered many deaths throughout the prolonged agony of their detention. The 26th Native Infantry being at Lahore, not Mianmir—then a cantonment in a desert—and gazed at like beasts in the Zoo by crowds daily, must have been driven to desperation before rushing upon certain destruction as they did. At Ferozepore the case was different; the troopers were laxly guarded, and when ordered to surrender their horses, preferred escape to what seemed hopeless confinement.

Throughout the rest of August no further sepoy attempts to break the coils surrounding them were made until towards the end of the month in Peshawar. The lot of the disarmed sepoys there was peculiarly terrible, for not only did they know that, surrounded by a bloodthirsty population of fanatical Musalmans, escape was hopeless, but many of them were guarded by Edwardes' levies, the cut-throats of hill and plain, of whom he retained 1650, and they naturally enough enjoyed baiting and terrorising their prisoners. When, then, those miserable Hindustanis were told that General Cotton was going to put them in irons,—he had prepared 2000 leg-irons for the purpose should they be wanted,—and soon after their lines were searched, the suspected sepoys became distraught. On August 28 the lines of the 51st Native Infantry were overhauled by some of the Afridi levies, who freely taunted and abused the "blacks." The work over, the sepoys were ordered to move out to a camp on the British side of the cantonment. Thinking they were to be killed, and seeing the piled arms of a newly raised Sikh regiment within reach, in a mad impulse for self-preservation they made a rush for the arms, fought desperately for a few minutes, and then broke and fled towards the Khyber. Then followed a wild chase by Sikhs and Afridis, headed by the colonel of the fugitives, who died next day from sunstroke. Before Jamrud was reached the last of the 700 panic-stricken sepoys had been shot down. "The example," Edwardes reported, "sufficed. The disarmed regiments were paralysed with the sudden retribution."

The cases of the 26th Native Infantry at Lahore and the 51st Native Infantry at Peshawar show what a baited life most disarmed sepoy regiments must for some time have been leading. For both escape was hopeless, destruction certain, yet in their desperation they rushed upon death. As the struggle between "white" and "black" before Delhi lengthened, race hatred intensified; and there is not a doubt that, given a pretext, English and Punjabis alike would have felt satisfaction in killing off the disarmed Hindustanis throughout the province. The massacre at Peshawar on August 28 was the last affair of the sort in the Punjab, for the end was now approaching at Delhi.

Nicholson with his column had reached the "ridge" about the middle of the month, not a day too soon, for although dissensions, confusion, and a general sense of depression prevailed inside the city, outside the daily wastage from death and sickness had reduced our effective numbers to under 5000 men. The arrival in camp of a fresh and thoroughly serviceable brigade nearly 2500 strong, under the most daring and resolute leader of the day, put new life and energy into our exhausted forces. General Archdale Wilson, commanding the Delhi Field Force—his predecessors, Anson, Barnard, and Reed, had one after the other succumbed—was at once constrained to authorise a vigorous offensive. At the time the Nimach and Bareilly brigades, the latest accessions to the enemy, were closing round in rear of our position, and once established astride of the Grand Trunk Road, would not only have cut our communications with the Punjab but, failing expulsion, might have intercepted the slowly approaching siege-train then nearing Karnal.

Within two days of his arrival Nicholson and his column had changed the whole situation. By smashing one of the rebel brigades and terrifying the other into hasty retreat without fighting into Delhi, he secured our communications, and enabled General Wilson to greatly extend his camp, and confine the disunited and now desponding mutineers to the city. On September 4 the siege-train, weakly escorted, reached camp, followed by the last reinforcements which Lawrence, without withdrawing cis-Indus from Peshawar, had dared to send—one more "Piffer" regiment, some levies, and the contingent of 2000 Dogras from Jammu—good raw material these last, but until blooded and hardened of little value for desperate fighting against odds. Hitherto the Anglo-Punjab force had been merely holding their own, now the siege was to begin in earnest, and the political situation demanded that the work should be done quickly and thoroughly. The final reinforcements raised the force before Delhi to 11,000 men; but of that total some 2000 were in hospital or otherwise unfit, and the Jammu troops had not yet received their baptism of fire. For breaching purposes the number and calibre of our pieces was ample, fifty-four of the heaviest ordnance in India, hence the battering work would be effectual; but for the actual assault, on which everything depended, not more than 4000 men, exclusive of the Dogras, upon whom little reliance was placed, would be available, and at a fair computation the "stalwarts" amongst the mutineers, who would fight to the last house and wall, would be treble that number.

The general who, practically without reserves, would launch his forlorn-hope upon such a venture required a heart and mind of steel. Unfortunately Wilson had never possessed either, and prolonged anxieties had further enfeebled him, yet he nerved himself into accepting the plans of the determined group of men advising and in a sense dominating him,—Lawrence, Neville Chamberlain, Baird Smith, and Nicholson,—and after forty-eight hours of incessant bombardment allowed the assault to be delivered (September 13). A footing on and inside the city walls was gained, but the cost had been great, a third of the strength of the columns actually engaged; then followed two days of comparative inaction, owing to the demoralisation of a large proportion of the surviving heroes of the assault, who were lying about literally "beastly drunk"—the enemy having designedly left casks of strong liquor in their way. On the 16th the attack was renewed, and the "stalwarts," who had already begun to leave, were gradually cleared out of the palace, mosques, and houses, until by the 20th the city was wholly in our hands, after which for three days it was given up to the vengeance of the victorious soldiers, and not until Lawrence himself, five months afterwards, went to Delhi did the indiscriminate hangings and systematic looting—an art in which Sikhs, Pathans, and Ghurkas were adepts—give place to order and justice.

Thus did the Punjab, unaided from without, under the strong will and wisdom of John Lawrence, recover Delhi for England from the mutinous Bengal army. But the debt of the Empire to the Punjab did not end on September 20, 1857; it continued for a year more. During that period the frontier province had under arms 80,000 men, of whom upwards of 35,000 were sent down to aid Lord Clyde and his slowly augmenting, slow-moving, baggage-encumbered English army in the great guerilla warfare, which lasted for many months after the taking of Delhi and the second relief of Lucknow (November 21, 1857). Throughout that long weary hunt after the scattered forces of the mutineers—a hunt compared at the time to bulldogs pursuing foxes—the Punjabi Irregulars, particularly light cavalry, were the hounds who usually ran down the fox. In our wars in India, Pindari, Mahratta, and even Sikh, the enemy were accustomed to play round our unwieldy armies, and in that against the revolted sepoys the old game would have been repeated, and the chase indefinitely prolonged, but for the mobility of our Punjabi troops.

Whilst the hunt was in progress Lawrence deported to their homes in isolated batches the bulk of the disarmed Hindustanis still interned in the province, all but a faithful remnant, the 55th Native Infantry at Peshawar, 59th Native Infantry at Amritsar, and certain scattered detachments of various regiments, who through the happy influence of their officers, their segregation, or other fortunate accidents, had escaped both epidemic and panic, and during their long ordeal, though never trusted, had conducted themselves admirably. The two regiments just named received back their arms with all honour, and the detachments were amalgamated into a new battalion called "the loyal Purbias."

Further, when order was restored in the North-West Provinces, and communications were once more uninterrupted from Delhi to Calcutta, the Government of India repaid in some measure the debt of gratitude owed by the Empire to the chiefs of the Punjab, Sikh and Muhammadan, but more especially to Patiala, Jhind, Nabha, Kapurthalla, and the Khan of the Khattaks (trans-Indus); and Lawrence, before he left his province, had the gratification of announcing to them increases to their principalities, jagirs, and dignities. About the same time, too, he repaid with interest at six per cent the loan levied early in the war, the exaction of which had delighted the peasantry and been useful both financially and politically, by replenishing a depleted treasury and securing the loyalty of our creditors. The amount of our indebtedness was £420,000, not a large sum considering the wealth of the commercial classes in the province. Of the subscribers, the Punjab chiefs alone had been willing contributors; every rupee lent by traders and bankers had been obtained by extortion. In regard to the business houses of Lahore and Amritsar, the official pronouncement was, "Their contributions were inappreciable. . . . Their niggard distrust of our Government speaks very unfavourably for their loyalty, and is in strong contrast with the eager co-operation of the rural population." At Peshawar, when the city fathers declared their inability to find any money, Edwardes assessed them at four lakhs and gave them a day to make their arrangements. The amount was at once produced. "The loan operated very well on public opinion," he reported. "The people enjoyed seeing the money-lenders brought to book, and respected the power which asserted itself in difficulties."

The loan paid off, the Mutiny crushed, normal tranquillity restored, "the man through whom Delhi fell," as Lord Canning recorded of Lawrence, received an instalment of his reward,—a G.C.B., baronetcy, Privy Councillorship, and, what was more useful, a special pension of £1000 a-year, whilst the army which took Delhi received a year's pay as *batta*, besides prospective benefits.

His great work accomplished, his peasantry prosperous and contented, his province acknowledged the saviour of the Empire, its boundaries extended to the Jamna so as to include Delhi, and its status raised to a lieutenant-governorship, John Lawrence, after a grand send-off from all classes—soldiers, civilians, and people—sailed for home, there to rest and recruit until India required his services once more.

Looking back over the events of 1857-58 and their causation, the mind wonders and is thankful that, with such a tool as the Bengal army, and the poor quality of the brains usually directing it, we not only achieved, but retained, dominion over Northern India. Now and again a civilian, only qualified to be the superintendent of an office, has been appointed governor of a province; but as a rule the civil heads of provinces, departments, and even divisions have been and are the best men in their respective official generations. In the Indian army before the Mutiny the contrary was the case, inefficiency in high places being the rule, efficiency the exception. The seniority system, untempered by age, health, or examination regulations, had long placed the immense close brotherhood known as the Bengal army in the hands of old men, invalids, or other incompetents, yet this army, for the most part poor in material, unsatisfactory in organisation, and in all gradations, down to regimental units, indifferently commanded, not only conquered Mahrattas and Sikhs but afterwards held them down. Further, when 800 of its English officers were serving away from their regiments, and those who remained were few and fatuous, this same army, discontented, tampered with, sole masters from Delhi to Calcutta, for years resisted every temptation to seize power, and at last only succumbed under the overpowering pressure of a caste-panic. Having mutinied, during the long war which followed, this same extraordinary army failed to produce a single leader of ability, enterprise, or influence. These facts, at first sight surprising, are perhaps explicable if the respective qualities and training of Englishmen and Hindustanis be remembered.

Whilst our Empire was growing, whatever our organisation, strategy, or tactics, they were almost invariably superior to those of our opponents, and when from inequality in numbers or other exceptional accident—*e.g.*, the disciplined bravery of the Sikhs and good generalship of Sher Singh—the issue was for a time in doubt, in the end the scale was always turned in our favour owing to the stiffening influence of our British troops and the devoted leading of the younger British officers of sepoy regiments. Afterwards, when empire had been achieved, the Bengal army remained faithful, from the habit of obedience to authority and belief in the power and good fortune (*ikbāl*) of the Company Bahadar, and when, eventually, it did run amuck, it produced no leaders and fought like spiritless dogs—except behind walls—because those upon whom it had always depended, its English officers and English comrades, were now its enemies, and, above all, because by heredity and environment Hindustanis are neither hardy nor warlike. With Englishmen, in every stage of their world-history, the exact contrary has been the case: we have always been an imperial race,—in other words, a grasping, organising, self-reliant people,—and as to leading, in every part of the globe, particularly in India, no matter the system, the occasion produces the man.

CHAPTER XV.

COLLAPSE OF PEASANT PROSPERITY.

WE saw in Chapter X. that when Lord Dalhousie, following his predetermined policy, had rounded off the north-west boundary of our Indian dominion by annexing the Punjab, he had by right of conquest a clean slate to work upon, and that he then, through the Lawrences, introduced changes in the land-revenue system which, however convenient for budgets and regular disbursements, were fraught with serious consequences for the rural communities of the province.

At that time the conception of individual property in agricultural land hardly existed, except to a limited extent in regard to areas irrigated from wells and a few private canals. The village community, not the individual, was the occupying unit. In Hindu and Moghal times the State had been the universal overlord; under the rapacious Sikhs it became the sole landlord, and appropriated all the profits of cultivation. In our turn we re-established the old view of state rights in land, limited our demand to the estimated value of from a fourth to a sixth of an average crop, and exacted payment on fixed dates, whether the yield had been good, bad, or nothing. Thus, whilst under the Sikhs the people had been treated as cattle—the property of the strong man of the day, whether Maharaja, jagirdar, or revenue-farmer—under us they were raised to the condition of intelligent freeholders.

Unfortunately for the intended beneficiaries, we went too fast. Their endowment with the rights and responsibilities of a restricted citizenship in the British Empire was too sudden. By presenting each member of a community—hitherto one of a herd abject and half-starved—with the fee-simple of his holding, subject to a considerable fixed quit-rent in cash, we created individual property, and its corollary, credit. Both soon proved fatal gifts, as crops were never certain, and necessity, coupled with the possession of marketable assets, induced borrowing. Thus, before long, the astute few began to make money out of the ignorant many; but, until some years after the Sepoy Mutiny, creditors were satisfied with good interest on their loans; the villager grocer had developed into the petty village money-lender, and nothing more; he was hardly yet a usurer, being still dependent on the community; earth-hunger he had none, for land, except when irrigated, was worth little or nothing; the legal system was embryonic, the administration paternal, and title-deeds to fields still under preparation; creditors, therefore, preferred to let an account run on, occasionally receiving handsome interest in grain or money, to taking over land as mortgagees, with all the consequent risks and obligations of landlordism.

In fact, for many years after annexation, ordinary rain-lands—*i.e.*, those not artificially irrigated—were hardly marketable. Whenever the crops failed, the owners, according to the Administration Report published in 1854, were "too ready to abandon their holdings, in the hope of escaping present liabilities, and returning at some future time when things looked better." Until towards the end of the 'sixties the competition was not between tenants for holdings but between yeomen-owners for tenants; even into the 'seventies, in many tracts the proprietary brotherhood would make over common land to outside cultivators on the mere condition that the lessees would pay the quota of land revenue which the village community had assessed thereon.

What Punjab agriculturists were in the early days of our rule is well summed up in the Administration Report for the two years preceding the Mutiny. "The cultivators," the Chief Commissioner wrote therein, "are essentially 'peasant proprietors.' There are no farmers or middlemen, and generally no great landlords. As a rule, each man owns and tills his own glebe, upon which he pays the revenue and pockets all the profits. . . . He is saddled with no rent. He has to provide for the cost of cultivation and for the Government demand; the rest of the produce he may devote to the maintenance of his family and the accumulation of his capital. But these men, while maintaining their individuality, do yet belong to village communities. A village is not inhabited by a certain number of ryots each unconnected with the other, but by a number of persons of common descent, forming one large brotherhood, having their own headmen, accustomed to joint action and mutual support. . . . The Punjab system . . . is therefore the village system."

Such were the agriculturists of the province in 1856. The disintegration of "the village system" began soon after; but the process was slow and insidious, and attracted little notice before 1870. About that time settlement officers now and again complained that the rigidity with which the land revenue was exacted, and the harsh character of the law of contract enforced by the civil courts, were undermining the strength of village communities, and reducing their members to a state of landless poverty. The Administration Reports of the period either ignored the question or merely mentioned the fact that "some officers took a gloomy view of the financial position of the peasantry," to point out that the horizon of such officers was too limited to enable them to grasp the bearings of beneficial economic changes affecting the whole province. All beliefs die hard, and nothing short of judicial proof or a revolution could kill the secretariat belief that as the condition of the peasantry was in 1855-65 "eminently creditable to British rule," it could not have materially altered for the worse by 1895. Indeed, up to the present time, when a revised assessment is imposed on a village—and none such is undertaken unless the preliminary forecast shows that a large enhancement of revenue will accrue to the Government from the operation—the official instruction is still maintained that the distribution shall be left to the village community, though in fact it is carried out by revenue officials in consultation with the most prominent landholders, who are frequently capitalist intruders.

The high-water mark of peasant prosperity, meaning thereby freedom from indebtedness and the possession of unencumbered holdings and a reserve of food-stuff, was probably reached in the Mutiny year, when the harvests were abundant, creditors too fearful to be exacting, and officials too preoccupied to act as debt-registrars and collectors. In the following year the harvests were short and the tide began to turn. About that time, too, the system of administration in the Punjab, enlarged by the acquisition of the Delhi districts and raised to the dignity of a lieutenant-governorship, was beginning to lose its early simplicity of character. The change from paternal to machine rule, of the type obtaining in the regulation provinces, was soon after accelerated, *inter alia,* by the reduction of the period of limitation for claims based on loans from twelve to three years, except in the case of money lent on registered bonds, for which six years were allowed. The new law, by forcing creditors into court at short intervals, brought about a flood of litigation, and appreciably embittered the relations between lenders and borrowers. Instead of being mutually accommodating, as formerly, each now depended on the law — creditors, because it favoured the longer purse and keener intelligence, debtors, from helplessness and the off-chance of gaining time by the law's delay. Abetted by the civil courts, the petty lender, under the new conditions, soon blossomed into the professional usurer. He obtained little real grip upon any of the peasantry until 1860-61, when the first of those famine calamities occurred, which have since, in combination with our "system," been the prominent causes of the ruin of a large part of "the finest peasantry in India." During the period of distress, loans at high interest—the peasant's necessity being the money-lender's opportunity—were freely incurred, and, with the money, revenue liabilities were met, food provided, and farm stock replaced. Happily, good seasons succeeding, and the power of recuperation being not yet enfeebled by previous indebtedness, only five or six per cent of the peasant-proprietors became hopelessly involved. Thus, by 1865, the Government was fairly justified in regarding the general condition of the people as satisfactory: their standard of discomfort was less wretched, not only had they more and better food, but some were indulging in mild extravagances, such as second wives. Still, the *facilis descensus* once begun, what the Government, by some extravagance of a flippant secretary's pen, called "this grand *battue* of litigation," went on, and increased in volume, until the number of lawsuits brought in the year rose to over 200,000, or more, in distressed localities, than one to every five families.

Foreseeing the evil days coming upon the Punjab should the reign of hard law be consolidated, the survivors of the Lawrence school of administration fought hard to resist its consummation, but were powerless. In 1866, for the second time in seventeen years, the Punjab had to submit to the yoke of a conqueror. In 1849 he had proved a deliverer, in 1866 he was a destroyer. In that year a Chief Court was established at Lahore, the regulation code of civil procedure was extended to the province, and lawyers were permitted to plead in all courts. By 1870, improvements in conveyancing, the hardening of the laws regulating contracts, and particularly the completion of the regular settlements of the cis-Indus districts, had greatly enhanced the value of agricultural holdings, and even made lands dependent on direct rainfall a profitable investment.

For the province generally, peasant expropriation

on a large scale by professional non-agricultural money-lenders may be said to date, for each district, from the first year of scarcity or famine succeeding the fixation for a period of twenty or thirty years of the land-revenue demand, and the preparation of what is called the "record of rights." That record showed respectively the right, title, and interest of the Government, owners, and tenants in every parcel of land in every village of the province, and as it was annually attested and corrected to date, and a transfer of interest could be secured by a simple mutation-order duly made by a qualified revenue officer, it gave land-investors the facilities of acquisition and security of title which had hitherto been wanting. Even then, earth-hunger on a large scale was not excited amongst the cautious commercial classes until the punctual payment of a competitive, as opposed to a customary, rent was assured by the certain action of the law and a sufficiency of labour from the multiplication of the rural population.

The establishment of the Chief Court, administering statute law without powers of equity, and exercising full control over all the civil judges of the province, gave capitalists, as soon as the law's supremacy and the court's ability to enforce it had been recognised, the inducements and opportunities which they required, before attempting to begin the systematic exploitation of the hereditary simpletons recorded at settlement as owners of the agricultural assets of the province.

Throughout the 'seventies the Government pronouncements on the condition of the Punjab agriculturists continued studiously self-congratulatory: they "had merged into vigorous manhood"—a hyperbole probably implying the belief that, in spite of Chief Court, law, lawyers, and usurers, they were able to take care of themselves; "the state of the peasantry is in general eminently prosperous"—a phrase later revised to "eminently creditable to British rule"; the peasant-proprietors of the Punjab "are the thriving and industrious cultivators of the soil"; the Government is "not disposed to regard this comparatively free resort to the courts in petty cases as an unfavourable sign." Such pronouncements abound in the Administration Reports of the period. Their frequent reiteration indicates a consciousness of the weakness of the position taken up by the Government: asseverations were not facts; the truth could have been ascertained at any time by means of local inquiries in selected areas, but that test was avoided.

In 1871, whilst the litigation fever—officially at the time "an indication of healthy progress and confidence in our courts"—was still rising, the Government of India, who, since the famine of 1866-67, had been considering the formation of a famine-insurance fund, called on the Punjab to contribute its quota to such a laudable object. In the eyes of the local government the peasantry were the class to be squeezed, they being "prosperous," lightly assessed, accustomed to bear burdens without murmuring, and, prospectively, the chief beneficiaries from the tax. The sum wanted was £120,000 each year. To enhance the land revenue *pro tanto* would have been simple but illegal, as the village contracts could not be varied except once in twenty or thirty years on revision of settlements. However, the money had to be got somehow, and from the peasantry. The legal difficulty was surmounted by calling the enhancement a "cess"; accordingly an additional "local rates" cess of 6 per cent on the land revenue was legalised and levied. Its imposition was morally indefensible, and the Government was roundly accused of a breach of faith. The distinction between a "cess"—a rate levied on the land revenue—and an enhancement of that revenue was explained; but such casuistic refinement was incomprehensible to simple Punjabis, who did not care what the collector might call the component parts of their rating, provided that its aggregate was not raised whilst a settlement was running.

The sense of wrong at the sudden increase to their burdens, the worries arising from growing indebtedness and never-ending persecution by creditors, courts, and court underlings, and, above all, the readiness with which *ex parte* decrees were given and executed, naturally created widespread dissatisfaction with the Government. Sayings contemptuous of the civil administration were now in every rustic's mouth, as, for instance, "To-day is the *rāj* [rule] of the money-lenders"; "The pen gives the land to the usurer, but the slipper [force] will take it back"; "A bond, a witness, a decree,"—indicating the popular view of the routine stages and uniform results of law-suits. Echoes of these grumblings rarely penetrated into the detached seclusion in which the Government—Lieutenant-Governor and his secretariat—lived and moved; but official facts and opinions had to be examined and disposed of, and in the 'seventies, as the elaborate settlement reports and reviews by Commissioners and Financial Commissioner were successively published, the concurrence of testimony was considerable, that the peasant proprietary of the country were becoming seriously indebted, and alienating their holdings to money-lenders. Perfunctory inquiries were instituted, but bureaucratic optimism was proof against all inferences which clashed with predilections. The conclusions arrived at were of a negative character: statistics of indebtedness and land-alienation to non-agriculturists were meagre and unreliable; even if the weakly were sinking, the fit were rising; the country was passing through a transition period (has it ever been otherwise?); the Punjab had the best of possible governments—if under good laws carefully administered the peasantry could not thrive, the Government could do no more. Thus, the decision was to fold hands and look on, trusting to the far-off moral and economic ameliorations which the spread of education might some day effect, if only the agricultural classes, who paid a compulsory school cess, would send their children to school—a preliminary to mind expansion which is, to the present day, almost wholly monopolised by non-agriculturists.

In 1874-75 two new kinds of civil courts, chiefly for the adjudication of claims for money lent, munsiffs and judicial assistants, were created. Their establishment was regarded by the commercial classes as a further step in the promotion of their interests, by the rural masses as additional evidence of the ascendency of "the *rāj* of the money-lenders." That common belief was strengthened by the facts that the *personnel* of the munsiffs was drawn from the trading and ministerial classes of the towns, that they were located—as was, of course, reasonable—wherever money-lenders congregated, and had—as was natural—little intercourse except with men of their own caste. Then, too, as they were bound to hear and decide actions in accordance with the provisions of the Civil Procedure Code, Evidence, Contract, and other Acts, their local ignorance and unfamiliarity with village life generally lent point to the common sneer that a bond and a witness, however worthless, secured a decree. Thus, the new debt-registering and collecting agency was hated by the people, and gave a further impetus to petty litigation. Within a decade the number of suits disposed of in the year rose to the unprecedented figure of 271,375 (1883), a carnival of litigation remunerative to the Government and pleaders, but ruinous for the peasantry.

Meanwhile, the recurrence of famine in 1876-78, beginning in Madras and spreading north into the Punjab, and an agrarian insurrection against foreign usurers (1876) in the Bombay Deccan, had constrained the Government of India — influenced to some extent by public opinion in England—to institute comprehensive commissions to inquire into both phenomena. In due course (1880) the Famine Commission, presided over by Mr (afterwards Sir James) Caird, an economist of European reputation, made public the appalling revelation that for British India generally "about one-third of the land-holding classes are deeply and inextricably in debt, and that at least an equal proportion are in debt, though not beyond the power of recovering themselves." The conditions elucidated by the more particular Deccan inquiry showed that the situation there was even worse, and that the insurrection had been induced owing to the intolerable exactions of foreign Mārwāri money-lenders supported by the action of our courts, and of the Government in the collection of its land revenue.

The conclusions arrived at, though in the case of the famine inquiry based more on opinions than proven figures, persuaded most unprejudiced minds that as the people of India were being exploited by comparatively a handful of usurers—men who escaped taxation and were from their calling and effeminacy held in popular odium—further persistence in *laisser aller* would eventually lead to some great catastrophe. No system, it was contended, could be sound which pauperised a whole people. It was the Government of India, not the 270 millions of patient toilers, against whom an indictment should be laid. Placed on the defensive, the Government repeatedly challenged and sifted and resifted the facts put forward by the two Commissions; but all in vain, for each subsequent investigation resulted in the accumulation of fresh evidence that the first generalisations were absolutely correct. This, however, is anticipating; we must go back a little.

Whilst the inquiries were in progress and the reports of the commissioners under consideration, the Punjab administrative machine had been improved into a beautifully finished and intricate arrangement of wheels, which, great and small, from Lieutenant-Governor to collector's bailiff, from Chief Court to munsiff's process-server, worked in frictionless subordination to the scientific ideal of perfection in a government — unsympathetic centralisation. Like God on the sixth day of the creation, the Government, *pace* commissions and pessimists, "saw everything that he [it] had made, and, behold, it was very good;" the land-revenue settlements had been completed and every field in the province mapped, registered, and assessed to a fixed sum exacted twice a-year, rain or no rain; then a Chief Court, with 500 subordinate courts, administering laws and rules adapted from every statute-book in Europe, regulated the affairs of everybody, and to interpret and misinterpret those laws and rules a multiplying locust-swarm of pleaders had settled on the land. As the Government, courts, lawyers, and money-lenders were satisfied, complaint was unseemly from the people, the mere producers, who refused to be educated or to take the trouble to understand the system under which they toiled and died: *sua si bona norint:* let the fittest survive, and grow fat on the sweat of the stupid many.

Judged by its action and pronouncements, such was the deliberate conclusion of the Punjab Government.

CHAPTER XVI.

MACHINE RULE.

As assertions, unsupported by evidence, are not convincing, a glance at indisputable facts will help readers to form their own conclusions.

Since the Mutiny — which roughly synchronised with the period when the peasantry of the Punjab were most prosperous, being then the unencumbered owners of their holdings, and recent harvests having been bountiful—there have in all been seven years of famine—viz., 1860-61, 1876-78, 1896-97, and 1899-1901; in addition, scarcities from short droughts in rain-dependent tracts have been frequent. During the earlier famines—four years in all—out of the annual land-revenue demand, apart from water rates on canal-irrigated lands, hardly two per cent were suspended, and the fraction ultimately remitted or written off as irrecoverable was infinitesimal. Since 1896, the destitution of a large fraction of the cultivators having been officially proved, the Government has been less niggardly in granting suspensions and remissions. Unfortunately, the relief given, coming too late, fails to reach the classes who most require it—the poorest of the peasant proprietary—and only saves the pockets of the capitalist-mortgagees and purchasers of holdings. If it be remembered that the average daily income per head of the Indian population is, taking the mean of the various estimates, less than three halfpence, and that fully 25 per cent of that population never attain that average, the hand-to-mouth existence, even in normal years, of a large part of the Punjab peasantry will be realised; if so, their general inability without borrowing to pay the land revenue, or even avoid death from starvation whenever a scarcity from drought occurs, let alone a famine period, requires no demonstration.

Now, turning to the assertion that since 1866 the Punjab has been increasingly law and lawyer ridden, we find that in that year five Bengal Regulations and seventy-seven Acts were in force therein, and that thenceforward, until about the middle of the 'eighties, the annual output of Acts applicable to the province averaged seven, and in the most active mid-period was ten. After 1885 production began to decline, and now it is inappreciable.

The hasty and inconsequent character of our Indian legislation in the 'seventies and early part of the 'eighties may be judged from the facts that in 1866—the year in which the Punjab was absorbed into the legal system of the regulation provinces—the Government of India, through Sir Henry Maine, the then law member of Council, publicly declared that, were the Council to dose India with English law, "one of the most cumbrous systems in the world," "there could hardly be any censure too heavy" for them, and that should the attempt be made, it would be "a most intolerable hardship" for the 250 millions of Indians, and that, notwithstanding, within the next few years not only was the attempt made, but it was persisted in for about fifteen years, until a symposium of selections and adaptations from the legal systems of Europe had become the statute law of India. The gradual return of the Government of India to sober-mindedness was the result of a combination of causes, —the exhaustion of raw material, the insistence of district officers, and to a small extent of unofficial English opinion, that the growing evils in the body politic were largely due to excessive and unsuitable legislation, and, latterly, the wise relegation of parochial subjects to the newly created provincial legislative councils. So long as the Indian masses were alone the *corpus vile*, the torrent of new enactments attracted little notice; but as soon as the comparatively wealthy classes, and particularly the small European community, became directly affected, the proceedings of the Government began to be subjected to scrutiny, and legislation likely to cause change or induce litigation was condemned. Probably but for the public clamour against the "Masters and Servants Bill" (1877) and the "Ilbert Bill" (1883), the legislative activity of the Government would have continued without a break until every conceivable cause of possible disagreement in the daily life of the people had been defined, classified, and its disposal regulated by law.

Of the many enactments in force in the Punjab—some 200—those connected with revenue, excise, rent, tenant-right, forests, village officers, and the like, having been gradually evolved to meet local circumstances, and being chiefly rules and practices already in force compressed into codified forms, either supply a real want or have some *raison d'être*;

moreover, having been first worked out and rough-drafted by the provincial revenue-executive department, to which jurisdiction under them is confined, their working is simple, smooth,—except under the heads "waste lands" and "forests,"—and inexpensive, hence lawyers, when permitted to plead, seldom make use of the privilege.

Such is not the case in the vast field of economic and social relations over disputes in which the Chief Court and subordinate judiciary exercise exclusive jurisdiction. Throughout that field the laws in force were conceived, shaped, and carried through Council by English lawyers ignorant of India but familiar with the civil-law systems of the leading countries of Europe. As a consequence, successive legal members of Council treated India, with her diverse nationalities and conditions, as if the whole continent were inhabited by a homogeneous and highly educated commercial people, all anxious that their inter-relations should be regulated by uniform up-to-date Western laws. Under these conditions India was deluged by the three energetic and fertile-brained successors of Henry Sumner Maine with a steady flow of intricate, technical, and sometimes even mischievous Acts, the want of which had never been felt, and the meaning of many of the provisions of which is a frequent subject of remunerative dispute to those who live by the law. Hardly any such Act, passed between 1870 and 1884, is comprehensible to laymen. In England no prudent man is his own lawyer; he effects his transactions through professional experts. In India every one managed his own affairs until we introduced complications,—technical law-courts, barristers, and pleaders, all recently congregated in respect of the Punjab by Lord Curzon under the contemptuous phrase "the complex paraphernalia of the Chief Court." Even now solicitors and conveyancers are unknown outside the Presidency cities of India, and yet the law governing the simplest of contracts —a loan, lease, or mortgage—is now so complex and artificial that all such ought to be referred to professional advisers. The masses have neither the intelligence nor the money to do so, which is one reason why the few who have both, aided by the law, exploit the many.

As instances of the vexatious legislation effected during the period referred to, the Specific Relief Act, 1877, and the Easements Act, 1882, may be cited.

When Sir Arthur (now Lord) Hobhouse introduced the former bill, so ignorant were his fellow-councillors of the meaning of the term "specific relief," that he found it advisable to explain that the object sought was not the relief of the famine, then prevailing in Madras and Central India, but of certain specified civil torts. After that the bill was passed without serious discussion, the case being one of *ubi tu pulsas ego vapulo tantum*. Many of the Acts of that period were of a similar character—measures introduced by a lawyer ignorant of India and passed by a Council ignorant of the measures.

Now, turning to the "Easements Act," 1882, except the lawyer who devised, drafted, and introduced it, hardly a civilian in India, Englishman or Indian, could have explained the nature of an easement, and not one could have translated the title or any of the provisions in any of the eight or nine official vernaculars of the country. In fact the terms in most of the exotic Acts in force in India are untranslatable in any of her recognised languages, and as to the other eighteen or twenty current, no combination of words could represent to the minds of the natives speaking those tongues the meaning intended to be conveyed. Under the Easements Act, if a villager finds his familiar pathway closed to his ancestral field, he must be told in English—translation into any Indian language, with or without a literature, being impossible—that he must sue "the dominant owner for a release of the servient heritage under chapters iv. and v. of the Easements Act." As he does not know English,—though even in English the words are hardly intelligible,—if the man means to fight and wants to win, he puts his case into the hands of a lawyer, and very likely a year or so afterwards has to mortgage land to meet his law expenses; if he is poor and simple, he removes the obstruction, whereupon an assault or riot ensues, with consequent complications, all involving expenditure.

Though the Act was applicable to the whole of India, the Punjab Government, wary by experience, pointed out that the people of the province were still too backward to benefit by such an advanced measure, and the plea for delay was admitted. Whether the Government of India would have been so accommodating but for the growing outcry against doctrinaire legislation, may be doubted. All beliefs die hard, and none was harder to kill than the conviction that congested cause-lists and a strong Bar indicated general prosperity and confidence in our courts. "As well," scoffed a critic at the time, "may we look upon the multiplication of doctors and undertakers and the increase of pawnbrokers' tickets as satisfactory proof of increased professional or commercial activity."

Though ridicule had scotched, if not killed, further

legislation of what was cynically called ruffles for the shirtless kind, vexatious Acts already in force were so numerous and comprehensive that the Chief Court of the Punjab became a byword amongst the people as "a court of quibbles [literally twists], not of justice" (*pench kā mahkama adālat nahin*). As each decision when published became, until superseded, a ruling, the mischief wrought when the law, as declared, was contrary to previous practice, custom, or popular sentiment, was considerable.

A few illustrations will give point to this assertion. For thirty years subsequent to annexation the rule of the Punjab courts was, that, until consummation, the breach of a marriage-contract between infants entered into by guardians entitled the aggrieved party to compensation only, as in the case of a breach of betrothal. In 1879 the legality of the practice was challenged and fought up to the Chief Court, which ruled on the *fiat lex ruat populus* principle, that an infant marriage was binding until lawful divorce by the husband on attaining his majority. This new departure was widely demoralising, as the following case will show. In 1876 a boy of ten was "married" to a young woman, who soon after induced her boy-husband's mother—his surviving guardian—to give her a divorce, whereupon the girl married her lover and had a family by him. In 1884 the original boy-husband, now a man, informed of the ruling of 1879, sued for restitution of conjugal rights, and obtained a decree. As the woman declined to live with him, he sought to execute his decree by imprisoning her for refusing, and charged her illegal husband, the father of her children, with adultery. In all his proceedings the law was with him, both the father and mother of the children had been guilty of adultery, and the children were bastards. Thus, by the ruling of 1879, not only was an approved practice of long standing upset, but confusion was created in family relations all over the province.

Now passing to another example. For many years the executive head of a district had usually described himself as "Deputy Commissioner," but as the administration developed, he also performed functions as "District Magistrate," "District Judge," "Collector," and "President of the District Board." In spite of their various titles some of the senior officers in the Commission, in the hurry of their multifarious duties, were still in the habit of subscribing themselves by the designation most familiar to them. The practice, though irregular, had never been challenged until in the 'eighties, when the Chief Court, on the revision side, quashed all proceedings in a civil case because the district officer, when deciding a civil cause, had written "D.C." for "D.J." after his name. The ruling invalidated hundreds of costly civil proceedings all over the province.

Perhaps the judgment which created the greatest demoralisation, as it converted thousands of simpletons into rogues, was one which gave precedence, irrespective of date, to registered over unregistered instruments. The premium thus put on dishonesty instigated debtors to repudiate their unregistered obligations by the hundred, and make use of the same security twice over. Again, the intricate and highly technical Contract Act, 1872, gave rise to a whole series of varying and sometimes conflicting decisions and rulings, chiefly on the constituents and effect of "consent," "ignorance," and "undue influence."

A decision of 1879 deserves mention for the benefit it conferred, until superseded, on unwary peasant debtors, to effect that, in cases of hard bargains, "undue influence" might be presumed from the bare fact that the borrower was an agriculturist and the lender a usurer. It was a ruling of heart, not of law, and stood, with changeful fortune, until a few years ago the hard letter of the Contract Act was softened, and courts were given an equitable discretion to vary the terms of unreasonable agreements.

On the criminal side, too, a whole host of unfortunate rulings might be quoted, some due to hair-splitting, some to the law itself. Of the former class was one which excited much comment at the time, to the effect that blank cartridges were ammunition, but loaded cartridges were not. Women cases always created awkward situations, Indian and English ideas materially differing. We have just seen how a civil decision upset domestic relationships in many families. In the following criminal ruling the consequences have been even more disastrous, yet the law on the subject is unassailable. The Chief Court held that in cases of offences against married women, such as adultery and abduction, unless marriage were preliminarily admitted or proved, the charge could not be sustained. Since then, as the accused, when sophisticated or defended by a lawyer, invariably deny the fact of marriage, and proof, when possible, is a costly and lengthy affair, aggrieved husbands, failing to obtain justice from the courts, are forced to take the law into their own hands—a proceeding prolific in offences of violence, and at the root of a large percentage of the murders and cases of arson and other mischief in the province. Except when woman is the cause, miscarriages of justice are infrequent. Perhaps unfamiliarity with the language most frequently brings them about, few English officers being masters of, if knowing, any Punjabi dialect. A case will illustrate the difficulty. In 1875 a well-known sessions judge, after a patient trial, acquitted a murderer on the ground that a conviction on mere hearsay was impossible; one "Sānu," to whom all the witnesses referred, had not been produced. The committing magistrate was called upon to explain his omission,—and his reply and the story attached to it went the round of the province, and is still remembered; it was that all the witnesses had given direct evidence, *sānu* being the local Punjabi for "We" or "I."

To return to the matter of unfortunate rulings: those given are a few out of scores which either offended against common-sense or were otherwise so unsuitable that they tended to bring our legal system into contempt. The fault did not lie with the learned judges—except when indulging in hair-splitting—but with the law which they had to administer, and that law was the product of a succession of up-to-date doctrinaire legal members of Council, whose acquaintance with India began late in life and was confined to Calcutta and Simla. Each in turn was permitted by his fellow-members, preoccupied as they were with the work of their respective departments, to devise, introduce, and pass a series of scientifically perfect general enactments applicable to "all British India," but wanted by no one except, perhaps, a few needy lawyers as a means towards subsistence.

The plague of over-legislation abated for a time

after the withdrawal of the Masters and Servants Bill (1878), broke out again virulently a year later, began to subside after the exposure and fiasco of the Easements Act—declined with thanks by more local governments than that of the Punjab—and ceased entirely about 1888, in which year a projected enactment on "Torts" died still-born.

About that time (1886) a book called 'Musalmans and Money-lenders'[1] appeared, which, depending for its statements on official publications, to some extent constrained the Government to consider the indictments formulated therein—viz., that the land-owning tribes of the Musalman or western half of the Punjab were generally indebted and sinking into the position of serfs or villeins to Hindu money-lenders, and that their degradation was directly due to our system of administration, particularly to the innovations of fixed assessments, freedom of contract, individual property in land, and the series of technical laws which benefited the rich and astute at the expense of the poor and ignorant. The remedies suggested were the substitution of elasticity for fixity in collecting the land revenue, the disabling of agriculturists from alienating land to non-agriculturists, and a reversion to simple equitable laws, courts, and procedure for the disposal of agricultural civil disputes. There was little new to district and settlement officers either in the charges made against our revenue and judicial systems or in the remedies suggested. Sir James Caird, already referred to, had in his official capacity as President of the Famine Commissions (1878-1880) summed up the

[1] Musalmans and Money-lenders. By S. S. Thorburn, I.C.S. William Blackwood & Sons.

case for the people of India in the following words:—

"The pressure on the means of subsistence is rendered more severe by the moral disorganisation produced by laws, affecting property and debt, not adapted to the condition of the people. In most parts of India, as shown by the late proceedings in the Legislative Council on the Deccan Ryots Relief Bill, and as is plain to any careful observer in the country, the people are not only dissatisfied with our legal system, but, while the creditor is not much enriched, the debtor is being impoverished by it. Those British officials who see this feel themselves powerless to influence a central authority far removed from them, subject to no control of public opinion, and overburdened with details with which it is incapable of dealing."

What 'Musalmans and Money-lenders' did was to help to focus attention upon the real issue not only for the Punjab but for British India generally—viz., whether we should persist in governing the 270 millions of Indians, in spite of their conflicting nationalities and varying intelligences,—a large portion of them unable to count over twenty, or think beyond their next meal,—as if they were all educated business men of one race, or should discriminate between educated and simple, legislate and administer in accordance with their respective requirements and capacities, and thus, by protecting the ignorant against errors due to their want of knowledge, partially revert to the "paternal" system of the early Lawrence school. The Famine Report, the book, the accumulation of evidence from many parts of British India, and the growing opinion amongst district officers that the "system" was largely responsible for the general declension in peasant prosperity, failed to rouse the Punjab Government to vigorous action. Instead, objectors were reminded that an approved working system could not be remodelled without proof that the evils imputed to it existed, and were due to it, and that, were both premisses established, even then no reforms could be introduced without reasonable certainty that they would be efficacious. Thus, ineffective discussion dragged on for years, and the seasons being propitious, the dead-weight of the "system" prevailed once more. The Government pronouncement now was that, even if masses of the old peasantry were sinking, it was too late to change a system which, judged by all the criteria usually applied to European countries, was successful,—cultivated area, production, revenue under all heads, consumption of spirits and drugs, all showing steady progress except during and immediately after famine visitations. Were the Punjab a single estate, and all the cultivators tenants-at-will with only one landlord, those criteria would no doubt indicate prosperity, —his prosperity,—but seeing that its lands are or were owned until some thirty years ago by a round million of peasant-proprietary families, their prosperity cannot be measured by the gross volume of production and consumption, but depends on the due diffusion amongst the producing masses of the profits of their labour. Statistically, the Punjab might be the richest country, yet its people the poorest, in India, if they were the rack-rented tenants of capitalists. That is the condition towards which our "system" was, until 1900, reducing the "finest peasantry in India."

In 1894 Lord Elgin succeeded Lord Lansdowne as Viceroy, and, unaware of the power of departments and precedents, announced his intention of redressing agricultural grievances. He laboured through the literature on the subject, compressed it into the compass of a comprehensive digest, and propounded his views upon a scheme of salvation. But the "system" was stronger than he; moreover, the execution of his good intentions was retarded by the famine of 1896-98 and the frontier wars of 1897-98.

Meanwhile, the writer had been allowed to carry out for the country between Rawalpindi and Lahore a proposal for local inquiries suggested by him in 1884, with a view to meet the standing preliminary objection of the Government to the introduction of reforms—viz., the absence of proof that the peasantry were generally indebted and alienating their holdings to money-lenders. The inquiry proved to the hilt that the gloomiest assertions of those, whom the Government had always regarded as pessimists, were within the truth.

The long controversy as to facts was at last over. Tardily repentant, the Punjab Government now showed contrition for its persistent refusal to admit the truth by publicly acknowledging that it was necessary "to provide a corrective for our own acts, and mitigate the almost revolutionary effects of British rule applied to land-tenures in the Punjab." Similarly Lord Curzon, who succeeded Lord Elgin as Viceroy in 1899, reaping where his predecessor had sown, in putting to his Legislative Council the reform measures indicated by the results of the writer's inquiry of 1896, acknowledged that "this canker of agricultural indebtedness, which is eating into the vitals of India, . . . has reached or is reaching the most dangerous dimensions" in the Punjab. . . . "We originated the present land system, which has had the unfortunate consequences that it is proposed to rectify, as well as the legal system which has given the usurer his opportunity."

The measure then passed was reactionary, almost revolutionary, for in a few clauses it superseded much of the elaborate legislation of the previous forty years, disabled non-agriculturists from acquiring permanent interests in agricultural land, created a peasants' jubilee every twentieth year, and confined jurisdiction under the Act to revenue officers, thus barring out pleaders, securing equity, and in a large measure restoring the paternal system by "protecting the ignorant from errors due to their want of knowledge."

The new departure, called "The Punjab Land Alienation Act," is satisfactory as a first instalment towards the solution of the great question of land-law reform. By partially destroying agricultural credit, maiming the professional money-lenders, and ousting legal practitioners from some of the courts, it has pulled down many fetishes. But, to be successful, demolition has yet to be followed by construction. Peasants have yet to be enabled to live as freemen through bad seasons, and to redeem their lost fields at reasonable cost, and that will be impossible until a disinterested substitute for the village usurer has been created, the rigidity of the land revenue system has been elasticised, and the courts and law administered by them have been simplified to the conditions of a rude and ignorant people.

The task before the Government of India is great, its disabilities many. For instance, no government can prevent famines—*i.e.*, rain-failures and the rise of food grains and fodder for cattle to prices prohibitive for the poor—because the possible extension of irrigation-canals is nearing its limits, and experience shows that, when a canal has converted a desert into a granary, the multiplication of mouths soon approaches congestion-point. Again, no government can check the continuous growth of population during non-famine periods: throughout a continent in which habit or religion requires boys and girls to be parents at an age when their English contemporaries are still at school, instruction in political economy and "moral" text-books has no effect. Further, the Government cannot reduce taxation, for ways and means must be found, and no equivalent can be devised for the land revenue or salt-tax, at least none which Great Britain, wedded to free trade, no matter how the term be interpreted, will tolerate. What is called India's "tribute" to England will probably be larger in the future than it is now. Whether it be twenty or thirty millions sterling, the larger part represents what are, unfortunately, under an alien government, unavoidable payments, interests on loans,—most of them incurred for productive works such as railways and canals,—pensions spent out of India, furlough allowances, home establishment charges, private remittances, and the like. However burdensome to the Indian taxpayer, this "economic drain without return" will continue so long as our dominion in India lasts. The cost of the white garrison—only 74,000 men—is great, no doubt; but were India independent, her defensive expenditure would be higher than it now is, for, even with internal tranquillity, in addition to land forces, she would require a powerful navy to safeguard her 3000 miles of coast, whilst up to the present she contributes practically nothing to the maintenance of the British navy, which renders her immune from attack.

Finally, for the Punjab, is the disability arising from the fact that, through the operation of our "system" during the last thirty-five years, fully a third of her peasant-proprietary—called by the present Viceroy, in the speech already quoted, "the flower of the population, and the backbone of the native army"—now till their ancestral fields as the tenants of their former dependents, the money-lenders. That so many are hopeless paupers is pity, that those who are not yet submerged should also go under would be worse than pity: such a catastrophe would disgrace our civilisation and stamp us as the Ruiners not Rulers of India.

To avert such a disaster the Government cannot, as seems intended, now sit still awaiting developments, before carrying what it calls the "experiment" in relief legislation to its logical conclusion. "Should we be successful in this enterprise," says Lord Curzon, "we shall be encouraged to proceed." If so, years will elapse, and before another step forward is taken half the still solvent peasantry will have disappeared as proprietors. Obviously, precious time cannot be wasted in waiting for far-off results. Obviously, too, a disinterested alternative for the professional money-lender —an honest some one who will sell money cheap and not dear—must be found. For years the Government have been coquetting with the idea of "agricultural banks"; but as our "system" has broken down the communal character of village institutions and substituted a sort of selfish individualism, the postulate for success—the coming forward of benevolent pioneers—is absent. Every attempt by the Government to shift responsibility in this respect on to the shoulders of private individuals is foredoomed to failure. Clearly, then, what has to be done must be done quickly and by the Government—*i.e.*, by ourselves. We are by our own admissions "the largest landlords in creation," and have hitherto so mismanaged our property that many of our tenantry are now discontented serfs, not, as they should be, prosperous right-holders. We have lately confessed our faults, and profess to seek in future to be good landlords rather than hard taskmasters. As a first reform, we have proscribed money-lenders; but as our peasantry, who are now, where still uninvolved, rather Crown tenants than proprietors, are too poor to pay rent when the crops fail, and can no longer borrow or get credit easily from their tradesmen, we have yet to adapt our rent or land-revenue system to the vicissitudes of seasons, and further, by advancing money at low interest for farming purposes, put ourselves as friendly landlord-bankers in the place of the disestablished village usurers.

When, if ever, these reforms are worked out and come into operation, and, in addition, the rules of recruitment for judicial and clerical posts—at present, owing to educational disabilities in rural parts, monopolised by the commercial and ministerial classes of the towns—are so amended that qualified agriculturists receive a reasonable share of appointments, our system of administration, instead of being the means of destroying the peasantry, will be their protection. That our reproach be speedily taken away from us should be the determination of every Englishman.

CHAPTER XVII.

TRAINING OF THE RIVERS—EASTERN PUNJAB.

WHILST morally our shortcomings as rulers are manifest,—our system benefiting the rich at the expense of the poor,—materially our success has long been conspicuous, cultivation, production, revenue, and population all having doubled, or more than doubled, since the 'fifties, whilst the external trade of the province has risen from practically nothing to many millions sterling.

To particularise: in the time of John Lawrence the cultivated acreage was thirteen millions, most of it rain-dependent; it is now twenty-eight, and of that total six are irrigated from canals and four from 350,000 wells, 80 per cent of which are masonry: at the first census (1855) the population was thirteen millions, at the latest (1901) it was over twenty-two; in the former year the revenue from all sources was roundly two millions sterling, in the latter it was but a little short of four,[1] five if receipts from rates since imposed under various denominations for certain local and famine-relief services be added, and

[1] As the gold value of the rupee was about 35 per cent higher in 1855 than now, the appreciation of our rupee revenue is really greater by that percentage than is shown in the text.

the whole of these additional millions are due to enhanced production, not higher assessments; for as a fact the land-revenue rates—allowing for the rise in prices—are now fully 30 per cent lower than they were during the first two decades of our rule, and the tendency is still towards reduction. Then as to trade, from beginnings so small as not to be held worthy of mention in the early reports of the Board and Chief Commissioner, the exports, chiefly cereals, now amount to ten millions sterling annually, and the imports, largely cotton piece-goods, to a like figure.

As a creator of wealth, then, our system[1] has worked admirably; its reproach lies in the fact that, instead of diffusing prosperity amongst the producing masses, it has operated to concentrate the fruits of their labours, over and above a bare subsistence, in the hands of capitalists, traders, money-lenders, lawyers, and in a sense the Government. If the Punjab be regarded as an estate, a unit, the often-repeated official pronouncement, that its condition "is eminently creditable to British rule," is justified; but regarded as the inheritance of several millions of hardy peasant-families, their decline and fall from the status of unencumbered right-holders in their fields to indebted serfs under their former dependents, ought to change our self-satisfaction into shame. In spite of our science, our unique experience in govern-

[1] The loss to India, without replacement, of her old village textile and other industries, and to some extent the increasing drain of her annual "tribute," are not due to "our system," which refers to that built up by administrators inside India, but to two outside influences—the subordination of India's commercial interests to those of Britain, and the monopoly by thrifty sojourning Englishmen of the most profitable appointments and occupations in the country, a condition almost inevitable wherever we rule Asiatics.

ing Asiatics, and the unselfish devotion to duty of our Anglo-Indian officials, we have failed to fulfil our primary obligation as rulers, the doing of the greatest good to the greatest numbers. On the one hand, throughout the last forty years, the wealth of the province has been steadily and rapidly increasing, and is now so great that even in famine periods it produces a superabundance of food; on the other hand, the peasantry have been gradually sinking into poverty, until fully a third of them are now leading lives but a little higher than those of the beasts of the field. The impoverishment of the producers proves the unwisdom of our methods of administration, the largeness of the products the ability with which we are extorting from blind nature a certain subsistence for the multiplying millions whom our system calls into life and keeps from death.

In the Hindu trinity Brahma creates and Vishnu preserves; but their work is spoilt by the third member of the godhead, Siva, who destroys. This Siva, until we English came and made war upon him, was supreme, more feared and worshipped than his titular co-equals were loved and adored. After a prolonged struggle we have at last succeeded—*pace* plague—in deposing, killing, and burying him, and our victory has been chiefly due to the persistent skill with which we have converted the great rivers of the Punjab into food-producers.

After collecting their strength in the Himalayas, and boring passages through the last of the mountain barriers between them and the open country, they sweep and tear through a submontane zone under the partial confinement of water-worn cuttings and fairly consistent banks. Southwards, at distances ranging from forty to eighty miles from the hills, the aspect of the country changes, rock, loam, gravel, herbage disappearing, and merging into a vast expanse of flat sandy plain, which in turn deepens into the deserts of Sindh, Bahawalpur, and Rajputana. Through that northern plain the rivers move south-west towards the Indus, a large part of their flow being underground; for downwards and laterally, as far as excavations have penetrated, no hard substratum has been reached—the spade encounters nothing but moist sand.

For thousands of years succeeding rulers had allowed those noble rivers, the Sutlej, Beas, Ravi, Chenab, and Jhelam, to traverse the great plain of the Punjab unutilised, although all were potentially as powerful life-givers as the Nile—in the hot months veritable floods of liquid gold, in the cold patchy and easily tractable streams, creeping sluggishly southwards but a foot or two below the levels of the broad depressions which limited their wanderings east and west. The inhabitants had aptly called their country "Punjab"—"five-rivers" land—and Runjit Singh, by pushing his conquests westwards to the foot of the Sulimans, had added a sixth, the Indus; but, if we except some small inundation canals in the south-west corner of the province made by that sagacious governor, Diwan Sawan Mull, rulers and people, instead of collaborating and drawing assured sufficiency from the rivers, had in their ignorance and ineptitude trusted to the luck of each season's rainfall for their food-supplies, scratching the seed into the thirsty soil, and leaving results to the caprices of the niggard heavens.

Even when, in the middle of the seventeenth

century, the Emperor Shah Jehan began to turn to account one of the neglected great rivers of his northern province, his inspiration was love for the beautiful, not pity for his sometimes starving people. That fountains might play in Shalimar, the royal gardens at Lahore, he cut a canal, the Hasli, from a point on the Ravi 110 miles north of his Punjab capital, and more than a century later Runjit Singh and his Sikhs extended it to Amritsar, there to fill the sacred tank about the Golden Temple.

After annexation one of Henry Lawrence's earliest self-imposed duties was the conversion of the Hasli into a great irrigation canal ;—if he could but intercept the Ravi under the hills, and spread its waters over the Manjha, the profits from plough and hoe would reconcile the disbanded Khalsa to the loss of sword and musket. His project materialised into the Bari Doab Canal, the head-works of which are at Madhopur near Pathankot. Excavation was begun in 1851, but for some years progress was slow and results unsatisfactory. At the time river hydraulics were a novel science in India, the Ganges Canal—the prototype of all its successors—was still under construction, and on it as well as on the Bari Doab our engineers had to acquire knowledge from the teachings of their mistakes. On the Ravi the heavy nature of the cuttings, the necessity for a series of falls to regulate a drop of 326 feet in the first twenty miles of the main, and a futile attempt by means of locks to make the canal navigable, added greatly to the difficulties and expenses of the undertaking. However, by 1861 irrigation began, and by 1889 the interest account was cleared, a remarkable achievement for the pioneer canal of the Punjab ; commercially its ultimate success had been assured early in the 'sixties. With an irrigating capacity of 800,000 acres, paying on an average five shillings an acre, the net annual return on the capital invested, a million and three-quarters sterling, is now 12 per cent.

On the political side of the account results have been no less satisfactory, for "the horde of barbarians who have overrun the Punjab," as we called the Sikhs before we fought them, have for two generations now been foremost amongst the prosperous farmers and loyal soldiers of the Empire. Their eminence in both capacities is owing to the happy combination in their national character of the acquisitive and fighting instincts, qualities conspicuous in them even during their prolonged struggle for existence when an obscure military commonwealth. Their love of gain and inherited shrewdness have, since the establishment of our reign of law, enabled them to avoid the pitfalls of the system of administration which has demoralised so many of the less efficient agricultural communities of the province.

Before the training of the Ravi had transformed the arid treeless Manjha into gardens and corn-fields, 110 miles eastward the breaking to harness of the greater Sutlej at Rupar, and eighty miles still farther east the more thorough bitting of the Jamna at Jagadhri, were being undertaken.[1] For both works the experience gained on the Ganges and Bari Doab canals was valuable to our Engineer officers. Though the western main of the Jamna Canal irrigates some

[1] There was a Jamna canal in Moghal times. Between 1814 and 1840 the Agra Government restored and reopened both its western and eastern branches. The Punjab Government began the remodelling and re-aligning of the western or Delhi branch in 1874.

of the districts of the Delhi division, transferred to the Punjab after the Mutiny, the river itself, as indeed is the case with the division, appertains more to the United—lately North-West—Provinces than to the Punjab proper. On the other hand, the Sutlej, or Sirhind Canal, as it is officially designated, is a purely Punjab work, and as such deserves mention in these pages.

The design was daring, almost doubtfully feasible, and certain to be immensely costly—to divert a large part of the Sutlej at its debouchure from the Sewaliks below Simla, convey its intercepted waters by a high-level main for thirty-nine miles through a very difficult country to Doraha, on the Grand Trunk Road near Ludhiana, and thence spread them over the Jat country lying between Ludhiana, the Bikaneer desert, and the Ghaggar stream. Of the commanded area, a tract larger than Wales, two-thirds were in British territory, and the rest divided between the native states, Patiala, Jhind, and Nabha. The crux of the enterprise lay in a few miles of the short distance between the head-works and Doraha. Below that point—the terminus of the main—the construction of the 2500 miles of branches and distributaries was simple. Above, strange and novel problems were encountered: in eleven out of the thirty-nine miles of the main the spring level was many feet above the bed of the canal; throughout its whole length the main had to be carried across drainages of great volume from a mountainous catchment area as large as Yorkshire, with twice its rainfall, all compressed into two mouths; then at the head-weir 6000 *cusecs*[1] had to be drawn off out of the 300,000 which in

[1] *Cusec* = cubic feet per second.

floods rush down the bed of the river, and finally the country, being uninhabited and unproductive, workmen and some of the materials had to be imported, the former by the attraction of good terms, —unlike Egypt, we have no *corvée* in India except for military transport in war-time,—the latter from distant places. To carry out the scheme, as finally approved in 1879, 1800 convicts and multitudes of free labourers, including during three famine years 15,000 relief workers from Sirsa and Bikaneer, were located in movable camps at different points along the line, and a temporary railway was built to feed them and convey material, much of which latter was obtained from the forests of the Himalayas and the quarries, brick-fields, and buried cities of the Punjab, particularly Sirhind. The question of the disposal of the cross-drainages was solved by taking them under or over the canal by means of masonry conduits. Of the former, the Dohar torrent siphon, which passes 5000 *cusecs*, is a good example; of the latter, the super-passages for the Siswan and combined Sugh-Budki torrent. The Siswan has a discharge during floods of 30,000 *cusecs*, the Sugh-Budki of 40,000, which latter is more than six times the designed volume in the main canal, and considerably more than the minimum of the Nile. The aqueducts which transported over and under the main the tens of thousands of tons of water, sand, mud, and gravel suddenly hurled upon it after every heavy downpour in the hills, are necessarily of a size and solidity compared with which the largest bridges in Europe are inconsiderable. That since 1882, when Lord Ripon formally opened the canal, the cross-drainage conduits have withstood the attacks of many floods, proves the high quality of the minds which designed, and the careful work of the hands which executed, those massive aqueducts. The successful carrying of the main over three miles of low-lying marsh-land was rather a triumph for dogged persistence than engineering skill. As the bed of the canal had to be excavated to a depth of fourteen feet below spring level and raised as many above it, the chief difficulty lay in counteracting the constant inflow of water into the excavations. This was effected by incessant pumping and the casemating of the sides and bed as work progressed. In addition, as the marsh had no bottom other than soft mud, a precarious stability for the masonry superstructures required at various points had to be obtained by sinking wells to considerable depths and surrounding them with stones and blocks of concrete. The capital outlay on the canal—long the least remunerative in India—has been nearly three millions sterling, of which roundly a third was debited to the native states benefited; but as the work commands 3500 miles of naturally sterile country, actually irrigates 1,160,000 acres, which pay on an average five shillings an acre, and the annual interest earned has reached during the last quinquennium 9 per cent, and will in the next rise to 11 per cent, the undertaking is now a success.

Apart from money considerations, the Sirhind Canal gives comparative affluence to a large population previously leading a hand-to-mouth existence, and in famine years feeds multitudes of starving refugees from Bikaneer and Sirsa. Even so, it is questionable whether the canalisation of the Sutlej should not have been postponed until one of the easier, more remunerative, and for the always dis-considered Muhammadan population of the Western Punjab, more necessary, Chenab and Jhelam projects had been carried through. Surveys, plans, and estimates for canals from those rivers as well as for the Indus were completed early in the 'seventies, and none of them presented the same classes of engineering problems as had been encountered in the cases of the Ravi, Jamna, and Sutlej.

As the Punjab plain broadens from 150 miles on its Jamna side to 450 along its Indus frontage, the Government, when training the rivers successively from east to west, had been constrained to begin the canalisation of the Jamna, Ravi, and Sutlej as they issued from the Himalayas upon the Punjab uplands, and consequently to construct falls, here and there locks for navigation purposes, and in addition massive conduits, to carry off the cross-drainages intersected by the mains of the canals. All of these were engineering difficulties peculiar to the cis-Ravi portion of the province. Then, too, by canalising the eastern rivers before breaking ground westwards the Government laid itself open to various charges—the continued neglect of Muhammadan for Hindu interests, the prior protection against famine of the less insecure half of the Punjab, the watering of submontane tracts already supplied with numerous wells, and blessed by a considerable and fairly certain rainfall, and the sinking of a larger capital on construction than would have been necessary for any of the western rivers. Trans-Ravi the canal-heads being situated in the flat plain, far south of the skirts of the Himalayas, the obstacles to economic construction and maintenance, so serious cis-Ravi, would have been absent. The Sirhind

Canal, no doubt, converted potentially troublesome Sikhs and Jats into well-fed, and therefore contented, farmers; but at the same time it, coupled with the Bari Doab and Western Jamna canals, gave, as just noted, the Hindu section of the community a great advantage over the Western Muhammadans, who were already, owing to their scantier rainfall and less self-helpful habits, the chief sufferers from fixity of demand and the unsympathetic inflexibility of our administration.

The three eastern rivers having been canalised, the Government early in the 'eighties turned their eyes westwards to the Muhammadan districts of the province, and resolved to successively divert the waters of the Chenab, Jhelam, and Indus over their respective doabs, and thus reclaim some 15,000 square miles of country. In all three cases the great depth of the level sandy plain had enabled our Engineer officers, when aligning the canals, to fix the position of their respective head-works from 80 to 120 miles south of the most southerly spurs of the Himalayas. By so doing large economies in construction and maintenance were secured, falls and cross-drainages being avoided. In addition, in each case the country commanded being comparatively rainless, with few wells or settled inhabitants, the dislocation of rural relationships, which the introduction of canal irrigation invariably produces, would, it was hoped, be so insignificant as neither to ruin well-owners nor derange the revenue system of neighbouring tracts.

In giving priority to the Chenab over the Jhelam the Government acted upon business principles. As the Rechna was more extensive than the Chaj Doab, and most of its waste—the loose inheritance of Muhammadan tribes—had already been appropriated as state property, its colonisation by peasant settlers from the congested central districts of the province would be more rapid and profitable than that of the less extensive doab to its west. There was only one objection,—the Chenab was a sand-carrier, and whilst irrigating, might also gradually sterilise, the soil; on the other hand, the Jhelam, rich with the drainage of Kashmir, would fertilise and renovate it. So far apprehensions have not been realised; but as the process of deterioration, if begun, must be slow, and the virgin strength of the Rechna Doab has not yet been exhausted, probably years will elapse before doubts can be definitively set at rest.

CHAPTER XVIII.

CANALS AND COLONIES—WESTERN PUNJAB.

DECIDED on, the Chenab project grew in the making from an inundation canal to the final concept of throwing the whole river, by means of a masonry weir 1500 yards long, built right across from bank to bank, upon the 4420 available square miles of the doab. Work on the first scheme began in 1882, on a more ambitious development in 1889, and three years later on the still bolder undertaking just mentioned. Its grandeur, though not apparent to the eye, nine-tenths of the work—the down-stream apron excepted—being below water, captivates the understanding. As we have succeeded in damming and turning to purposes of agriculture a wide and foundationless river, which in flood has a flow above and below ground equal to that of the Nile, it would appear that no force in nature useful to man will be capable of resisting subjection to him. Naturally, in the Chenab case the whole problem centred in the question whether a weir, sufficiently stable and massive to wall back the river, could be raised from a bottom of fine and always unstable sand. The weir, as made, consists of a shallow core wall protected by a bulwark or breakwater of packed stones and blocks of concrete surmounted by a line of falling shutters, six feet in height. The under-sluices rest on deeply sunk masonry wells, on whose equilibrium and stability the safety of the whole superstructure depends. The successful construction of similar weirs in Southern India, and perhaps of the Alexandra Bridge over the Chenab, eight miles above the great weir, warranted our engineers in their bold experiment of damming the whole river.

When the weir was built (1889-95) the railway-bridge—its wells and piers occasionally buttressed and strengthened—had stood the test of many years, trains creeping cautiously over it even during the highest recorded floods. That fact is a happy augury for the permanent stability of the weir. Once only has there been apprehension of catastrophe, in 1895, when the serious subsidence of a section indicated that the work was not secure against the danger of being undermined, and, once pierced, the whole structure would have been wrecked. Further mischief was immediately arrested by extending the width, depth, and mass of the sunken defences. As the beginnings of evil, though occurring sixty or more feet below surface-level, are at once in evidence above it, the experienced and resourceful staff, maintained at the head-works, are confident of their ability to preserve the weir intact against the assaults of any floods; indeed, the history of our railway-bridges and canals throughout India warrants the conclusion that, as the conflict between man and nature proceeds, the former will not only retain the fruits of his past conquests, but will continuously extort new victories, until eventually the whole water-supply of the Punjab—that of great floods excepted—will subserve agriculture, and in a secondary degree industrial enterprise.

That this is no unreasonable anticipation is easily shown :—within the last six years the Jhelam Canal, taking off from Rasul, close to the battlefield of Chillianwala, has been made and opened, and as its irrigating capacity is greatly in excess of the area commanded in the Chaj Doab—1,400,000 acres—projects have been elaborated for utilising its surplus waters, by throwing them across the Ravi or into the Chenab above the head-works of the present canal; in other words, the intention is to interchange the water of the great rivers of the country, much as well-owners manipulate the trickling streamlets in their little water-courses. Then, too, the Government is only awaiting the conclusion of a satisfactory arrangement by which about two-thirds of the Sind Sagar Doab—the country between the Jhelam, Lower Chenab, and Indus—will become State property, to throw a weir across the Indus at Mari, just above Kalabagh, and spread that river's waters over the greater part of the doab, an area of about 9500 square miles. When completed, which should be within the next generation, the Indus Canal should do more in a few years to tame and civilise our frontier tribesmen than has been accomplished, without canals, by half a century of British rule or domination.

Besides diverting the great rivers from their beds in the lowest levels between their respective doabs into canals dug down the watershed of each, and thus giving large tracts perennial irrigation, the Government, not only in the sub-Himalayan districts,—in which the rainfall three years out of four is timely and sufficient,—but also in the wide alluvial valleys of the Sutlej, the Indus, and the Lower Punjab, has for many years been promoting the development of the minor irrigation resources of the province, directly, by making and extending inundation canals,—short shallow channels which fill when a river is in flood,—and indirectly, by granting advances at nominal or very low interest to enterprising proprietors for wells, reservoirs, embankments, and the like. By the former means a million of acres have been reclaimed and bear spring crops, by the latter the rainfall has been supplemented and crops made safe over four millions of acres.

Up to date the total cost of Punjab canals—exclusive of the share contributed by native states—has been under seven millions sterling, and the annual net return on that outlay now averages 11 per cent, and in another decade may rise to 18 per cent. The Chenab Canal already gives that rate of interest; the Jhelam Canal, when colonisation shall have been fully developed, should pay a higher dividend; and that from the Indus should ultimately yield a return of 12 per cent, for, whatever the cost of construction, its irrigating capacity and commanded area will be double that of the Chenab, at present the largest irrigation canal in India, if not in the world. At Mari—the point selected for the head-works of the Indus Canal—where the great river has the appearance of a narrow loch in the Highlands of Scotland, and moves between mountain walls with majestic stillness over a hard bottom, the weir will not be more than a third as long as that of the Chenab, and will rest on firm natural foundations, factors which make for cheapness. On the other hand, the cold-weather volume of the river is large and subject to sudden rises from rain-storms in some part of its immense catchment basin; then the rock-cuttings in the first few miles of the canal will be considerable, and the soil of the doab is in parts poor and sand-hillocks are frequent. All these are elements which mean heavy expenditure on construction and maintenance. They have given rise to apprehensions which will probably not be realised; for instance, as the river carries in suspension quantities of fertilising matter, it will in time, the writer is convinced after ten years of personal observation of the effects of Indus silt in Mianwali, make its own soil, and if so, sterile sand will change to good loam, and then crops will be heavy and ratings high.

Again, experience proves that, by the gradual consolidation of banks, the strengthening of head-works, and the introduction of economies in the application of water, both the limits of irrigable area and the maximum discharges of canals become enlarged. In proof thereof is the fact that the discharges of the Bari Doab, Sirhind, and Chenab, originally calculated at 19,000 *cusecs*, have already increased to 25,000, whilst their powers of irrigation have risen still higher. Treating the Jhelam canal-lands as fully colonised, the five great perennial canals of the Punjab now irrigate over five millions of acres—an area approximating closely to that from the Nile; further, according to the figures of experts, the limit of irrigating power will not be reached until the five millions rise to seven: *e.g.*, the present capacity of the Chenab is two millions of acres, but a few years hence it will be three.

In another direction, too, there will be expansion—the charges for water will be enhanced. The handsome direct return on capital invested in the Punjab canals—11 per cent now and 14 to 16 in the near future—is calculated on current rates and methods of assessment; but, as both are unsatisfactory, they will be revised for each canal as existing agreements expire. Under the present modes of assessment the whole of a commanded area is usually treated as a unit or revenue circle, and every irrigated acre inside it is charged on a uniform scale, so much for each watering, or differentially according to class of crop grown. Neither system discriminates between variations in soil, rainfall, levels, and distances to sources of water-supply—the last two of primary importance in a flat country, as affecting flow and deposition of suspended matter. The cumulative effect of these influences is so potent that, where all four are favourable or adverse, the value of similar areas identically rated on the same canal differs as much as does good well-land from poor rain-land fifty or more miles farther south. Presumably, then, as existing settlements expire, the Government will better adjust the demand to the value of the outturn.

In 1898 the writer advocated the splitting up of the commanded area on each canal into zones, the classifying of the squares or fields in each with reference to the factors just named, and the adoption of a sliding-scale for the several ratings, which would, during the frequently recurring periods for rain-lands of lean and fat years, proportion the demand to the market prices of the time. Had some such system been in force during the recent famine and short-food years, 1896-1901, the State might have recovered from canal-irrigated lands as much additional revenue as it was constrained to remit on rain-lands, and this equilibrium might have been obtained without undue interference with the reasonable expectations of canal-assessees at such times.

If we apply the view here taken to the Chenab colonies, and, selecting wheat as an example, assume that for assessment purposes the estimated average acreage yield was commuted into money at 35 lb. a shilling,—a fairly liberal valuation even for times of plenty,—we should find that, during the five years above referred to, producers sold their wheat at an average rate of 21, not 35, lb. a shilling, and that consequently each cleared nearly £1 an acre in excess of the estimate of the profits on which his assessment had been based. If so, had the Government arranged its assessments on a sliding-scale principle, and collected, let us say, one-third of what was in fact "an unearned increment," all or the greater part of the revenue foregone on rain-lands would have been recouped from that gained on canal-lands, and the canal-assessees would have pocketed about 13s. an acre in excess of their rights. When, then, perennial canal expansion shall have reached its limit, provided that existing assessments are meanwhile revised on the lines suggested above,—and no one will dispute the right of the Government as canal-owner to sell water to best advantage compatible with the continued prosperity of those buying it,—the net annual direct profit on the capital invested will be fully 20 per cent. In the case of the Chenab it will certainly be over 25 per cent. Indirectly, too, there will be in every cycle of years a handsome return, as the saving in famine-relief expenditure will be considerable—viz., the difference between the cost of relief with and without canals. Thus, whether considered as a series of commercial or famine-protection measures, the canalisation of the Punjab rivers is proving progressively more and more successful. When completed, we shall have accomplished the most beneficent, comprehensive, remunerative, and difficult work ever undertaken by any Government within historic record.

The railways of India are large distributing, consolidating, and civilising agents, and have cost many more millions than all the canals of our great dependency put together, and some of their bridges attest our victory over physical obstacles thought unsurmountable fifty years ago. The Alexandra Bridge already mentioned is a case in point,—a grand achievement, no doubt, yet, as a conquest over nature, not to be compared with the canal-weir a few miles lower down the same river. The bridge hardly narrows the flood-way; it merely acts as a cut-water, and supports the weight and downward thrust of trains moving slowly over it; the weir, also erected upon sand, resists the lateral onset of the whole mass of the river's floods and the additional strain caused by their setting back for some ten miles above the great dam.

The world has read much about the training of the Nile; its great *barrage* just below Cairo is one of the sights of Egypt, and for years the European press has made "copy" out of the lately completed Assuan dam and reservoir. Though, from an engineering standpoint, the mighty works on the Nile are inferior to those of Northern India, except officials on duty few visit the latter, and, outside officials, not many know of them. Compare for a moment the difficulties of Nile canalisation—mostly, by the way, the work of Indian engineers—with those of the Chenab, or, for that matter, any of the other five great rivers of the Punjab, whose harnessing has been, or shortly will be, accomplished. The Nile has for more than five thousand years been a sort of embanked canal, being considerably above the level of the country which it irrigates; it has always flowed in a confined manageable channel, and from Assuan to the sea, a distance of 750 miles, its course is through a country so flat that the fall is only four inches in the mile; it rises slowly and regularly; its rocky bed gives perfect foundations wherefrom to build superstructures, and the *corvée* has always supplied the State with cheap and unlimited labour.

Those favourable conditions are wanting in the Punjab. There, the rivers flow in constantly shifting channels in the lowest levels between their respective doabs, and with rapidity—the fall in the submontane uplands being very great, and even in the flat plain treble that of the Nile: they rise suddenly and overwhelmingly a foot or more in a night and without warning, whereas the Nile swells inch by inch and on foreseeable dates; some of them —*e.g.*, the Chenab—have no firm bottoms, and their underground movement is immense; then, finally, their weirs and regulators are built from unstable artificial foundations forced down to great depths.

Colossal, productive, and life-creating and preserving though the irrigation works executed and projected in the Punjab are, our self-satisfaction should be discounted by the reflection that had the Government decided to continue what in these pages is called "our system" in the administration of the canal-commanded areas of the Chenab, Jhelam, and Indus, most of the wealth created by us in those regions would have passed, in a decade or two after the opening of each canal, from the producing peasantry to the soft-handed, machine-rule-made capitalists of the towns. Happily for the former, the unfortunate consequences of our system were demonstrated for the Punjab in time to induce the Government to take measures to safeguard its colonists on the Chenab and later canals against a fate similar to that of their unprotected brethren in their home districts.

The scheme of Chenab colonisation was simple: the doab below Khanki—the head of the canal—was first divided into blocks corresponding with the areas commanded by its several branches. The blocks were then successively demarcated into, roundly, 70,000 permanent squares, each containing 27·7 acres, the size and shape believed the most convenient for irrigation, revenue, and allotment purposes; and, then, parcels of squares, up to about 10 per cent of the whole number, were set apart as a reserve for reward grants to meritorious Indians—chiefly Punjabis—and for disposal by auction to capitalists. By these means the Government not only satisfied persons with claims upon the State, but advertised and valued its property, and tested the popular view of the pitch of the intended assessments which had been previously published.

By the middle of 1893 the competition for land amongst capitalists and officials, not only throughout the Punjab but beyond its limits, had become very keen, a proof that, in the opinion of intelligent men, the margin for profit, after payment of the expenses of production, including the Government demand, would be large. The full awakening of the slower-witted and home-tied peasantry to the certain competence awaiting settlers came a little later, and was at first confined to the central and most congested districts, particularly Sialkot, Amritsar, and Hoshiarpur. Even in them there had been hesitation at first, for the conditions on which allotments were offered were strange and forbidding,—alienation, non-residence, and failure to cultivate, one and all entailing summary forfeiture of holding; and, further, provision was made against unreasonable *morcellement* by restrictions on partitions by inheritance. Such unprecedented innovations filled the ignorant peasantry with vague apprehensions. To many the freedom to ruin themselves and their children—exercised for generations in their old homes—appeared preferable to the shackled abundance now promised. Happily, the Government knew its own mind, and was determined that, in spite of "system," with its laws, lawyers, and enforcement of the letter of so-called contracts, colonists should be at the start, and always continue to be, prosperous and unindebted. Reflection soon convinced the more industrious and thrifty that the Government was acting as their best friend in protecting them and their heirs from prospective declension and poverty. When, then, the struggle for allotments began in earnest, the Government was in a position to select tenants on its own terms, and in doing so took only substantial men from the most industrious castes and tribes in the congested districts of the Punjab. As all settlers throve amazingly, and many were in a short time able to redeem mortgaged fields in their home villages, evidence soon accumulated that, had the acreage ratings approximated nearer 12s. than the 8s. taken, there would have been neither appreciable diminution in the competition for allotments nor serious lowering of the widely diffused prosperity in the different colonies.

Though the scheme as devised and executed has proved grandly successful, that success will not justify the Government in applying purely business principles to the development of the Jhelam and Indus canals. In the case of the Chenab the Government sacrificed, or at least postponed, local Muhammadan interests for large and quick returns. As the canal penetrated southwards, converting waste into corn-fields, the Musalman tribes on either bank in its vicinity—the hereditary possessors of the country—were not only denied participation in the abundance flowing by their doors, but were required to stay at home, cultivate their now profitless wells and rainlands, and pay their fixed revenue assessments. The instinct of self-preservation, however, proved stronger than the fiats of the Government, and soon, for a depth of thirty miles on either side of the canal-irrigated country, wells were abandoned by the hundred, and a large part of the rural population migrated to the canal villages, working there as farm-labourers, artisans, and menials. In this way the fabric of estimates and measurements, on which the assessments of considerable tracts in the districts of Gujranwala, Montgomery, and Jhang were based, was destroyed, and numbers of previously well-to-do peasant and yeoman families were reduced to want.

If we remember that the Bari Doab, Sirhind, and Western Jamna canals had given the eastern or Hindu half of the province a start towards security of livelihood of from ten to thirty years, according to priority of irrigation, over the Musalman half of the country, the three districts just named should have received, on the broad principle of equality of treatment for all Punjabis, large allotments on the Chenab, and the fact that the canal was cut through those districts should have enhanced their claims upon the Government. Instead, their peasantry were at first treated as pariahs and outsiders—in their own country too —and a great wedge of industrious foreigners was established in their midst. As Commissioner of Rawalpindi, and later as Financial Commissioner of the Punjab, the writer pressed their case upon the consideration of his Government, and latterly with some measure of success.

The Musalman tribes of the Chenab were doubtless politically negligible, being poor, ignorant, and some still semi-pastoral; but for the Jhelam and Indus canals conditions are different. The former cuts deep into the heart of the country held by powerful and capable Musalman communities; the latter—when made—will pierce the region where those tribes meet and commingle with our frontier Pathans and Baluches. If the claims of the weak Chenab Muhammadans were considerable, those of their more influential and powerful co-religionists farther west should be irresistible. What was good business, judged by dividends, on the Chenab, would be bad policy and rank injustice on the Jhelam and Indus.

CHAPTER XIX.

THE FRONTIER UNDER PUNJAB MANAGEMENT.

HITHERTO only incidental reference has been made to our troublesome North-West Frontier, the Indus valley, and mountains beyond; but a borderland which in the last fifty years has been the scene of forty wars and expeditions deserves more than a passing mention. Apart from the interest always excited by bloodshed, the Afghan fringe of our Indian Empire has other claims to attention:—it extends for 600 miles from the neighbourhood of the icy Pamirs in the north to the scorched deserts of Sindh in the south, possesses every variety of scenery and climate, is inhabited by four millions of Musalmans, all armed, all priest-swayed, the majority what we call fanatical, and they are held in subjection or restraint by a garrison of 25,000 soldiers, supported by levies, militia, and police, cantoned or locked up in stations, forts, and posts at intervals along the eastern skirts of the wall of mountains which, until recently, abruptly stopped our further expansion towards Afghanistan. True, this book concerns the Punjab in peace and war, and since the beginning of 1901 its Pathan districts have ceased to belong to it, having been formed into a new province under the direct control of the Viceroy. That fact seems, however, rather to enhance than weaken the claims of the lost territory to a place in this volume, because up to the time of its divorce it had been successfully, economically, and unostentatiously administered by the provincial government, and the separation, though ostensibly based on the inefficiency of the local management and peculiar fitness for the duty of the supreme Government, was in reality due to Lord Curzon's abuse of the *force majeure* of his position as Viceroy.

Geographically, ethnically, and administratively the trans-Indus valleys and highlands referred to are part and parcel of Afghanistan and Baluchistan, their dominant inhabitants being Pathans and Baluches speaking respectively Pashto and Baluchi, and their history being that of a number of small semi-independent democracies or feudal states, each generally standing alone, but one or more of them frequently owing loose subordination to the power ruling at Kabul, Delhi, or Lahore.

When in 1809 the Government of India fixed the Sutlej as the Rubicon for Sikh expansion eastwards, and Runjit Singh was thus headed off from Delhi, the Khalsa, under his inspiration, turned their conquering energies upon the Muhammadan states north and west of Lahore, and continued to push their dominion to and even beyond the Indus, until further progress was arrested by the same forces which have for the last twenty-five years baffled most of our attempts to extend our effective occupation to Lord Lytton's imagined "scientific frontier." The imperviousness to outside influence, whether of arms or bribes, of the trans-Indus hill-tribes is as determined to-day as it was fifty or a hundred years ago.

When, after Sobraon, we attempted to administer in the name of the Durbar the Pathan remnant of Runjit Singh's mushroom kingdom, we found that both in Hazara and trans-Indus—except for part of the Peshawar valley—the Sikh supremacy had not been that of a settled government, but of a marauding organisation, whose forces periodically swept through the country, nominally "collecting arrears of revenue," but really consuming or carrying off what was portable, and destroying what was not. Between 1846 and 1848 we, too, "collected revenue"; but we did so as sympathetic intermediaries between Durbar and people, and by our justice and moderation gained the goodwill of most of the Muhammadan tribes west of the Jhelam. After Gujerat we continued the work for ourselves, as conquerors of the Sikhs; but the only change perceived by the peasantry was a more scrupulous protection of their rights, a more systematic exaction of a reduced revenue demand, and generally a closer administration, in which the vagaries of personal rule by each district autocrat gradually disappeared under the levelling power of fixed regulations. Up and down what was now our frontier we took effective possession of the constructive acquisitions of our predecessors. The vindictive tribesmen of the Indus valley, though formerly never at peace amongst themselves except when fighting a common enemy, readily obeyed the firm but mild-mannered incarnations of powerful justice who, now living in their midst, were devoting all their energies to the welfare of their charges.

The civil administration was soon organised: the

long extent of frontier was divided into two commissionerships, Peshawar and the Derajat, each with three districts, of which the five northern were inhabited by Pathans, the sixth and most southern—a mere strip of desert between the arid Sulimans and the Indus—by Baluches. Soldier-politicals, most of them young, were appointed to all the eight charges thus created, and each was given a backing of troops and directed to enforce order, protect British subjects from raids by hillmen, and collect the revenue. Outside this general instruction, and the rules from time to time issued by the Board of Administration, each had a pretty free hand, and played the Earthly Providence as he pleased. Though the governing machinery, from commissioners to revenue-collectors and village revenue establishments, was on the same model as that introduced cis-Indus, its working in the frontier districts was cheaper, rougher, and, because of its simplicity and distance from Lahore, even more effective than in the interior of the province. In the case of the trans-Indus districts and Hazara, the indifference of the central authorities to what is officially called "moral and material progress" —stagnation, waning and waxing, depending largely on the amount expended on education and works of utility—was due to the fact that until after the Mutiny our Pathan districts were looked upon as a bad investment, an objectionable legacy from the Sikhs, only retained because honour forbade their relinquishment. Lord Dalhousie had pledged himself, as has been stated, to make the Punjab "a profitable possession," and both he and the Lawrences, for financial reasons, would have been glad to have stopped short at the Indus, India's traditional boundary. As that had not been feasible, they hoped to keep expenditure trans-Indus within reasonable limits by starving public works, avoiding entanglements with the hill-tribes, and preserving peace and order with the minimum of force considered necessary to obtain the desired ends. Under those conditions the lines of local development depended primarily on the idiosyncrasies of the Peshawar and Derajat Commissioners, but more particularly on those of their respective district officers.

The fact is that, in those days Punjabis and their rulers regarded their trans-Indus appanage very much as a well-regulated family would a scapegrace stranger thrust permanently upon their hospitality. Ethnically, Pathan and Baluch districts had nothing in common with the Punjab proper, the land of the Sikhs and good husbandmen; fiscally, they were a burden, yielding little and costing much for policing; administratively, their peoples were savages, aliens in race, manners, customs, and sentiments to the well-ordered peasantry on the hither side of the Indus. Influenced by those considerations, Lord Dalhousie, with John Lawrence's full approval, was about to detach the frontier from the Punjab and transfer its management to a chief commissioner directly subordinate to himself, and had even selected the first holder of the new office, Colonel Mackerson, when that officer's assassination at Peshawar in September 1853 led to the pigeon-holing of the scheme. When, four years afterwards, the Mutiny occurred, and the loyalty and valour of the frontier districts and their local army were instrumental in enabling the Punjab to take Delhi and, afterwards, help in the re-establishment of the British power in

Oude, the feeling that in sentiment and interests the Indus valley had proved itself one with the Punjab was so strong that all further talk of its severance was dropped for the next twenty years. Not until Lord Lytton came out to India as Viceroy, with orders to push the new forward policy, was the project revived, and, what is more, it was on the eve of accomplishment, and Sir Frederick (now Lord) Roberts had been selected as the first Chief Commissioner of the new province, when the outbreak of the Afghan war of 1878-80 and the consequent semi-insolvency of India put an end for a time to the grandiose schemes of the pushful politicians then mismanaging the affairs of India. After that second failure India's "creaking gate" continued to hang from its Punjab post for twenty more years, until the other day Lord Curzon by brute force tore it from its hinges.

As in the early days of misrule, so in 1900 the proposed assumption of the direct control of frontier affairs by the Government of India was not unpopular with the civil officers trans-Indus: it meant immediate and handsome recognition of services for themselves and less niggardly expenditure on their charges, a quickening of life all round, and a jump from seclusion into prominence. In the 'fifties our trans-Indus civil officers—the majority of them young soldier-politicals, zealous and self-reliant—cared little which master they served. To most of them political work, the influencing of the tribes immediately beyond the border, was more interesting than the comparatively humdrum details of district routine. Throughout the Peshawar division a practice grew up of dealing with our hill neighbours through middlemen, usually local Khans or notables, each of whom naturally put his own interests before those of his Government, some of them occasionally going so far as to procure assassinations or the raiding of villages in the pursuit of a blood-feud or hope of reward for exertions in settling a trouble of their own creation.

To the Pathan revenge is a duty, the taking of life a mere incident, a nothing; but to our officers killing was murder, hence our modes of enforcing the *pax Britannica*, instead of promoting friendly intercourse between ourselves and the tribes encircling the Peshawar valley, more frequently shut them out from it altogether. Thus, when the Mutiny surprised us, and we wanted the help of every dare-devil who could sit a horse or wield a sword or spear, Edwardes, the Commissioner, reported that "for one crime or another almost every powerful tribe beyond the border was under a blockade."

In the Derajat middlemen were eschewed from the first, and district officers were in the habit of meeting tribal *jirgas* or councils of greybeards and personally discussing affairs with them. Results, however, were much the same as in Peshawar. Both north and south our hill neighbours quickly realised that, whether manipulating them through agents or directly, we preferred to forgive rather than to punish; and that raid, burn, and abduct as their young bloods might, the damage they inflicted was a trifle compared with the expenditure we incurred when attempting retaliation; further, that even if hitting back we contented ourselves by merely "lifting their *purdah*"—*i.e.*, marching troops up their hillsides, doing a little burning and surveying, and then hurrying back into our own territory closely followed by the enemy. If, by that time, terms had not been arranged, the pre-existing blockade would be re-established. Eventually, forced by hunger, the tribe would come in, often grass in mouth and halters round necks,—the outward symbols of submission,—and we would accept, in lieu of the money compensation outstanding, a number of stunted under-nourished cattle at fancy prices, cry quits, and give good lodgings and liberal allowances to some scores of families sent in as "hostages" for good conduct. The settlement effected, British territory would be reopened to all comers, and a new account begun. With the Mahsuds the competition for the lucrative honour of being "Government guests" was always keen, so much so that, repeatedly, unrepresented sections would go on the war-path to enhance their importance in our eyes and gain the coveted recognition. Though reprisals and punitive expeditions were frequent in the Derajat, the losses resulting, judged absolutely, were never serious. The tribesmen being wretchedly poor and miserably armed, had neither property to destroy nor ability to fight. Occasionally a few *ghāzis* devoted themselves or rushed a weak or careless picket; occasionally, too, we captured a few goats, blew up towers, or burnt some hovels. Whenever our rear-guard left a halting-place, then only did the enemy show in force—their women and children, followed discreetly by their men, creeping out of caves and other cover, and joining the crows, kites, and vultures in searching the abandoned bivouac for our leavings.

Except for the Peshawar valley, the system of

border defence was uniform all down the frontier. We built strong blockhouses at intervals at our end of the chief passes leading into the hills, and connected them by a bridle-road and a line of small defensible posts or towers. The blockhouses were held by detachments drawn from the "Piffer" garrison—usually two regiments of infantry, one of cavalry, and a mule battery—congregated at the headquarters of each district, the intermediate posts by local levies of no fighting and small patrolling value, but useful as guides and messengers; moreover, their pay served as a retaining fee to the headmen of each locality, who had the right of nomination. The "Piffers," as explained in a former chapter, were the Punjab Irregular Frontier Force, raised soon after annexation—one garrison and four mule batteries, four regiments of cavalry, eleven of infantry, and the Corps of Guides, in all about 13,000 men, and for some years they were supplemented by several battalions of military police. The gunners and infantry were mostly Punjabis, many of them at first old Khalsa soldiers; in the cavalry the Hindustani element was considerable. It was the creation of this irregular force which to some extent excited the apprehensions of the Purbia regulars in 1856 and early months of 1857 lest their occupation should soon be gone, and when they did rise, but for the "Piffers" the Punjab would not have taken Delhi.

For the Peshawar district, border defence was entrusted to the Bengal army, the 2500 Britishers and 7500 Purbia sepoys, who with the 1500 Guides, horse and foot, at Hoti Mardan garrisoned the valley. This large force—veritably "the head of the lance," as John Lawrence called it—was penned up in the most malarious tract in Northern India, more with a view to pierce and repel the Afghan hordes, should their ruler throw them upon Peshawar, than to overawe the Afridis, Mohmands, and other tribes encircling our territory.

In hill-fighting the garrison was only strong through numbers and discipline. In fact, no troops in the Bengal army were adapted for guerilla warfare in the mountains: Britishers and Hindustanis alike were plainsmen, not cragsmen, and neither moved unless accompanied by immense baggage-trains. Owing to these disabilities expeditions launched from Peshawar were infrequent, and when undertaken were rather costly, formal, and ineffective campaigns carried on close to a base within our border than the rough-and-ready sort of marching customary in the Derajat. The fact that, for nearly thirty years after annexation, except in and about Peshawar, throughout 600 miles of wild borderland the hill-tribes never saw a British soldier, yet never, whether in time of peace and plenty or of famine and feud (*badi*), caused our villagers as much material damage as is sometimes effected to this day by a gang of dacoits operating in the heart of one of our oldest provinces, proves that the Punjab system of policing its border and maintaining relations with the hill-tribes beyond was generally not unsuccessful. The whole work—except in Peshawar—was done by the local officers and Punjabi troops under the orders of the Punjab Government, and the average cost of blockades and expeditions up to 1880 was small compared with the expenditure incurred in the last decade, during which time the Government of India has been solely responsible for frontier management.

Moreover, in spite of the enormous outlay of those years, the tribes to-day are less in touch with us than at any previous period in our fifty years of connection with them. Until Lord Lytton's baneful viceroyalty (1876-1880) the Government of India, influenced by John Lawrence's non-interference system, had treated border management as more a provincial than an imperial concern, and the vague but grandiose terms, so frequent in Blue-books since the "forward policy" came into being, such as "imperial considerations," "sphere of political influence," "the larger problems of foreign policy," had not yet been introduced into Indian State Papers. But even in those days, although the Lieutenant-Governor of the Punjab had large powers of initiative and control, and the "Piffer" force obeyed his orders, no punitive proceedings, more serious than a blockade or counter-raid, were undertaken without the previous sanction of the Viceroy.

For the Peshawar valley the conditions were different; its large garrison being directly under the orders of the Commander-in-Chief, and the Amir of Afghanistan and Viceroy corresponding with each other without the intervention of the provincial ruler, the Government of India necessarily closely supervised Peshawar frontier affairs, and, owing to local ignorance, sometimes burnt its fingers badly—*e.g.*, in the Ambela war of 1863. Our misfortunes in that campaign, though immediately conducing to the appointment of John Lawrence as Viceroy, contributed later to supply forward politicians with arguments for replacing his close-border system by one of aggressive activity. Had we not, they contended, shut ourselves up behind a Chinese wall of forts and pillars, we should have known something of the country and its inhabitants between ourselves and our objective, Ambela, and our force would not have been hemmed in and held in check for months by a coalition of hostile tribes just beyond our border, but would have destroyed the nest of Sitana fanatics in a week; therefore, it was urged, we should extend our influence trans-frontier and gradually absorb the hill-tribes. There was truth in the statement of fact, but not in its corollary. Knowledge was possible without aggression. By degrees the new yeast began to work, and the inert dough gradually rose until an over-aerated loaf was produced in the person of Lord Lytton, whose *rôle* was, by bribes, blandishments, or brutality, to quicken reluctant Amir and independent tribes into acceptance of our friendship and protection. Meanwhile Königgrätz had roused us to the advantages of superiority in weapons, and the small-arms of our Indian soldiers were progressively improved, Brunswick rifle, Enfield, and Snider successively replacing Brown Bess. The desire to establish "friendly relations" with tribes and Afghans grew proportionately with the increase in our offensive strength. The inevitable ensued, hostilities with both, and in 1878, in spite of famine, deficits, and falling rupee, the grasping politicians then in power, whilst endeavouring to obtain a "scientific frontier" —that mirage of a disordered imagination—and force a protectorate upon the Amir of Afghanistan, plunged into a protracted war with that country, and emerged from it two years afterwards the poorer by 25 millions sterling, the richer by a few square miles of worthless territory.

The discovery that we should have strengthened

our defences inside India before advancing into space outside her limits, now induced us to pause in our policy of aggression, and we spent the next decade in erecting fortifications and linking up our cantonments trans-Indus. For thirty years we had neglected the work; the money wasted in Afghanistan would have more than sufficed to complete it, and then we might have laughed in security at the raging of the heathen beyond—Russians, Afghans, or both. But, as man is constituted, entrenched positions, roads, railways, bridges, and telegraph-lines are poor equivalents for war, which gives ambition scope, whilst spade-work does not. When, after the madness of the war, the imminent insolvency of India enforced a return to common-sense in our councils, the railway was only open to Jhelam, the Indus was nowhere bridged, and beyond it from Peshawar to Sindh communications were almost in the same embryonic condition as they had been in 1849. So prehistoric were they, so isolated were the various garrisons all down the frontier, that whenever the rivers were in flood some of our cantonments —*e.g.*, Bannu — were cut off from all connection with the outer world frequently for a week at a time. In 1870, when the Muhammedkhel Waziris of Bannu rebelled, news of their ambushing and shooting down a detachment of our troops did not reach the Punjab Government at Murree until a fortnight after the outrage had occurred. By 1890, so vigorously had road- and railway-making been pushed during the preceding ten years that, except for Bannu, reinforcements could be concentrated at any point upon India's Ultima Thule almost as rapidly as was the case for any interior station.

The opening up of the frontier districts, besides materially increasing our military strength and keeping down the cost of future expeditions, brought prosperity to the population of the country. In India, under our system, the chief beneficiaries from improved communications had previously been—besides the Government—the money-lenders and grain-dealers, who as creditors or mortgagees were already absorbing the margin of profit in excess of the cost of production. Happily, trans-Indus and in the Hazara hills, the peasantry were in the beginning of the 'nineties less indebted and less expropriated than in the interior of the province, as in the frontier districts the refinements of our legal system were still sitting lightly on rulers as well as ruled, and popular opinion, expressed by the dagger, still deterred Hindus from the risks of landlordism and the enforcement of unconscionable contracts. Happily, too, for our frontier peasantry, their land-revenue settlements—the latest taken up in the province—had still many years to run, hence, most of the profits arising from better prices, wider and newer markets, and expanded cultivation went to the producers and not to the money-lenders and the Government. Thus, so far, the more direct assumption of political control trans-Indus by the Government of India was bringing good to people, including hill-tribes, and local government alike. So long as the non-interference policy had continued—*i.e.*, until the period of the Afghan war, 1878-80—the Supreme Government had contributed very little to public works of a civil nature in the frontier districts; and, naturally, the local Government, with its small resources and many obligations, allocated its expenditure amongst its rich, populous, interior districts. After the war the mouth of the horn of plenty was turned trans-Indus—the poor man's starveling had become the millionaire's darling. Not only were people and local government enriched, but in 1880 "nobody's child," as "Piffer" officers called themselves, found a wealthy stepfather in the Commander-in-Chief, *vice* their fond but pauper parent, the Lieutenant-Governor, now supposed to be breaking up from senile decay. Superficially that transfer of authority merely ended an anomaly—civilian control over a large military force—but, in effect, it deprived the ruler of the Punjab of most of his direct authority in frontier politics, and reduced him from the position of Lord Warden of the Marches, with large powers of initiative, to that of head of one branch of the foreign department of the Government of India. Thenceforward every question, whether imposition of a tribal fine, movement of troops, proclamation of a blockade, counter-foray, or the launching of an expedition, had to be referred to the Viceroy. The descent from ruler and war-lord to adviser and "channel of communication" was not announced in words, but was felt in acts.

As the views of the Government of India materialised and expanded—imperialists being ever pushful —"friendly relations" with our hill neighbours were rigorously cultivated at the point of the bayonet. On five occasions between 1888 and 1893 we sent our troops as schoolmasters into their mountains; but though the lessons taught cost the Indian taxpayers over a million sterling, the pupils learned nothing,—they preferred freedom and ignorance to subjection and education. As expedition succeeded expedition, again and again did the moribund old man of the Punjab warn his inexperienced but headstrong superior that the new imperial mixture, bribes and bullets, was an irritant, not an anodyne. But no remonstrance had any effect; the adviser was courteously informed his views were parochial, those of the Government of India world-embracing; the Sandeman system—lavish expenditure and enlistment of levies with the birch in the background—had tamed Baluches, the same treatment was bound to succeed with Pathans, human nature being everywhere amenable to the same influences. The Punjab Government rejoined, that whatever the results of the Sandeman system for mild-mannered, chief-obeying, religionless Baluches, Pathans were different—being truculent, fanatical, grasping Ishmaelites, who would take everything and give nothing, and that already, owing to the outpouring of treasure upon them, the province was suffering, public works being starved and the land revenue being enhanced, to the injury of agricultural interests. The protest availed nothing; imperial projects were still growing, and were not to be denied; the further impoverishment of the peasantry of the Punjab—for that matter, of all India—was of minor importance compared with the establishment of the British protectorate, with administrative control as its aftermath, over all the tribes right up to the limits of Afghanistan proper, the affairs of which kingdom, belonging as they did to the domain of "high politics," were outside the horizon of a provincial government.

CHAPTER XX.

THE FRONTIER UNDER VICEREGAL MANAGEMENT.

LORD LANSDOWNE was Viceroy at the time (1888-1894). A Conservative in politics, high-minded, courageous, and a thorough gentleman, he had been sent out to promote the imperial mission of England beyond India, vaguely known as the "forward policy." Its chief objects appeared to be the education towards citizenship in the Empire of the tribes outside the north-west frontier of India northwards up to the confines of the Pamirs and Tibet and westwards to the lines of Lord Lytton's fanciful "scientific frontier," and further, the conversion of the Amir of Afghanistan, always suspicious of our good faith, into our exclusive ally and dependent, in which position we should be enabled to use him and his people as bulwark and buffer against Russia in her progress towards India. The new Viceroy did all that was possible within his limitations, but, until nearly the end of his term of office, failed—failed egregiously, as Punjab men had foreseen: the tribes had taken his money but still hated the donor, latterly the Amir had taken nothing—not even his subsidy of twelve lakhs—but was sulking in dignified dudgeon in Kabul. We had encroached upon his territory by occupying New Chaman,—now the Candahar terminus of our Baluchistan railway,—had bribed clans hitherto sometimes politically dependent on him to accept our exclusive protection, had pushed our tentacles into independent tribal territory all up and down the borderland, and finally had sought to belittle him, the God-guided ruler of Afghanistan, in the eyes of all his subjects by pressing on his acceptance a mission headed by Lord Roberts, his betrayed father's destroyer, and escorted by a brigade of Highlanders to boot!

The position seemed hopeless, and Lord Lansdowne's policy of pin-pricks a failure, when, hey! presto! at the eleventh hour the whole situation was changed and cleared by a word from a Mr Pyne, an English employee in the Amir's arms-factory at Kabul; a military mission was intolerable, but if an unescorted civilian were substituted his Highness's prestige would be enhanced, and, what was of equal consequence,—and here the little man, a Court favourite because of his capacity and frank jovial manners, waxed confidential,—his Highness might make money out of it and increase his armaments as well. The suggestion being acted upon, the "Durand agreement" was its result; and a happy issue out of immediate difficulties it proved for all concerned; for Lord Lansdowne, Durand, and that astute employee it brought honours and rewards, and for the Amir £60,000 a-year as additional consideration money, and the right to import through India munitions and military stores to his heart's desire.

So Lord Lansdowne, successful statesman now instead of discredited politician, departed from India amidst coruscations of congratulations, and Lord

Elgin, earnest, plodding, conscientious, but a Liberal and wholly inexperienced in affairs, was installed at Calcutta in his stead. Durand (now Sir Mortimer Durand, K.C.S.I., and ambassador designate to Persia) had already gone, and in his place was a new foreign secretary, who had spent most of his official life on a stool in the Indian Foreign Office and had never been west of Lahore. Now external affairs in India are practically in the hands of the Viceroy and his foreign secretary, hence upon those two men fell the responsibility of giving effect to the "Durand agreement." Had not Mr Gladstone been a very old man, and his waning powers concentrated on his Irish Home-Rule project, action upon the agreement might have been deferred for some years; but soon after Lord Elgin's arrival in India Lord Rosebery became Prime Minister, and in foreign politics he was an imperialist. Being called upon to give practical effect to the agreement by delimiting the hinterlands of the independent tribes according to the Durand maps now within our protectorate, Lord Elgin elected to begin with the Mahsûds, they being weak, divided, scattered, and badly armed, and Mr Bruce, the Derajat Commissioner, anticipating no serious opposition. After palavers and payments that officer gained the verbal assent of the less lawless half of the tribe, and was still negotiating and reporting when on October 25, 1894, his camp was rushed, 103 men, sepoys and followers, 7 British officers, and many transport animals being killed and wounded, and considerable loot, including 36 Martini rifles and 15 horses, carried off. A retaliatory expedition of 10,000 troops was at once despatched, Mahsudland overrun in every direction, everything destructible destroyed, and the tribe reduced to abject submissiveness for a time. The boundary was then demarcated, but whether the cairns were allowed to stand or at once demolished no Englishman or Indian knows to this day.

Having paid dearly for his little experience, Lord Elgin was inclined to stay his hand, at least until a more convenient season; famine was widespread, the treasury was empty, and the tribes about Peshawar buzzing like irritated hornets over the rumours then prevalent that the Sarkar was going to annex their countries. The Viceroy's advisers were still divided; the Punjab Government and two of his Excellency's councillors were opposed to further interference with the tribes, the three others were advocates of vigorous action. Unhappily for the perplexed head of the Government of India, his party had now disrupted, and the Conservatives were again in power supported by the Liberal-Unionists. Lord Elgin had now either to resign or to be prepared to carry out measures distasteful to his principles. He chose the latter alternative, and, though dimly cognisant of the risks, decided to carry out the demarcations to the bitter end. His view was that, as Viceroy, he was a servant and had to obey the "mandate" of the Ministry of the day; when accepting his high office he had, as he afterwards plaintively explained, "inherited" certain "obligations," one of which was the execution of the previously concluded "Durand agreement." Whatever the consequences, imperial consistency seemed to require that they should be faced; if the pillars could only be put up, a *succès d'estime* would be obtained, and once up it mattered little what became of them. He had succeeded with the Mahsuds, after considerable loss and expenditure no doubt, but they were a graceless tribe, and had been a thorn in our flesh ever since our first contact with them. North of Mahsudland was Dawar and the upper reaches of the Tochi River, a valley raided on by both Mahsud and Darwesh Waziris, and that valley might some day be useful as a new route into Afghanistan.

Led on by the local political officers, Lord Elgin and his advisers now discovered that the inhabitants along either bank of the Tochi were longing to make a voluntary cession of their country to the British Government, and recorded that "it is desirable to extend military protection to the Tochi tribes." The grounds for this extraordinary conclusion were contained in a statement which the Commissioner of the Derajat had obtained from 394 "responsible men" of the valley, "expressing their willingness to remain (?) under the British Government," provided that liberal personal allowances were made to them. The prayer—a form of application as easily procured by British as by Russian officers in Central Asia—was at once granted, and the country was occupied. The sequel will presently be seen.

Meanwhile, the sequence of events takes us farther north, for there our successive encroachments—the establishment of sepoy garrisons in Chitral, Chakdara, and Malakand, the annual march of the Chitral relief force through Swat and Bajour, and the despatch of a mission to Kunar with a view to arrange the partition of the Mohmands with the Amir—were filling the minds of the ring of tribes surrounding the Peshawar valley with a common desire to free themselves from the coils of the great Kafir python who was now strangling them. Knowing that to touch them might be to put our hands into the mouths of tigers, Lord Elgin had postponed the northern demarcations until settlements had been effected with the Mahsuds, Tochiwâls, and Darwesh Waziris. He had full knowledge that the tribes about Peshawar and Kohat, particularly Orakzais, Afridis, and Mohmands, were numerous and well armed,—at least for hillmen,—and that, unless heavily bribed and tactfully manipulated, they might deny us the barren satisfaction of putting up our pillars. The Orakzais had in 1891 received real punishment from us, and we had since built and garrisoned a chain of forts and posts along the crest of the Samāna mountain, whence we dominated their chief valley; the Afridis had been our friends for more than fifty years, their young men serving in our armies,—1600 of them in Oude during the Mutiny,—their old men drawing pensions from the Peshawar treasury, and well-paid representatives from all their sections guarding the Khyber Pass on our mutual account. With both of them arrangements for delimitation work might be possible; but, as Nature had erected her own pillars in the wall of snow mountains known as the Sufaid Koh, demarcation by British officers might perhaps not be necessary.

With the Mohmands the case was hopeless from the first. Some of their lowland clans held lands and jagirs inside British territory, and had been fickly friendly with us since annexation; but of their upper sections we knew little, the very geography of their country was problematical. True, in our agreement with the Amir we had boldly divided them, the common line between the Kabul and Indian Governments being the supposed watershed between the Panjkora and Kunar rivers, and rather than cause a hitch in the negotiations our envoy's reply to a pointed question from his Highness, who claimed the whole tribe as his subjects, had been evasive. After studying the map put before him the Amir had asked, "Then do I understand that I have the whole of the upper Mohmands?" and the perplexed head of the mission had replied, "The map is on too small a scale to show your Highness the exact line of demarcation." After that the agreement was signed by the contracting parties; but, oddly enough, the Amir did not affix his signature to the map illustrating the line of boundary. When, afterwards, he discovered that we had pushed our boundary—on paper at least—well into his Naboth's vineyard, and had annexed half the Mohmands, he thought himself tricked, but for his bribe's sake took no overt action. His diplomacy knew other methods, and, soon after, we found that although the Mohmands readily took our money, they would not have our boundary: for centuries they had lived a united tribe, except when quarrelling amongst themselves, which was always, hence vivisection was intolerable to them. The *impasse* was protracted.

About the same time still farther north a fire-eating agent of ours, Dr (now Sir George) Robertson, disregarding his vaguely worded instructions, was trailing his coat in Chitral, thus flaunting our flag almost in rear of the Kunar valley. This last aggression added Bajouris, Swatis, and, later, distant Bonerwâls to the list of tribes, all Pathans and blood-brothers, up and down the borderland, who only required leaders to rise and strike a blow to preserve their threatened independence. Now it so happened that, a little previously, the Amir, very inopportunely for us, had published a treatise on holy war (*ghaza*) against infidels, and after discussing the subject—academically, no doubt—with a great convocation of Mullahs drawn from all parts of his kingdom and the Anglo-Afghan borderland as well, had dismissed them to their homes with gracious words and substantial presents. At the time the restiveness of the tribes, caused by our machinations to partition the Mohmands and obtain the control of Chitral, thus opening the Amir's backdoor to Kunar and Jalalabad, was beginning to attract the closer attention of Lord Elgin. The Amir was addressed in regard to his attitude, and at once gave such satisfactory assurance that we sent a boundary mission, under his safe-conduct, to Kunar, with instructions to make concessions, if necessary, and arrange some sort of a settlement of the Mohmand question, which would give us "peace with honour." Whilst our Commissioner and his escort were under surveillance in Lower Kunar, nominally the Amir's honoured guests, but really his closely guarded suspects, an unscrupulous adventurer named Umra Khan, once our *protégé*, but now no longer trusted by us, was in Upper Kunar intriguing all round for his own hand. Some short time previously, in one of the palace revolutions frequent in Chitral, the ruler of the hour, one Sher Afzal, a snuffy elderly little gentleman, addicted to sleep, cards, and prayers, had been forced to flee, and had been granted an asylum in Kabul by the Amir, who, having formerly ear-marked Chitral for himself, detained the refugee until he should be wanted. When, then, the Amir discovered that we had forestalled him in Chitral,—action within our rights, according to the Durand agreement,—Sher Afzal incontinently escaped from his easy restraint, and passing our helpless Commissioner's camp, presented himself, bags of rupees in hand, as a suppliant before Umra Khan. That upstart was easily persuaded to play king-maker and reseat his petitioner on the throne of his ancestors.

After that the interest of the situation was shifted from the Mohmands and our mission in Lower Kunar to Chitral, some sixty miles up-stream. Whilst Umra Khan with his *protégé* advanced from the south, Dr Robertson, our political agent at Gilgit, advanced from the north-east with a strong escort. Umra Khan seized the Drosh fort in Lower Chitral and proclaimed Sher Afzal the Mehtar or king, Robertson countered by throwing himself into the Chitral fort and proclaiming a child, a cadet of the ruling family, as Mehtar. After that the two king-makers defied each other. The imbroglio was exciting enough for the two bold adventurers who had brought it about, but undignified and compromising for the Government of a great empire. The situation was now critical and curious. The Amir was popularly supposed to be backing Umra Khan—covertly, Lord Elgin to be backing Robertson,—also covertly; but, in reality, his Excellency knew little about that officer's proceedings, for communications between Chitral and Calcutta were slow and liable to long interruptions, and in those days of imperial spread-eagleism the horses drawing the Government coach, having no capable driver on the box-seat, had their heads, and ran the lumbering vehicle as they pleased. Naturally, then, Robertson, high-couraged and precipitate, took the bit between his teeth, and challenged his rival to mortal combat. The gage was picked up with alacrity; the forces of either side advanced, met, and ours, few in number and overmatched, were badly beaten and driven helter-skelter back into the Chitral fort with the loss of 70 men, a third of the number engaged—a result due to the possession by Umra Khan of 200 breech-loaders, most of them said to have been given him by Lord Lansdowne in 1892-93 during the period of tension with the Amir, and to the presence amongst the invaders of numbers of Afghan soldiers, absent with or without leave from the Amir's camp in Lower Kunar. After his victory Umra Khan sat down before the fort and closely invested it. He had a clear month wherein to take it by assault or starve its somewhat demoralised garrison into surrender. Inside, we had over 400 sepoys, of whom only one-fourth were Sikh regulars; but with that stiffening, coupled with a dozen resourceful Sahibs and native officers, the little garrison could be trusted, so long as food and ammunition lasted, to hold their own behind loopholed defences against ten times their number of besiegers.

For some weeks India was without certain news from Chitral; the gravity of the situation was at once realised, for the fall of the fort would have convinced the tribes south of the Pamirs that in Umra Khan they had found the Allah-granted deliverer of their prayers, who would free them from the encroachments of the infidel Feringhees; and in that event the Amir of Afghanistan would have been constrained to side with his co-religionists and lead in the holy war, or—suspected, despised, and rejected by his people—take refuge with one or other of the enemies of Islam at his gates. As soon as Robertson's position was known in Calcutta all India was in commotion.

A business-like Government, before plunging into a policy of adventure amidst independent Moslem communities all up and down a long frontier, and in the case of Chitral 150 miles beyond it, would have counted the cost and prepared plans to meet the probable consequences of its rashness. But Lord Elgin and those in his confidence had thought out nothing; having informed the Secretary of State for India of the risks of simultaneous forward moves along the whole north-west frontage of India, they appear to have washed their hands of the consequences, and to have considered that their duty and responsibilities began and ended in blindly executing the supposed "mandate" to carry out the "Durand agreement." The object-lesson given by the Mahsuds at Wana, when the Derajat Commissioner's camp was rushed, had been disregarded, and the Upper Tochi valley had afterwards been imprudently occupied. The Government had next courted disaster at the other end of its frontier, 400 miles north of Mahsudland, and 150 beyond the limits of roads and telegraphs, and, when the inevitable catastrophe had occurred, neither troops nor transport were available to meet the crisis.

On hearing the news Sir William Lockhart, the general who had just reduced the Mahsuds to temporary good conduct, offered to transfer the major part of his seasoned and well-equipped little army of 10,000 men, most of them Punjabi Indians, to Hoti Mardan, force a passage through Swat and Bajour, and relieve Robertson within twenty days;

but his offer was rejected—it involved risks, and in the interests of the army at large, the employment of corps and commanders, who had not yet seen active service on the frontier, was advisable.

During the next three weeks troops, war material, supplies, and upwards of 30,000 transport animals with 10,000 drivers were conveyed from all parts of India to Peshawar. By the end of the first week of April 1895 the expeditionary force, 15,000 strong, with its long trains of followers and animals, had entered Swat, and when they had forced their way to the hither side of the Lowarai Pass—the Indian portal into Chitral—they heard (April 25) that the relief of Chitral had just been effected by Colonel Kelly, commanding the Gilgit district, with 400 Mazbi Sikhs of the 32nd Pioneers, 200 Kashmir Rifles and Sappers, and some Hunza-Nagar levies, supplemented by two 7-pounders.

Even discounting the effect on the *morale* of Umra Khan's men of the approach of the army from the south, the fact that Kelly with 650 Indians, most of them sweeper-caste Sikhs, compelled the raising of the siege, will always live in history as a great achievement. Had he and his handful been lost—a not unlikely contingency, for to win they had to overcome hostile gatherings, snow, cold, and want of supplies and transport—their leader would have been called a foolhardy lunatic. He took the risk, and succeeding, thanks largely to Captain Borradaile's determination and resource in pushing over the snow-bound wind-swept Shandur Pass, was a hero. In the case of the southern army there was neither risk nor undue haste, but a well-ordered advance in overwhelming force after elaborate preparations. However, the luck was with the daring 600 from the north, and they deserved it.

The besiegers dispersed, Umra Khan a refugee, living at first in Kabul on the Amir's bounty, the Amir himself ostensibly our friend, Chitral garrisoned by Indian troops, a road from British territory thereto under construction, Malakand, the key to Swat, in our hands and held in force, the Panjkora bridged at Chakdara, the fighting ardour of the Swatis and Bajouris quenched, a watchful truce ensued for a time between Christians and Moslems. The tribes had shown their teeth, we our strength; but its collection and manifestation had cost India half a million sterling, so the Government, prudent after the event, decided to postpone further attempts at delimitations, and consolidate, if possible, our precarious hold on Chitral. The remaining seven months of 1895 and the whole of 1896 passed without incident, except that what was to prove the largest and most widespread famine of our Indian record had begun. When, then, in the spring of the following year,—1897, that of our late Queen's diamond jubilee,—the garrison left in Chitral had been relieved and not a hostile shot fired, there was reason to expect that the passions roused by Robertson's daring escapade had subsided. Had not the peace of the border been undisturbed for more than a year, and the exasperating demarcation policy definitely abandoned? Under those circumstances the softening influences of subsidies and trading facilities would soon harmonise all discords. So thinking, Lord Elgin and his advisers were concentrating their energies to fight the enemy within the gate—famine—when outside it, far away in the

Derajat, Nemesis asserted herself in an unexpected form and quarter.

Down south conditions were supposed to be eminently satisfactory: Baluchistan was ours; the Kurram valley was occupied, its population peaceful and friendly; the Mahsuds had been beaten and bribed into submission; Wana, a supposed strategic centre in Mahsudland, had been annexed and garrisoned; there only remained the completion of the protective work lately begun in the Tochi valley, which, as already explained, we had taken over at the prayer of its inhabitants to save them from Mahsuds and Darwesh Waziris. There, at least, our presence was welcomed; there we might safely consolidate our influence right up to the delimited boundary. In that belief, throughout the spring of 1897, careless of the drama being played at Chitral, our self-confident politicals explored routes, made surveys and roads, and bought the lip-service of the scattered tribesmen of the Upper Tochi. On June 10 the local political, combining pleasure with business, arranged for a picnic at Maizar, a village about four miles beyond Dattakhel, our most advanced military post. The inhabitants appeared friendly, presenting goats and other offerings, and even inviting our officers to take lunch on their village-green, right under the many-towered walls of their *kots* or fortified hamlets. Luncheon over, the Sahibs, completely off guard, were taking their ease under trees, while at a little distance their escort were also enjoying a smoke and siesta, when suddenly two signal-guns were fired; away scuttled the "friendly" villagers like frightened rabbits, out popped a hundred heads from the overlooking walls, forth protruded the barrels of a hundred matchlocks, and in a twinkling the village-green was a shambles. The few survivors, shot at by the men, and even stoned by the women and children of the *kots*, withdrew upon their surprised sepoys, and whilst the war-drums were beating and the tribesmen gathering to join in the extermination of the infidels, made hasty dispositions for retreat. For the four miles to Dattakhel the little force fought its way over broken ground, overlapped at respectful distances by ever-increasing mobs of wild men yelling and firing, all individually brave, but incapable of a united rush. At last safety was reached. That picnic cost us 72 casualties, including six out of seven British officers, caused the Government to march into the valley in mid-June an expeditionary force of 7000 soldiers accompanied by 10,000 transport animals and 3000 followers. Arrived near Maizar, they lay and rotted there until the setting in of the cold weather without seeing a hostile tribesman; for the Maddakhels—the leaders in the treachery—slipped across their recently delimited frontier and waited on its Afghan side in security until we should tire of the whole business. After five months of inaction, during which period a fifth of the force died or were sent back from fever and bowel-complaints, we withdrew to Lower Dawar. Whilst stagnating on the Tochi the sickness and mortality in the only two British battalions with the expeditionary force —the 2nd Argyll Highlanders and the 3rd Rifle Brigade—was fourteen times greater than amongst the Indian troops. The Argylls, country lads of good stamina, recovered when the cold weather set in; the Rifles, mostly Londoners, had no powers of recuperation—in fact, as a fighting unit the battalion, after burying a tenth of its strength and invaliding a third, ceased to exist in October, and the remnant was sent back to India completely broken down. It entered the field 799 strong, and within six months lost about half its strength from disease.

The Maizar massacre, to avenge which British troops had been unwisely marched from Peshawar and Rawalpindi to Bannu, thus publishing our disaster, weakening the local garrisons, and needlessly exposing our men to mid-June heat and fatigue, was the spark which ignited into a blaze the long-smouldering fires of Pathan hostility all up the frontier. The Mullahs in every tribe seized their opportunity and preached a holy war: this time, they announced, Allah was with the faithful and against the infidels and their big battalions: this time, to worse confound their knavish tricks and exhaust their resources, He had sent famine and plague upon India, and had turned the wisdom of the Sahibs into folly, for who but fools would lock up an army in a distant desert of disease, death, and desolation like the Tochi country? Now, then, was the time to strike for freedom; for the next four moons or more, whilst the heat was great, the white soldiers would be sick and barrack-tied.

A month passed: the manhood of each tribe was in consultation: Afridis and Orakzais knew the measure of their Mullahs, and, without aid from Kabul, would not fire a bullet: deputations were sent to the Amir; the Oracle was hospitable but non-committal: he was certain that the shells were charged, and that some would burst without his lighting the fuse; he foresaw, too, that the Sahibs, when they had burnt their fingers a little more, would apply cold-water dressing and avoid explosives for a time; he wished them well,—after a further lesson,—at their worst they were safer neighbours than the Russians—Allah's blight on both!

CHAPTER XXI.

NEMESIS, 1897.

Presently, as the Amir had anticipated, a shell too confidently handled did explode. Swat had been quiescent since the experiences of 1895, and might have remained so had not the political officer at Malakand, mindful of his *raison d'être*, the cultivation of "friendly relations" with the tribes of his agency,—in other words, the rendering of our self-imposed protectorate effectual,—thought fit to invite the Upper Swatis to a conference: village opinion was divided; the Sahib would at least be hospitable, would also distribute turbans and rupees, after which they would return home and discuss his proposals; some refused, fearing treachery or the bestowal of favours upon hated rivals to their own exclusion; the Mullahs—and Swat swarmed with them—became alarmed, for to them English influence meant priestly nothingness, so with one voice they advised their flocks to have no dallyings with the crafty Sahib. In spite of admonitions, counsels remained divided, traders and men of property generally favouring a closer connection with the English, the ignorant masses agreeing with their spiritual guides. Whilst Swat was still undecided, the inevitable "mad

Mullah" appeared, ranting and promising. To the simple his fervour was inspiration, his promises—immunity from bullet-wounds and aid from heaven—the word of Allah himself. By a common impulse the labouring manhood, including boys, of every village, poured out into the routes to Chakdara and Malakand, and gathering strength as they advanced, without organisation, many without arms, hurled themselves, with the reckless courage of *ghāzis*, upon our defences. Throughout the first night (July 26, 1897) the fighting was desperate, for we had been taken by surprise; at dawn succour came from below,—the Guides, first always,—and then gradually the attacks became less fierce, less frequent, until the assailants, left in the lurch by the Mullah and his hosts of fighting angels—who never appeared after all—dispersed to their homes, disappearing as rapidly as they had collected. Once more Swat was quiet, waiting for the further punishment which we proceeded to inflict in leisurely fashion. Swati action had been premature. Had it been possible for all the tribes, whose distrust of us had been materialised by our small aggressions and delimitations, to have risen simultaneously, the Afghans, with or without their Amir, would probably have been added to the list of our enemies. Happily for us, the tribes rose successively in local groupings, each forming a detached self-contained aggregate of little democracies, only connected with its neighbours by a common religion;—combined synchronous action was hardly possible for them.

Swat troubles over, the Mohmands suddenly poured down into the Peshawar valley, sacked and burned a small town therein, captured a weakly held outpost, and next morning (August 8) were driven back into the hills by troops hurriedly sent out from the Peshawar cantonment. Amongst their slain were soldiers in the Amir's uniform. The damage done by the raiders, some 2500 in number, was small, the insult great—they had pulled the great Sarkar's beard within sight of all Peshawar. Our prestige demanded their immediate punishment. They expected it, the Khyber tribes were sure of it, for delays were dangerous, and in and about Peshawar we had 15,000 troops. But we made no sign of movement. What we did was to fill the outposts with soldiers, and let them show their uniforms on the hither side of the passes,—and red rags to bulls that foolish coat-trailing was. Not only did we pack the outposts with regulars, but in a little time the cantonments of Peshawar, Naushera, and Hoti Mardan were also crowded with them, but still there was no movement on our side.

Amazed at our inaction, Afridis and Orakzais began to exchange views: if the Sarkar did not punish a second-class tribe like the Mohmands why should others hold back? As good Musalmans, and the premier fighting clans of the borderlands, duty and honour bound them to start a row of their own; besides the general delimitation grievance, they had their own special causes of complaint—our occupation of the Samana ridge, our recent quadrupling of the tax on "black" salt, the asylum given by us to faithless wives; by showing their teeth they might get a few knocks,—in time,—but eventually they would be gainers from larger subsidies, better service-terms, and increased respect from Sarkar and hill neighbours as well; at bottom the Sarkar and they were friends, necessary to each other, still the Feringhees were Christian dogs, not Moslems: a little blood-letting would remove causes of irritation on both sides; their chief difficulty would be with the Khyber Rifles, their own flesh and blood, who might be true to their salt and fight; if so, Allah's will be done.

Whilst the fermentation was rising in the hills overlooking Peshawar, down in the valley the chief local authorities, the Commissioner and the Brigadier,—no plan of action having been pre-arranged,—were sitting in their darkened office-rooms in constant communication with each other, with those whom duty kept in the Khyber or at one of the outposts, and with their respective official superiors recessing in the Himalayas, the Lieutenant-General commanding the Punjab army corps at Murree, and the heads of the imperial hierarchy at Simla, the Viceroy in Council, the Commander-in-Chief, and the Lieutenant-Governor of the Punjab. From the pass, from Landi Khana, our fortified serai at its farther end, where were the headquarters of the Khyber Rifles under the command of Captain Barton,—a battalion of Afridis "very similar in organisation to a regiment of the native army,"—and from Ali Masjid, the historic fort just inside the pass, every message urged the necessity of supporting our garrison with regulars, because, unless reinforced, a rising was certain; and if the clans rose, the Rifles would either be overwhelmed or, losing confidence in us, would be forced to join their countrymen. The Commissioner of Peshawar recommended that if possible Ali Masjid at least, if not Landi Kotal as well, should be held by troops; but the Brigadier—influenced perhaps by his preparations for the already sanctioned Mohmand expedition—met the suggestion by a *non possumus*, insufficiency of troops, of transport, and of water, also the awful heat in the pass. The Commissioner acquiesced in the force of these objections, and even pointed out to his Government that by the letter of their agreement of 1881 the Afridis, not the British, were responsible for the safety of the pass. Meanwhile precious time was being wasted; the five authorities, or six, if the Viceroy's Executive Council be included, amongst whom the decision lay, discussed points by wire, letter, and minute, noting, questioning, surmising, arguing, suggesting, doing everything, in short, but acting—each shirking responsibility, and waiting on one of the others to take the bit in his teeth and say the pass must be held, otherwise, if we vacillated longer, we should not only lose it but our honour as well.

In a multitude of counsellors there may be wisdom, but there is certainly weakness, and the wisdom, as a rule, shows itself too late. In the twelve precious days following the pulling of our beards by the Mohmands, the local, provincial, and imperial circumlocution-offices were in painful labour, but, alas! produced nothing, not one MAN. To the Commissioner of Peshawar—who to the last was an optimist, holding that the reports of intended risings were "exaggerated," and even up to the eve of the catastrophe sending the Government "reassuring news"—the position of Captain Barton at Landi Kotal was now causing anxiety. That officer, whether supported or not, intended to stick to his men—his duty was with them, and he trusted them though others did not. In the dilemma the Commissioner called

Barton down to Peshawar and detained him there. That was on August 20, the date on which the Secretary of State for India afterwards complained that the Viceroy had wired him "reassuring news."

The end was now at hand, *dies iræ* were upon us, days of pain and humiliation for every Englishman in India, such as never before had been experienced by the race which had achieved empire by taking risks and daring fortune. The race was the same, self-reliant, audacious, determined; but its men in authority were degenerates, desk-tied, vacillating, fearful, shirkers of responsibility, scribblers and talkers, not doers. Does any one suppose that in August 1897, had Peshawar, Murree, or Simla possessed a Lawrence, Edwardes, Nicholson, or Roberts, the events of that shameful week, with its costly consequences to Indian taxpayers and English prestige, could have occurred? No; Barton would not have been abandoned, and the Khyber Rifles, deprived of their British commandant, would not have been sacrificed.

What happened is soon told. On August 22 the Afridis collected, swarmed about the forts and posts in the pass, attacked, captured, and burnt Fort Maude and Ali Masjid—the former within sight of our patrols from Jamrud—and then invested Landi Khana. It fell on the 25th, being taken by assault after twenty-four hours' continuous fighting, in which the tribesmen were reported to have lost between 200 and 300 men. The defence, without being desperate, was creditable: amongst our casualties were Barton's munshis and servants, some of whom were killed, some circumcised: of the Khyber Rifles the majority made good their escape with their arms; 134 of them reached Jamrud in a body, and as they entered jeered and taunted our men as cowards—a reasonable enough conclusion, seeing that the Brigadier had five days previously sent out there a force of 2000 men, including two batteries and a regiment of British cavalry. To fight? No; in the foolish hope that "their presence might act as a demonstration to overawe the tribesmen"!

On the same day that witnessed our disgrace in the Khyber, the Orakzais gathered and attacked our posts on the Samana range. We cleared the ridge, reinforced our garrisons, and retired, closely followed by the enemy. Within a fortnight, the Afridi successes in the Khyber having been noised abroad had quickened Islam and compelled all good Musalmans of the hills to join the popular cause. In conjunction with bands of Afridis, the Orakzais now surrounded and attacked forts Gulistan and Saraghari on the Samana, both held by detachments of the 36th Sikhs. The former was successfully defended; the latter, being small and structurally defective, was taken, its defenders killed to the last man, and their cooks seized, trussed, and roasted alive by the exultant victors.

Such in outline were the events of August 20-26, 1897, in the Khyber, and August 25 to September 12 on the Samana, events disgraceful to us, but creditable to the Khyber Rifles and glorious to the gallant 36th Sikhs.

The contrast between British imbecility and Afridi devotion is better brought out in Sir Thomas Holdich's description of the conduct of the Khyber Rifles at Landi Kotal. He writes in his 'Indian Borderland': "The outbreak commenced by a fierce attack on the serai and fort at Landi Kotal. There was the spectacle witnessed of Afridi fighting Afridi. . . . It would not be fair to say that the mere weight of the rupee kept the Khaibar Rifles steady to their engagements. There is a quaint sense of honour amongst Pathans of all degrees which acts more or less strongly in keeping a man true to his salt. The Khaibar Rifles did all that could be expected of them. They fought splendidly . . . till they could fight no longer; and then they effected a retreat in good order to Peshawar. But, alas! whilst the Afridi fought for us we failed to fight for ourselves; 9500 troops about the Peshawar frontier looked on while 500 Afridis maintained British honour in the Khaibar. Over that little episode of the withdrawal of the British officer who should have headed the Khaibar defence, and the abandonment of the pass to its fate, it is best to draw a veil. There *can* be no excuse for it."

It only remains to add that on receiving news of the catastrophe the Government of India, in the agony of their shame, ordered the pass to be retaken; but it was then too late: what the Jamrud garrison could have prevented up to August 22 two divisions could hardly repair after the 25th.

CHAPTER XXII.

THE WAR AGAINST THE AFRIDIS.

WAR on a large scale against Orakzais and Afridis was now unavoidable. The country of the former had already been thoroughly explored by our troops in 1891, but Tirah or Maidan, the hub and heart of Afridiland, with its approaches, was a *terra incognita.* We knew that it was very difficult, had never been penetrated by an invader, and that the Afridis had more breechloaders, were better marksmen,—hundreds having served in our army,—and would make a more determined resistance than any foe yet encountered, the Afghans not excepted, in the annals of our trans-frontier wars. Whilst collecting troops, transport, and stores for the Tirah campaign, we hurriedly settled accounts with the Mohmands and their supporters—with the former easily, as they had few breechloaders and our terms were little more than nominal; with the latter, the Mahmunds in particular, only after severe fighting, in which we lost heavily. The Mohmand expedition was a mere *levée de rideau:* on the return of the troops it rose again for the real drama. Had the enemy been Russia herself, and not some 7000 or 8000 hillmen, of whom perhaps one in seven had a breechloader and twenty rounds of ammunition, our preparations could not have been more elaborate or extensive.

For the third time since 1894—the other occasions being Chitral in 1895 and Swat three months previously—the civil executive of the Punjab was converted into a vast organism for the impressment of transport to meet the military requirements of the hour. By law impressment had always been criminal; yet for all purposes great or small, from a military expedition to the annual reliefs or the cold-weather tour of a commissioner, it had been the only means by which the official requirements of peace or war could be satisfied. For peace movements inside India the people bore commandeering without a murmur; forced labour had always been exacted from them, only professional carriers were taken, and for short distances and periods, and the hire was liberal. But impressment on a large scale for war purposes outside India was unknown before our Kabul wars, as external campaigns had not been previously undertaken. In 1838-42 the people had been ignorant of better things and were submissive as slaves; in 1878-80 they had some knowledge of their rights, and, since then, repeated lessons and the omnipotence of law and lawyers had taught many of them sophistication. In 1878, during the first phase of the campaign in Afghanistan, the Punjabis had lost, from starvation, cold, and general neglect, 80,000 camels and other animals, and unascertained numbers of drivers. The sufferings then endured had so impressed owners with the risks and horrors of service trans-Indus that, without compulsion, transport of any kind had never since been procurable. As a consequence, whenever an expedition took place, the Punjab Government—inducements to voluntarism having failed—had been constrained to seize wholesale not only baggage-animals but their owners as well, and as the work was a penal offence it had never been regulated; hence it was done haphazard without discrimination or organisation. So long as camels and their owners were only requisitioned, the routine of village life was undisturbed; but when, as for Chitral and Swat, fully equipped carts, ponies, mules, pack-bullocks, and even donkeys were swept up from all parts of the province, driven to distant depots, weeded there, and the fit residue taken for service, the patience of the many-burdened peasantry was sorely tried; for every family was a sufferer, arrangements for marketings and the distribution of food being dislocated. Thus, besides the hardship for individual owners, the whole rural economy of the province was thrown out of gear, and the Government, compelled to break its own laws, had to stoop to the official subterfuge of concealing its wrongdoings by softening the terms "seizure" and "impressment" into "hiring" or "assistance rendered by civil officers to the Commissariat-Transport Department." To meet the military demands in the emergencies of 1897 the civil power collected roundly 160,000 animals and carts and 40,000 attendants; but eventually less than one-fourth of these numbers were pronounced fit and sent to the front.

The pressgang operations carried on in the villages, supplemented by rumours of what was commonly reported as the invasion of Peshawar by the Mohmands, and a fortnight later the fall of our forts in the Khyber and the long inaction which followed, brought home to the whole Punjab that their Christian masters were confronted with a serious war against the still independent Moslem tribes trans - Indus. Of the tribes themselves, their names, constitutions, and absolute and relative strength, the masses knew nothing, the well-informed little. For two months they daily saw trains filled with troops, animals, followers, war-material, and supplies steaming northwards through their drought - afflicted land, clear evidence of the magnitude of the struggle before the *sahib logue*. The Hindus, including Sikhs, were rather pleased than otherwise that their Sarkar was about to wage a great anti-Moslem campaign; but our seven millions of Musalman fellow-subjects west of Lahore, slower in intelligence, indebted and depressed, believing that Hindu exaltation and Moslem degradation were due to our Kafir preference for idolaters, usurers, and land-grabbers, viewed our troubles differently. They had no love for Pathans as such, swaggering, bullying savages that they were. But the Pathans were of their faith, and all Musalmans were brothers; and as, throughout the world, Islam was sinking under Christian domination, their sympathies went out to Swatis, Mohmands, and Afridis in their struggle to free themselves from our infidel yoke. To a large part of our Punjabi Muhammadans, then, the news of the abandonment of the Khyber was only less pleasing than would have been that of our expulsion from Peshawar. That the disturbances gave satisfaction, even vague hope, to masses of the peasantry in the Western Punjab was evidenced by their bearing throughout the worst period of tension in August and September. During those weeks they threw off much of their characteristic apathy, moved alertly, talked loudly, prayed less negligently, less irregularly, discussed politics less incuriously, and entertained less grudgingly those propagators of lies and treason, wandering fakirs and holy men—all practices at variance with the habit of sullen indifference to mundane vicissitudes observable in our depressed village-communities trans-Ravi.

When the preparations for the campaign had been completed, Sir William Lockhart—the only general since annexation who had administered real castigation to Mahsuds and Orakzais—arrived at Kohat from England, and took over the command of the expeditionary forces, 60,000 fighting men with their complement of transport and followers, the fittest, largest, and best-equipped army ever put into the field in India. The plan of campaign was simple: two divisions, supplemented by a third to hold the line of communications, and supported by a strong force in the Barah valley near Peshawar, were to advance from Kohat *viâ* our positions on the Samana ridge by the shortest route through Orakzai direct upon Maidān or Tirah proper, the summer headquarters of the Afridis right under the snows of the Safaid Koh. Established there, strong columns were to be sent out to search the various glens radiating from our central camp, destroying stores, blowing up towers, burning hamlets, and generally devastating the country: finally, the army was to emerge upon Peshawar in two columns down the Barah and Waran valleys.

Lockhart reached the Samana ridge on October 12, but he was not the Lockhart who, by the rapidity and unexpectedness of his movements, and the thoroughness of his punishments, had in a week or two reduced Orakzais in 1891 and Mahsuds in 1895 to abject submissiveness. The sound judgment and determined will were there, but not the physical and mental activity, without which the greatest measure of success possible, under the conditions of the campaign, could alone be attained. That a much-encumbered, heavily shod army of plainsmen fighting a guerilla war against well-armed, nimble-footed cragsmen amidst their own mountains, never before traversed by an outsider, should have many casualties whilst forcing a passage through their country was a foregone conclusion; but, that the war should begin with a check to our arms and end with a small disaster, were unanticipated mishaps which should not have occurred.

The first serious fighting took place on October 18, when the heights of Dargai were captured, and the tribesmen, moving rapidly towards the sounds of firing, were heavily beaten. That day we had 57 casualties, but towards evening we retired, thus throwing away all the advantage gained and disclosing our intentions to the enemy. Two days afterwards we began our advance in earnest, but were stopped for the greater part of the day at Dargai. The enemy, who had re-occupied it immediately on our withdrawal, were not dislodged until after seven hours of fighting, during which we lost 172 men. Whilst the heights which commanded the line of our advance were being stormed, the mass of the army was at a standstill, and as the track was rough and narrow and the mountain-sides precipitous, the jam and confusion throughout the day were considerable.

The rush of the "gay Gordons" under Mathias, well backed by the 3rd Sikhs and 2nd Ghurkas, over the bare bullet-swept neck of rocky ground which formed the only approach to Dargai is historical. After the action the army halted for a week at Karappa, four miles beyond Dargai. When ready for a fresh start, the plan of campaign was carried out without serious *contretemps* for the next five weeks. Maidan was reached early in November, and whilst palavers with Afridi *jirgas*—the Orakzais had by now practically submitted—were in progress, the valleys of Tirah were explored and their numerous hamlets destroyed by fire and dynamite. The Afridis, of whom more than 1000 were never seen in one locality, fought independently, the men of each clan and section defending their own homes as best they could, on opportunity boldly rushing rearguards and convoys and cutting off stragglers. Our main position, which covered acres of ground, was the nightly target for numerous snipers, each of whom, ensconced in his own lair, would fire careful bullets at long ranges into the silent and lightless camp until his ammunition was exhausted, or he himself was stalked and shot by our improvised cragsmen, the Ghurka scouts, whose services during the war were invaluable. Soon, shortening days and increasing cold reminded invaders and invaded alike that the Afridi highlands were unsuitable quarters for a winter bivouac. The discussions between *jirgas* and politicals continued; but although our terms, especially in regard to the number of breechloaders to be surrendered, were more than once lowered, no progress towards a settlement was made. At last Lockhart, warned by the first falls of snow, informed the expectant *jirgas* that he was going to winter his troops in their valleys, but would return in spring unless, meanwhile, his conditions were accepted. Our withdrawal was carried out in deliberate fashion between Dec. 7 and 17. Most of the troops, retiring by successive brigades, ran the gauntlet successfully down either the Waran glen or Dwatoi defile to the lower valley of the Barah. Naturally the Afridis viewed our departure as a flight: naturally, too, they concentrated their efforts on the last of the retreating brigades, Kempster's. With him was the mass of baggage, hospitals, and followers. On December 9 and 10 rain, sleet, and snow fell all night, numbing and exhausting drivers and animals, and converting the rice-fields into partially frozen bogs. On the 11th the rearguard, only 350 men, chiefly 2nd Ghurkas with 70 Gordons, after fighting all day, were benighted, together with large numbers of their helpless charge. A general massacre was averted by the steadiness of the soldiers. On the 12th Kempster, who had accompanied the leading portion of his brigade, returned with reinforcements, and on the 13th the march was resumed. During the retreat the rearguard lost a third of its strength; but there is no record of the numbers of the wretched followers and animals who were killed or died from cold and exhaustion. Had that guard been very strong, as the circumstances required, and had the brigadier been with it, as he should have been, our final exit from Tirah would not have been the inglorious flight it appeared.

Such, in brief, was the Tirah campaign—the destructive progress from south to north-east of an overwhelming force through or over an unexplored tangle of rocky ridges, glens, torrent-beds, clefts, and gullies, every coign of vantage secreting agile, well-armed marksmen. From start to finish our casualties were about 1500 soldiers, some hundreds of followers, and a considerable portion of our baggage-animals and stores. Proportionately, the enemy's losses—except in life and limb—were greater, as their possessions were small, and what was destructible we destroyed. The net result was fairly satisfactory—inviolate Tirah and her inmost sanctuary, Maidan, had been penetrated and desolated, and were now almost defenceless should we return in spring. In unveiling the mystery of Afridiland—"lifting the *purdah*," as it is called—we had suffered much, but that was hardly avoidable. If a herd of mahouted elephants attacks scattered wolves in a bad country, the assailants must get some falls and injuries.

Once out of Tirah, the second division, on whom the brunt of the fighting and losses had fallen, was given a long rest, whilst the first was transferred to the Bazar valley, which it exploited, and the reserve column re-occupied our abandoned positions in the Khyber Pass. Whilst these comparatively bloodless operations were in progress, the Afridi *jirgas* were negotiating in Peshawar for a settlement. On January 29 peace prospects were momentarily darkened by a blundering attempt of ours to outwit the wily Afridi at his own game,—a surprise capture of his flocks and herds grazing on the Kajauri plain, a stiff march west of Peshawar. Four columns of our troops suddenly converged on the pasture-ground: three saw nothing, but the fourth was intercepted in the Shin Kamar Pass, and, before extricating itself, lost 27 killed and 32 wounded, including 8 British officers. The affair, initiated by a political officer, was peculiarly unfortunate, because at the time the representatives of the Afridi clans were our guests in Peshawar, and hostilities were inferentially suspended; then, too, as luck would have it, the blow fell on a portion of the war-worn second division, the Yorkshire Light Infantry, and two companies of the 36th Sikhs, the regiment which had fought and suffered most throughout the campaign.

As it happened, the Shin Kamar mishap proved an asset for peace—the *jirgas* fearing that we might decide to avenge our reverse, we that success might induce their fighting men to defy us once more. At bottom both opponents desired peace, the only question was that of terms. Shin Kamar was an argument for lowering them. After much haggling and bluffing on both sides, our latest irreducible minimum was whittled down to conditions so light that the enemy's *jirgas* agreed to them. Their satisfaction with the settlement, which gave them continued independence, renewal and increase of allowances, and ultimate recovery of the guardianship of the Khyber, was at once evidenced by deeds. When, on April 5, it was known that General Lockhart, always popular with his tribal enemies, was starting for England, some hundreds of his Afridi admirers—including Zakkakhels, the most hostile clan of the whole confederacy—surrounded his house, dragged his carriage to the station, gave him a rousing send-off, and swore that every man and boy amongst them would fight his future battles in any part of the world; and they were as good as their word, for Afridi enlistments in our service that spring were so unprecedentedly numerous that our recruiting officers rejected scores of young men who would physically have done credit to our Grenadier Guards.

CHAPTER XXIII.

DISMEMBERMENT OF THE PUNJAB.

Before the return of purgatorial heat, just within a year of the first outbreak at Maizar, old conditions had been restored; the troops had been distributed to their stations, and were lazing in the perpetual afternoon of barrack-room existence under punkahs, and the tribes were without a grievance, happy in the enjoyment of peace and payments, with the prospect of increased service and allowances, and the gradual disappearance from their territory of the offensive uniforms of our sepoys—symbols of subjection and discipline for savage freemen. They did not regret the past, not a bit; their dead, like animals, they had already forgotten; the struggle had been forced upon them, as their independence was being filched away, and practically they had gained what they had fought for: the Sarkar would now attempt no more demarcations or encroachments. As for ourselves, those responsible for the most recent developments of the forward policy, particularly the occupation of Chitral, Wana, the Upper Tochi valley, and the delimitations, first persuaded themselves—the wish for self-exculpation fathering the thought—that "fanaticism" had been the cause of the risings, and then,—shutting their eyes to the truth and deliberately ignoring the recorded warnings of their few dissentient advisers—announced the fact to the India Office and the public; and in his reply the Secretary of State, after suggesting the existence of other contributing causes, endorsed the view taken by Lord Elgin, writing, "I entirely agree with your Excellency in Council in regarding fanaticism as the principal motive for an outbreak, which has been unprecedented in its suddenness and in the simultaneous action of distant tribes or sections of country affected."

As for the Indian taxpayers, they were inarticulate as always; although famine was afflicting eighty millions of them, and had already killed the weaklings and sent five millions to the relief camps, those who had the means or could borrow, paid the heavy bill of war-costs and continued their lives of ceaseless toil and semi-starvation: whether the Sarkar annexed new countries or not was all the same to them; it was theirs to labour, exist on dry crusts, and find money to enable the Sahibs to fight and become great Lord Sahibs. For once, however, in Anglo-Indian history, the generally strictly "correct" English dailies of the country did not support the official view that fanaticism was the root-cause of the troubles of the previous year. The vernacular papers, having no first-hand information, and having recently been muzzled on account of their utterances upon the plague proceedings of the Bombay Government, were prudently silent, or only indulged in guarded comments upon extracts translated from English journals. Of those of the first rank, 'The Civil and Military Gazette' (Lahore) and 'The Pioneer' (Allahabad), both of which, with numerous correspondents at the front, had been cognisant of all that had occurred, were outspoken in their criticisms. The former concentrated its scorn on the abandonment of the Khyber, and even gibbeted individuals as responsible for our shame; the latter, habitually cautious because dependent on the Government for favours, was less pointed in its denunciations. The Viceroy was naturally distressed at what appeared to him the disloyalty of the most influential leaders of public opinion: clearly, unless new matter should divert attention, the fourth estate was in no humour to condone the mistakes and shortcomings of his frontier administration, and if so, the publication of the Tirah Blue-book, however discreetly its contents might be selected, would prove awkward for the Government.

Whilst the press was still worrying at the subject, an officer of some eminence as a soldier and war-correspondent, who held an appointment at Simla—the brain of India—asked for permission to give a lecture on "Tirah and its Lesson." As the final draft ascribed the risings to fanaticism, and only dilated on uncontroversial points in the conduct of the campaign, such as the comparative merits of Afridis and Anglo-Indian soldiers as marksmen, the reading of the paper was authorised. For a fortnight before the appointed day Simla was placarded with invitations to the public—*i.e.*, officers of the Government and their families—to attend the meeting and discuss the lecture. On the afternoon of June 18, 1898, all Simla, from Viceroy to newly arrived griffin, flocked to the town-hall, and listened with signs of boredom to the already threadbare version of the story, which, as expected, endorsed the supposed official view of the causes of the risings, was silent in regard to the

Amir's share in fomenting them, passed lightly over the happenings in the Khyber, and generally lauded the wisdom and foresight of the Government, both before and during the campaign. When the lecturer sat down, the writer rose and quietly pointed out that what had been called "fanaticism" was merely the inspiration to brave deeds, and that the Mullahs might have preached to doomsday without a trigger being pulled, had not our own actions forced the tribesmen to fight; when they saw us giving bribes to their leaders, marching troops through their countries, surveying and mapping their hills, and erecting cairns of stone along the Afghan side of their hinterlands, they concluded that annexation was intended; as for the Afridis, they would not have risen had we not abandoned the Khyber Rifles and the pass; now that our attempts to establish "friendly relations" with the tribes, at the point of the bayonet, had failed, the impressment of the peasantry would cease, and that would be a blessed deliverance, for the indiscriminate seizures practised imposed intolerable burdens on our own people, four times the number of men and animals being collected and herded about the country to the fit residue finally despatched to the front.

Every word in that short speech was absolutely true: the whole press of India, English and vernacular, endorsed the statements as true; the speech was made at a public and unofficial meeting in which all men present were there as simple citizens, and at which discussion had been invited, and yet, because the truth was disagreeable to the Government, and the speaker of it was an official, he was soon afterwards compelled to apologise for having, "whilst a

Government servant, used expressions which have been regarded as an attack on the Government." Admitting that, officially viewed, the speech was an indiscretion, the lapse was a mere peccadillo compared with the sin of the Government in authorising and countenancing such a lecture—to be followed by discussion too. Officers in India as "servants" are, doubtless, bound to support their master or be silent, but, at the same time, it is the duty of the master to be careful not to strain their discipline and forbearance to breaking point. It is obvious, too, that discussion, unless free and honest, is a farce.

Now, to return to the Punjab frontier.

The tribes soon found that, as anticipated, they had done well in resisting their virtual annexation; for not only had they gained their immediate object, but their strength and unanimity were forcing us to reconsider our whole frontier policy. No sooner was Lord Curzon installed as Viceroy (January 1899), than our financial and military exigencies constrained him to advise and inaugurate a complete reversal of the practice initiated by his two predecessors of segregating Indian troops in negligible localities off the only two important lines of land-communication between India and Central Asia, the Bolan and Khyber routes. He saw at once that by locking up several brigades in Chitral, the Samana, the Kurram valley (Pārachinār), Lower and Upper Dawar, and Mahsudland, we were dissipating strength, increasing expenditure, inviting attacks, and generally weakening ourselves. Unable to wholly withdraw from the false positions already occupied, Lord Curzon fell back on the old Punjab system—first practised in the Derajat and later in Baluchistan and the Khyber—of endeavouring to enlist the goodwill of the tribes themselves in the cause of order and border defence by making it worth their while to behave as friendly neighbours and protect their own caravan-routes. Having the resources of the Empire at his disposal, he was able to be more thorough than the provincial government, with its narrow means, had ever been. Instead of employing levies—*i.e.*, undisciplined and ununiformed tribesmen under their own headmen—he converted the raw material in each locality into a militia; in other words, he extended and improved the Khyber system by organising levies into local regiments, each under British officers. Thus, for the Khyber, he increased the number of Rifles by one-third, raising their strength to 1250 men, and, instead of one British commander, gave them in addition a British adjutant and two other British officers. The new departure, or rather development of the old Punjab system, economises troops and money, enriches the tribes, placates their susceptibilities, and though in a sense a step backwards,—a drawing in of our tentacles,—is politically and financially a stride in the direction of business-mindedness, until then for many years a stranger to our counsels. If the experiment stand the test of troubled times, when they recur, the authorities of the day will marvel at the short-sightedness of their now discredited push-forward-the-military and damn-the-taxpapers predecessors. If it fail, as here and there it may, little harm will ensue:—a few months of anarchy in Chitral, Swat, the Kurram and Tochi valleys, or Mahsudland, however regrettable, would hardly affect our strength in localities of first-class importance to our military position trans-Indus.

The change of system sanctioned and introduced, time was found for the audit of the accounts of the later phases of the meddle and muddle period. In due course the balance-sheet was published—on the debit side a clear loss of some millions sterling, and of our good name as well with the tribes; on the credit side—nothing.

The audit proved that the affairs of John Bull & Co. had been grossly mismanaged, and that the directors had done their best to throw dust in the eyes of the shareholders, but had failed;—that balance-sheet proved their incapacity, for it showed that millions had been squandered on a rotten form of insurance against accidents. As the shareholders were dissatisfied, and the home directors anxious for the reorganisation of the trans-Indus branch of their business, Lord Curzon promptly decided to partially revive Lord Lytton's long pigeon-holed scheme, detach the Pathan districts from the province, and constitute them into a separate government directly under his own control. The difficulty was to establish a good case against the Punjab, and in favour of himself. The tracts in question had been part and parcel of the Punjab for fifty years, had shared in her triumph before Delhi and later in Oude, and, after all too, his immediate predecessor in office had been more to blame for the events of 1895-98 than any of his numerous advisers. Those factors, however, were hardly material;—the Lieutenant-Governor had always been an obstructionist, and Lord Elgin's misfortunes demonstrated the rottenness of a system, not the possible incapacity of a Viceroy.

As for the Punjab, it would be easy to prove that successive office-holders had not only possessed large powers of initiative and management upon their trans-Indus frontier, independent of the Government of India, but that they had so misused those powers as to demonstrate their unfitness for the trust reposed in them. Nothing if not thorough, Lord Curzon began his task by giving figures, which showed that with a cumulative service of 151 years, 20 months was the aggregate period spent trans-Indus by the last five holders of the office of Lieutenant-Governor, and that their chief secretaries had never, or only in their griffinages, seen parts of the Indus valley. From those premisses he deduced the conclusion that, "as a rule, neither the Lieutenant-Governor nor his Chief Secretary knows anything about the frontier at all." If right, he might analogously have argued that "not one of our Secretaries for Foreign Affairs, Secretaries for India, or Viceroys has ever known anything about his duties, because in spite of a cumulative service of a thousand years, 999 have been spent by them in England." Having proved the ignorance of successive rulers of the Punjab, Lord Curzon considered that he had also proved their incompetence as frontier administrators by asserting that in the fifty years, "during which time the frontier has been under the control of the Punjab Government, there have been no fewer than forty military expeditions, or one expedition for every fifteen months of the entire period."

The implication was that those repeated wars had been due to the faulty administration of the Punjab Government; but the truth is, as already shown, that from the time when the pushful policy took the place of John Lawrence's close-border system, the initiative, until then vested in the subordinate Government, was appropriated by the supreme Government. Until the Afghan war of 1878-80 the Lieutenant-Governor of the Punjab had been, for his own frontier, a sort of Deputy Viceroy, but, during and after that war, his authority was curtailed: from 1880 to 1887 he had acted as moderator, mentor, and executive officer for the Viceroy of the day; after 1887 his position became that of neglected adviser, and latterly he had merely been "a channel of communication."

The comparative success of frontier management by the local and supreme Governments may be gauged by the facts that, up to 1887, the aggregate cost of roundly twenty blockades and frontier expeditions, exclusive of Ambela (1863)—which was directed by the Government of India—was less than half that incurred after 1892, and that the tribes are to-day as little amenable to our friendly offices as at any former period—1897 excepted—in our long connection with them. True, in the domain of world-politics, such as imperial expansion, the influence of the Punjab—perhaps as the aftermath of Lord Lawrence's system—has always been on the side of peace and economy and opposed to push and expenditure. That, however, should have been counted for righteousness and not offence. If the literature on frontier affairs for the last twenty years be examined, it will be seen that the subordinate Government, when consulted, almost invariably gave advice, which, if followed, would have saved India from the misdirection of energy and waste of resources which culminated in the troubles and humiliations of 1897.

Having proved to his own satisfaction that the Government of the Punjab was ignorant, blundering, and obstructive,—a mere "ladder of delay" is the picturesque phrase used,—Lord Curzon boldly asserted the general competence of his own Government to directly manage the frontier, and in particular his own peculiar fitness for the task, in corroboration of which latter contention he rather prematurely cited the success of his new policy, including "my own scheme" for its application to Waziristan, both in reality extravagant reversions to old Punjab types. Finally, after a passing sneer at the parochialism of Punjab rulers, which disqualified them to "deal with the larger problems of foreign policy," he stated what in reality are the substantial justifications for eliminating the Punjab from part or lot in frontier administration—viz., the administrative convenience of subjecting Pathan tribes inside as well as outside our actual frontier to the same controlling authority, the advantages gained by the abolition of "the ladder of delay," and the concentration of all direct responsibility on the always ultimately responsible authority, the Viceroy of the day and his Peshawar agent, and, finally, the practical good to be expected from the rescue of Pathan districts from the over-refinement or, as Lord Curzon comprehensively put it, "the complex paraphernalia" of our Indian civil justice system.

Lord Curzon's Council—a member of which was an old Punjabi, and is now the first ruler of the dismembered province—tamely forwarded their chief's minute to the Secretary of State, "with an expression of our unanimous and hearty agreement with its main propositions." The scheme was sanctioned (December 20, 1900) as a matter of course, and so hurriedly and high-handedly had the whole proceedings been rushed that the office-holder chiefly concerned, the then Lieutenant-Governor of the Punjab, was given no opportunity of seeing and answering the charges made against him and his predecessors. So well disciplined were the Members of Council under Viceroy and Secretary of State that not one in India, and only one in London, had the courage to defend the man who had thus been condemned unheard. That one was Sir Dennis Fitzpatrick, the preceding ruler of the Punjab, at the time a member of the India Office Council; and not only did he vindicate the Punjab administration from the contumely heaped upon it by Lord Curzon, but he showed that some of his Excellency's statements and inferences were "of such a nature as to convey an erroneous or distorted impression," and secured that his own opinion should not be burked—as obnoxious opinions sometimes are —by prefixing to it a request that it should be "entered in the minutes of the proceedings."

Even without that outspoken independence which had always characterised his utterances, Sir Dennis Fitzpatrick might safely have ventured to dispute Lord Curzon's facts and conclusions, for he had reached the haven of rest and comparative ease for good Anglo-Indians—the Council of India, Whitehall. But the case for the official members of the Viceroy's Council in Calcutta and Simla was, and always will be, different. Being all practically nominees of the Viceroy of the day or his predecessor, and candidates for provinces, honours, or appointments in the India Office, they naturally incline to subordinate their own views—when they have time to form any—to those of an opinionated Viceroy. Their dependence is sometimes evident even to the public; for instance, in

1877, when Lord Lytton was forcing war or vassalage on the ill-starred Amír of Kabul—Sher Ali Khan—his whole Council concurred in all the crooked doings of their chief; again, when Lord Elgin, acting on his "mandate" theory, advised the exclusion of Manchester piece-goods from import-duty,—the only class of goods financially worth taxing,—the official members of his Council, the majority, voted with him against the clear interests of India. If, even twenty-five years ago, the Council was weak and compliant, it is still less independent now, for since then the evil of centralisation has grown to excessive dimensions, and, what is more, the development of the idea of the Cabinet system has so advanced, that members act as if they were absolved from responsibility in subjects outside their own individual departments.

Had Lord Curzon in his separation minute avoided personalities, adhered to facts, and based his proposal on administrative convenience alone, he would probably have achieved his purpose. The advantages from fixing personal responsibility, facilitating the rapid transaction of business, and detaching Pathan districts from the "complex paraphernalia" of the civil justice system of India are great. On the other hand, the Viceroy of the day, normally a man who "knows nothing about the frontier at all,"—or India, for that matter,—has been deprived of his only expert and independent counsellor, the Lieutenant-Governor of the Punjab, an official who—whether with or without previous trans-Indus training—had hitherto, necessarily, for the previous thirty years or more, been conversant with frontier affairs, and personally intimate with every officer, English and Indian, serving in the Pathan districts. So long as Lord

Curzon remains Viceroy the elimination of the Punjab expert from his counsels is of small importance, as he has local knowledge and inspires confidence; but in the long, long afterwards the case will be different. The Peshawar agent will often be an ambitious man "in a hurry," in which case he will push the forward policy, and amongst future Viceroys Aucklands, Lyttons, Lansdownes, and Elgins will be more frequent than Lawrences and Curzons, and then we shall have complications, coat-trailings, warlike movements, perhaps even wars, and they mean, as was the case through the 'nineties, extravagance trans-Indus, and crippling retrenchments or tax enhancements cis-Indus. That, under a capable Viceroy, the new arrangement will work satisfactorily has already been demonstrated. No sooner was the new province constituted than the most ill-conditioned of the Mahsuds—who for the last fifty years have alternately lived by looting or died from fasting enforced by blockades and expeditions—committed a series of outrages in British territory. The old Punjab device of a blockade, enlivened and accentuated by counter-raids on our part, was adopted and rigorously carried out for a year, when, in the absence of the Viceroy in inaccessible Manipur, the usual preliminaries to an expedition—the concentration of reinforcements at Tank, the portal of Mahsudland—were ordered. Had Mahsudland been then invaded, annexation would have followed. Happily, Lord Curzon, rejoining the telegraph line, peremptorily vetoed the whole programme, and, after six months of further starvation, the Mahsuds submitted for the seventh or eighth time since 1857, and truce conditions have since been restored, and may continue for a year or two.

Looking back for twenty-five years, remembering the causes of the Afghan war of 1878-80, the straining of our relations with the Amir 1890-93, the subsequent thrusting of "friendly relations" and a protectorate upon the independent tribes beyond our frontier, the enforced delimitations of some of their hinterlands, the futile consequential wars of 1897-98, unprejudiced minds must recognise that the taxpaying masses of India have received scant consideration, and that some of the heads of governments and subordinate officers, answerable for the blunders and wastage of the different periods, should have been discredited instead of rewarded. So long as the Government of India is practically an irresponsible despotism, and the Indian public merely a powerless mass of uninformed and inarticulate taxpayers, muddling, misrepresentation, and waste in the conduct of India's foreign affairs will not cease, and high-placed blunderers in authority will never be called to account. Until some force in India arises with the power, the will, and the ability necessary for securing a common-sense management of affairs, business-like prudence will not always be practised.

Present methods suit a bureaucracy: unless forced from the outside, reforms from inside are hopeless. Without the certainty that the truth will come out and be intelligently examined and judged, no Government will proclaim its mistakes or alter its ways. The fear of public opinion is the force which secures right-mindedness in men in power in England; but in India there is no public opinion—at least published opinion—except to some extent on domestic matters entering into the daily life of the people—*e.g.*, plague regulations—hence the Government of India in their foreign proceedings are irresponsible, and in pursuit of the chimeras of "high politics"—sometimes a mere mount for vaulting ambition—they plunge light-heartedly into adventures and wars which may benefit a few individually, but injure the people of India collectively. When things go wrong in India hardly a voice is raised against the wrong-doers: officials may not speak, the press has little information, and if it had more, is timid, the line between treason and criticism being finely drawn; and as for the masses, their horizon is the evening meal and the next instalment of the revenue demand. Outside India, nobody cares. John Bull is ultimately responsible; but as he does not pay the bills, and his immediate concerns engross him, he is not exacting, and accepts without scrutiny whatever statements the Government of India may lay before him. Take instances: Lord Lytton in 1877 forces a war on Afghanistan; it costs twenty-five millions sterling; India bleeds silently. Again, from 1890 onwards push and pin-pricks upon India's north-west frontier plunge her into many wars; the proceedings cost six or seven millions sterling; once more India bleeds silently. To particularise, an agent trails his coat in Chitral, a war follows, India pays, and the agent is knighted and promoted, and there the matter ends. Again, some of the trans-Indus Pathan tribes, mistaking our intentions, are frightened into fighting for their independence; the Khyber Pass is abandoned, the events of August 23, 1897, take place, a serious war follows: once more India bleeds, this time, happily, not quite silently. The

Viceroy in Council calls the risings "fanatical outbreaks"; no one objects until an official indiscreetly speaks the truth: eventually the blunderings are condoned, the blunderers rewarded, and the Secretary of State for India endorses—with hinted qualifications—the Viceregal fanaticism myth, and records in a despatch to Lord Elgin his entire agreement "in regarding fanaticism as the principal motive" for the tribal risings, and "on the part of her Majesty's Government their high approval of the manner in which your Excellency's Government has met an arduous crisis."

Is that the way in which Indian foreign affairs should be administered? Would not any private business, conducted on similar lines, be soon in liquidation? Is it unreasonable, then, to hold that there can be no remedy until some force comes into being outside what in Lord Lytton's time was irreverently called "the Simla Mutual Adulation Society," and does the work which public opinion and the press, working together, perform in England?

APPENDIX.

ARMS USED IN THE SIKH WARS AND MUTINY.

To realise the fighting in our two campaigns against the Sikhs, and later in the Mutiny, the combatants' weapons and their ranges must be appreciated. In the war on the Sutlej (1846-47) the Sikhs, like the Boers in 1899, brought a large part of their heavy ordnance into the field, whereas we rushed to the attack with nothing more powerful than field and horse artillery, 8- and 6-pounders, and a few mortars, mere pop-guns compared with the big pieces used by the enemy. At Ferozeshah, where the Sikhs defended their position with upwards of seventy cannon, their shot fell amongst our men at a distance of 1500 yards from their entrenchments, whilst ours were ineffective at 800 yards. After the battle, their captured guns showed few marks of shot or shell, whereas nearly a third of ours were disabled. Not only did the Sikh guns vastly outrange ours, but where both were of equal calibre, theirs having more metal in them, and being all made of "brass"—*i.e.*, gun-metal—and excellently finished, threw heavier projectiles. In the open, our superior mobility and dash would have more than counterbalanced the enemy's advantages in range and weight; but as the Sikhs prudently confined their efforts to the defensive, not until we had learnt our lesson at Ferozeshah, and brought up our siege-train, was the balance turned in our favour.

In small-arms, and more especially in their manipulation,

the superiority was with us from the first. Our troops were armed with the converted "brown Bess"; the Sikhs, at least their regular infantry, with a similar weapon of their own manufacture. Both were percussion-muskets, and made fair shooting, allowing for vagaries due to windage, at from 120 yards down to close quarters; but beyond the longer distance, to an extreme range of about 250 yards, the flight of the spherical bullet, the only kind then known, was so erratic that, at target practice over 100 yards, if one ball in a dozen struck a mark 10 feet square, the shooting was considered good. In musketry encounters on equal terms our infantry, sepoy as well as British, better in hand, better trained, and using better finished, balanced, and adjusted weapons and more reliable ammunition, could always count on defeating the best regiments of the Khalsa, so long as the fighting was confined to shooting. Besides regulars, the Sikhs put many thousands of irregulars into the field, whose firearms were their ancestral match- and flint-lock muskets, both noisy and ineffective, except for a first discharge up to 100 yards. In the excitement of battle the Sikhs often preferred sword to musket, and, like the Scottish Highlanders in the eighteenth century, after firing once, would drop their smoking weapons and charge sword in hand. Such rushes unnerved our sepoy battalions, except when their waning courage was sustained by a line of their steadfast British comrades.

In our second Sikh war (1848-49), though the arms of both combatants were the same, the Sikhs began the campaign at a serious disadvantage, having lost most of their best artillery and trained gunners in the battles on the Sutlej two years previously.

The equality of armaments in 1846-49 between ourselves and a small obscure, ignorant "horde of marauders," as we had called the Khalsa—a people with no mechanical contrivances, and no scientific training in the manufacture of guns and muskets, other than that supplied by the adventurous waifs from Europe who took service with Runjit Singh—appeared to the writer unaccountable, until he looked into the history of the development of firearms. That history gave facts, but it did not explain why Europe should have stood still in the art of ballistics, not only whilst in the grip of the feudal system, but well into the nineteenth century, in spite of the general mental quickening which followed the French Revolution and the rise to almost supreme dominion of a war-genius like Napoleon. For fifty years before Waterloo the most advanced nations of the West—or some of them—had been almost continuously at war, yet none of their great men ever directed the attention of the highest intelligences of their time to improving the means by which men could kill or maim each other: even the fertile and comprehensive mind of Napoleon himself, with all the learning and science of Europe—such as it was—at his command, rested satisfied with the clumsy firearms he found in use when he was still an unknown subaltern.

The doubtful honour of leading the way in advancing the art of killing by gunpowder is held by a clergyman, the Rev. Mr Forsyth. In 1807 he took out a patent for priming with a fulminating powder, which exploded when struck sharply with metal or indeed any hard substance; but, even so, the two centuries of stagnation were prolonged for thirty years more. At last, in 1834, it struck some one that by the simple device of screwing a nipple into the stock end of a barrel of a flintlock, and exploding the powder by striking the hammer of the gun on a copper cap, containing a little of the Forsyth composition, a great improvement in shooting would be secured. Tests tried at Woolwich proving successful, in 1839 the flintlocks of the British army were altered to the percussion-cap muskets, commonly called "brown Bess," a name already applied to the superseded weapon. By 1842 our army was generally supplied with the converted "brown Bess." The percussion principle appears to have been already known to some of the Sikh Sirdars, who possessed arms factories and employed European artificers in them, and in the wars of 1846-47 and 1848-49 the larger part of the Sikh regular battalions were armed with percussion-muskets.

The next great advance was in the practical application of rifling to the hitherto smooth-bore fire-tubes of the day. The actual invention of rifling was almost as old as that of gunpowder; but, so long as spherical bullets were alone used, windage was great, and reloading after the first discharge progressively slower and more difficult from the fouling of the barrel. In 1800 his Majesty's 95th Foot, now the Rifle Brigade, were armed with "Baker's rifle." It made fair shooting up to 800 yards, but, from fouling and the amount of ramming necessary to force the balls home, became unserviceable after the first few shots had been fired. The "Brunswick rifle," throwing a belted ball, was introduced into the army in 1836, but was soon condemned for the same faults as those of its predecessor. Next came Captain Minié's great invention, the substitution for the ball of a conical bullet with an iron cup in a cavity at its base, a contrivance by which ramming was made easy and expansion, after the explosion, secured. It was adopted in 1851, used by our army in the Crimea, and superseded in 1856 by the Enfield, which threw a cylindro-conoidal bullet made up in cartridges and lubricated. Shooting by it was accurate up to 800 yards. It remained the service weapon of our infantry until the introduction of the breechloader. As well known, the Enfield's "greased cartridges" were the immediate cause of the Mutiny. Pandy's rejection of the Enfield, and Thomas Atkins' possession of it, told immensely in our favour before Delhi and later. Had the sepoys accepted the Enfield and mutinied afterwards, our difficulties in suppressing their revolt would have been enormously increased.

In guns, improvements, as a rule, followed those in small-arms, and were worked out on similar lines.

PUBLICATIONS READ OR CONSULTED.

Period of Runjit Singh and the Sikhs, 1800-46.

Adventures of an Officer in the Punjab. (Major H. Lawrence.) 2 vols. 1846.
Forty-three Years in India. (Sir George Lawrence.) 1874.
History of the British Empire in India. (E. Thornton.) 1841-45.
History of British India. (James Mill, 1805-35; continuation, 1835-48, by H. H. Wilson.)
History of the Punjab and of the Rise of the Sikhs. (Anonymous.) 2 vols. 1848.
History of India. (Hon. Mountstuart-Elphinstone.) 1866.
History of the Sikhs. (Captain Cunningham.) 1853.
History of the Sikhs. (W. L. MacGregor.) 2 vols. 1846.
Military Annual. 1844.
Narrative of Various Journeys in the Punjab, &c. (C. Masson.) 3 vols. 1842.
Original Sketches in the Punjab. (A Lady.) 1854.
Our Relations with the Punjaub. (Sir C. M. Wade.) 1823.
Ranjít Singh. (Sir Lepel Griffin.) 1892.
The Punjaub. (Colonel Steinbach, late of the service of the Maharajah Runjeet Singh.) 1845.
The Punjab and the Indian Army. (General Caulfield.) 1846.
Thirty-five Years in the East. (Dr J. M. Konigberger, late Physician to the Court of Lahore.) 1852.
Tracts on the Punjab collected by the Court of Directors H. E. I. Company.
Travels in the Punjab. (Mohan Lal.) 1846.

Period of our Wars with the Sikhs, 1846-49.

Annual Register, 1846-50.
A Year on the Punjab Frontier, 1848-49. (Herbert Edwardes.) 2 vols. 1851.
Autobiography of Sir Harry Smith. 2 vols. 1901.
British Empire in India, 1844-62. (L. Trotter.) 1869.
Calcutta Review. (Contributions during the period on Punjab affairs.)
Despatches and General Orders during our Sikh Wars, 1846-49.
Diary of a Subaltern. (From 'The Times.') 1848-49.

Journal of a Cavalry Officer. (Captain Humbley.) 1859.

Journal of the Sutlej Campaign. (Rev. J. Coley.) 1856.

Life of Hugh, First Viscount Gough. (Professor Raits.) 2 vols. 1903.

Narrative of the Second Sikh War, 1848-49. (E. T. Thackwell.) 1849.

The Punjab Campaign, 1848-49. (Capt. Lawrence-Archer.) 1878.

The Bengal Artillery. (Colonel Malleson.) 1848.

The Sikhs and our Sikh Wars. (P. Gough, V.C., and Arthur Innes.) 1897.

Tracts, being Essays and Pamphlets, published 1846-51, collected by the India Office. 52 vols.

Period of the Lawrences and Mutiny, 1849-58.

Crisis in the Punjab. (Fred. Cooper.) 1858.

Dalhousie's Administration of British India. 2 vols. (Edwin Arnold.) 1862.

District Gazetteers of the Punjab (under Authority). 20 vols. 1883-92.

Essays, Military and Political, written in India. (Major H Lawrence.) 1859.

First Administration Reports, 1846-54 and 1854-56. (The Chief Commissioner.)

History of the Mutiny. (J. W. Kaye and Colonel Malleson.) 1888.

India under Dalhousie and Canning. (Duke of Argyll.) 1865.

Life and Opinions of Sir Charles Napier. (W. Napier.) 1857.

Life of Hodson of Hodson's Horse. (L. J. Trotter.) 1901.

Life of John Nicholson. (L. J. Trotter.) 1897.

Life of Lord Lawrence. (Bosworth-Smith.) 2 vols. 1883.

Life of Sir Henry Lawrence. (H. Edwardes and Herman Merivale.) 2 vols. 1872.

Lord Lawrence. (Sir C. Aitchison.) 1892.

Lord Lawrence. (Sir R. Temple.) 1889.

Present Condition of the Bengal Army. (John Jacob.) 1851.

The Jhelunder Doab. (H. Lawrence.) 1848.

The Punjab Mutiny Report. (By Authority.) 1858.

The Mutiny of the Bengal Army. (Colonel Malleson.) 1857-58.

The Mutiny in India. (Charles Ball.) 7 vols. 1858-59.

Thoughts of a Native of Northern India on the Rebellion. 1858.

Twelve Years of a Soldier's Life. (Ed. G. H. Hodson.) 1859.

Two Native Narratives of the Mutiny in Delhi. (Translated by C. T. Metcalfe.) 1858.

Punjab Administration after the Mutiny, and General, 1858-1902.

Administration Reports. (Annual, by Authority.) 1860-1901-2.
Asiatic Neighbours. (S. S. Thorburn.) 1894.
Bannu; or, Our Afghan Frontier. (S. S. Thorburn.) 1876.
British Dominion in India. (Sir Alfred Lyall.) 1894.
Chitral. (Sir G. Robertson.) 1898.
District Gazetteers (under Authority). 1883-98.
Egyptian Irrigation. (W. Willcocks.) 1899.
Famine Commission's Report. (The Commission.) 1880.
History of the Punjab. (Moulvi Mahomet Latif.)
Indian Baggage Corps. (Sir Charles Napier.) 1850.
Irrigated India. (Alfred Deakin.) 1893.
James Thomason. (Sir R. Temple.) 1893.
Land-Revenue Administration Reports. (Financial Commissioner.) Annual.
Land Systems of British India. 3 vols. (Baden-Powell.) 1892.
Lockhart's Advance through Tirah. (L. Shadwell.) 1898.
Moral and Material Progress of India. (Blue-book.) Annual.
Musalmans and Money-lenders. (S. S. Thorburn.) 1886.
Notes on Irrigation Works in the Punjab. (Official.) 1900.
Operations of the Mohmand Field Force. (Blue-book.) 1897.
Operations of the Tochi Field Force, 1897-98. (Major Kemball.) 1900.
Papers regarding Military Operations on the N.W. Frontiers of India, 1897-98. (Blue-books.) 2 vols.
Papers regarding British Relations with the Tribes on the N.W. Frontier of India. (Blue-book.) 1901.
Punjab Census Reports, 1881, 1891, 1901.
Punjab Records, containing Chief Court Judgments issued as Rulings.
Record of Expeditions against N.W.F. Tribes. (Colonel Paget and Lieutenant Mason.) 1885.
Report on the Colonization of Government Waste Lands on the Chenab Canal, 1897.
Report of the Indian Irrigation Commission. (Official.) 1901.
Report on Peasant Indebtedness. (S. S. Thorburn.) 1896.
Selections from the Records of the Government of the Punjab from 1871 onwards.
The Campaign in Tirah. (Colonel Hutchinson.) 1898.
The History of Small-Arms. (By Authority.) 1880.
The Indian Borderland. (Colonel Sir T. Holdich.) 1901.
Treatise on Military Small-Arms. (Colonel Bond.) 1884.

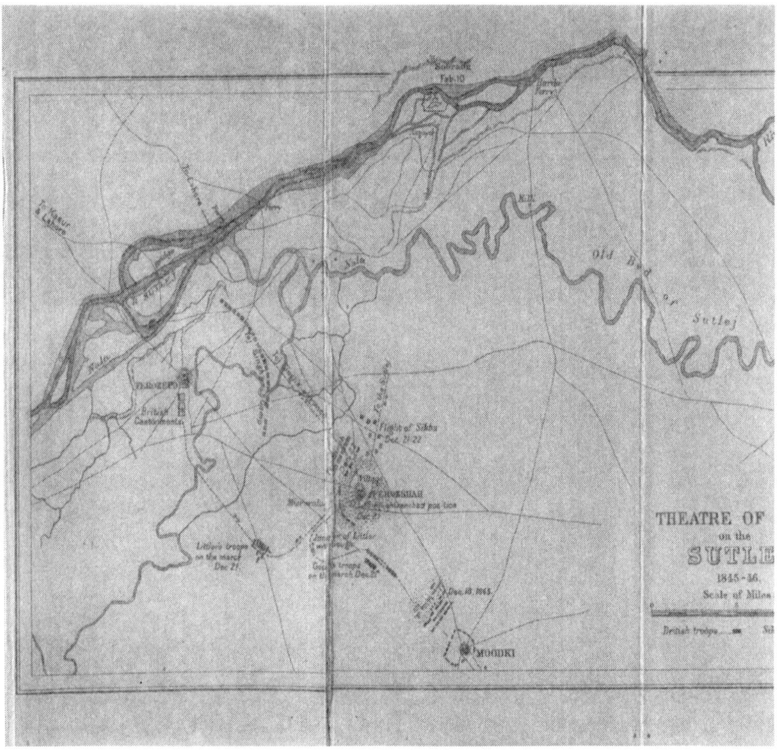
THEATRE OF
on the
SUTLE
1845-46.
Scale of Miles
Old Bed of Sutlej
Flight of Sikhs Dec. 21-22
Dec. 18, 1845.
MOODKI
British Cantonments
Littler's troops on the march Dec. 21.

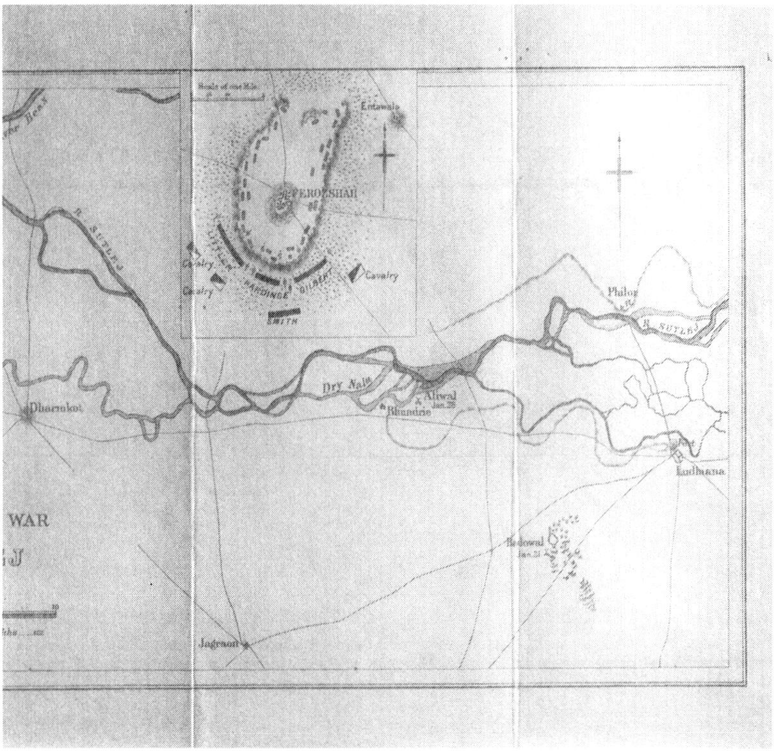

Scale of one Mile
Entawala
FEROZSHAH
LITTLER
Cavalry
Cavalry
HARDINGE
GILBERT
Cavalry
SMITH
R. SUTLEJ
Dharmkot
Dry Nala
Aliwal
Jan. 28
Bhundrie
Philor
R. SUTLEJ
Ludhiana
WAR
EJ
Badowal
Jan. 21
Jagraon

RIVER SUTLEJ
Camp of Sikh Regulars
Kote
Gurian
Flight of the Sikhs
Sikh Regulars
Bhundrie
British
Road to Jagraon
BATTLE OF ALIWAL
January 28th 1846.
REFERENCE.
British Infantry
" Cavalry
Sikh Infantry
" Cavalry
English Miles
0
½
1
2

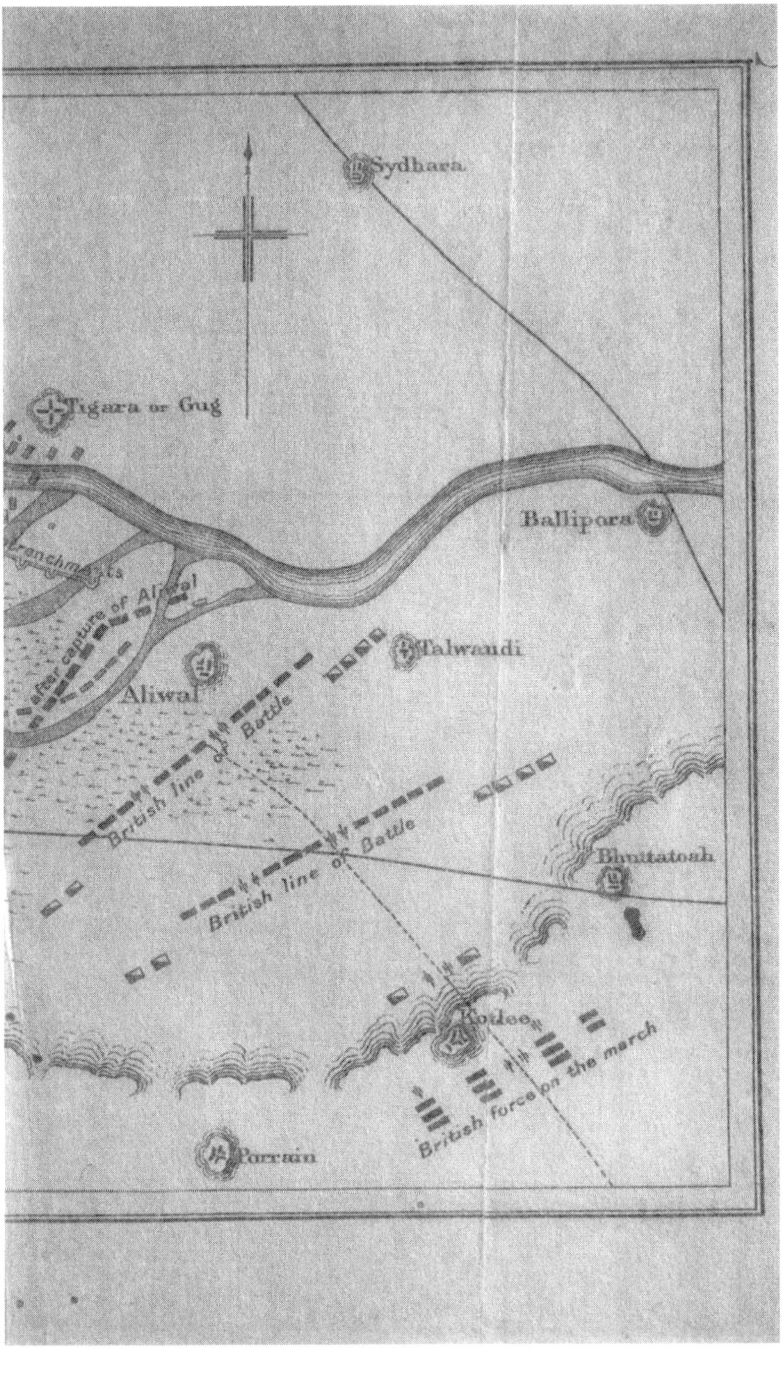
Sydhara
Tigara or Gug
Ballipora
Talwandi
Aliwal
British line of Battle
British line of Battle
Bhuttatoh
British force on the march
Porrain

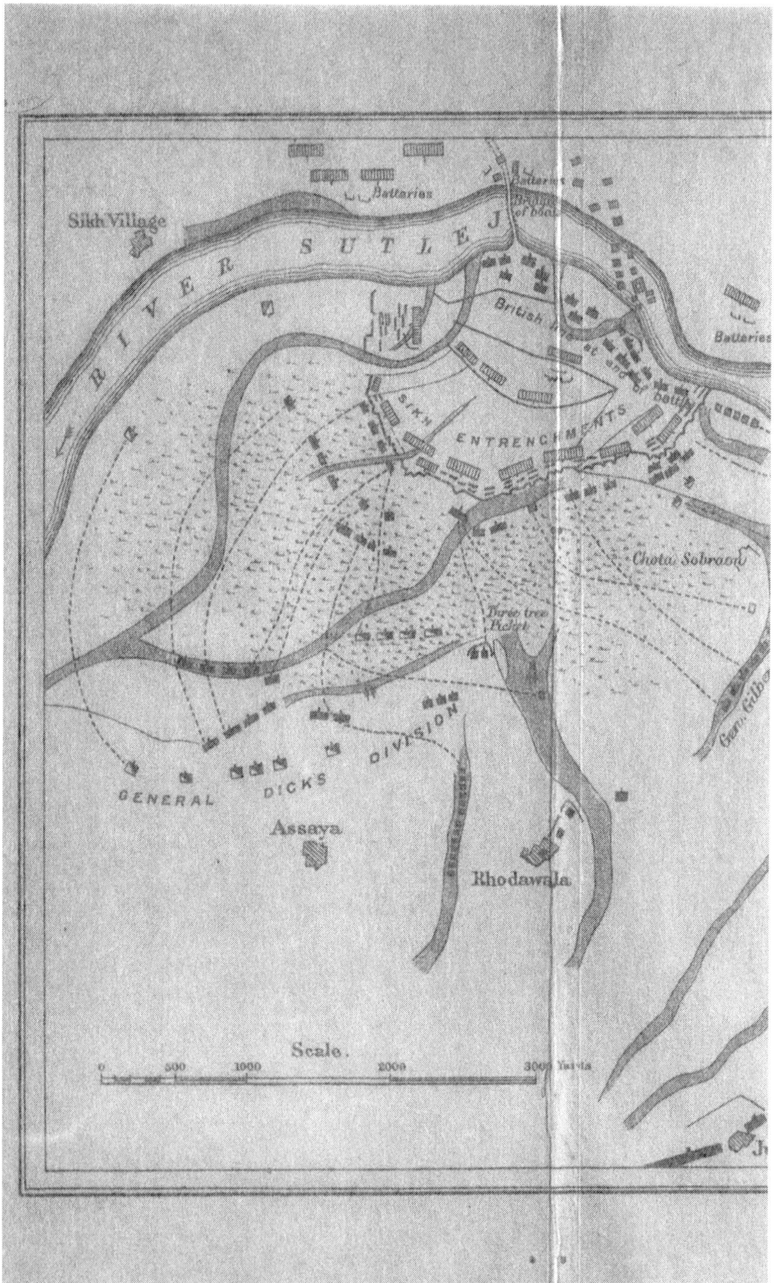
Batteries
Batteries
Batteries
Sikh Village
RIVER SUTLEJ
British line
SIKH ENTRENCHMENTS
Chota Sobraon
GENERAL DICKS DIVISION
Assaya
Rhodawala
Scale.
0
500
1000
2000
3000 Yards

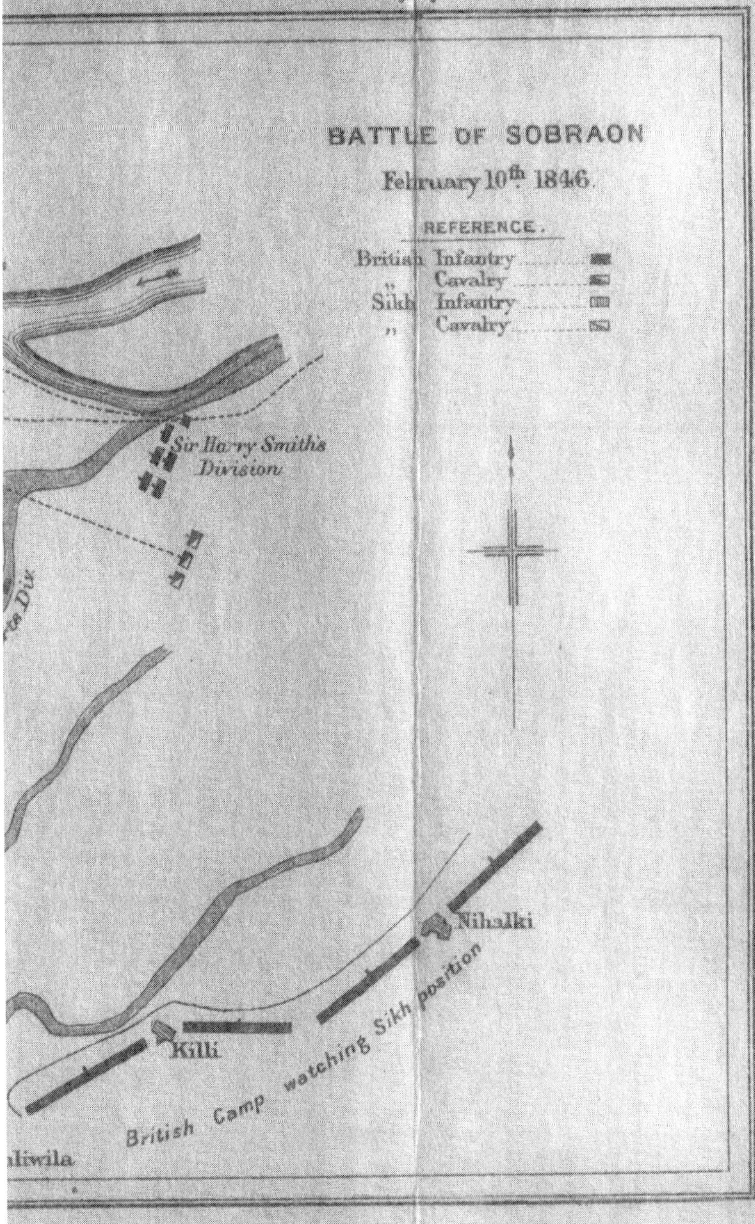
BATTLE OF SOBRAON
February 10th 1846.
REFERENCE.
British Infantry
„ Cavalry
Sikh Infantry
„ Cavalry
Sir Harry Smith's Division
Nihalki
Killi
British Camp watching Sikh position

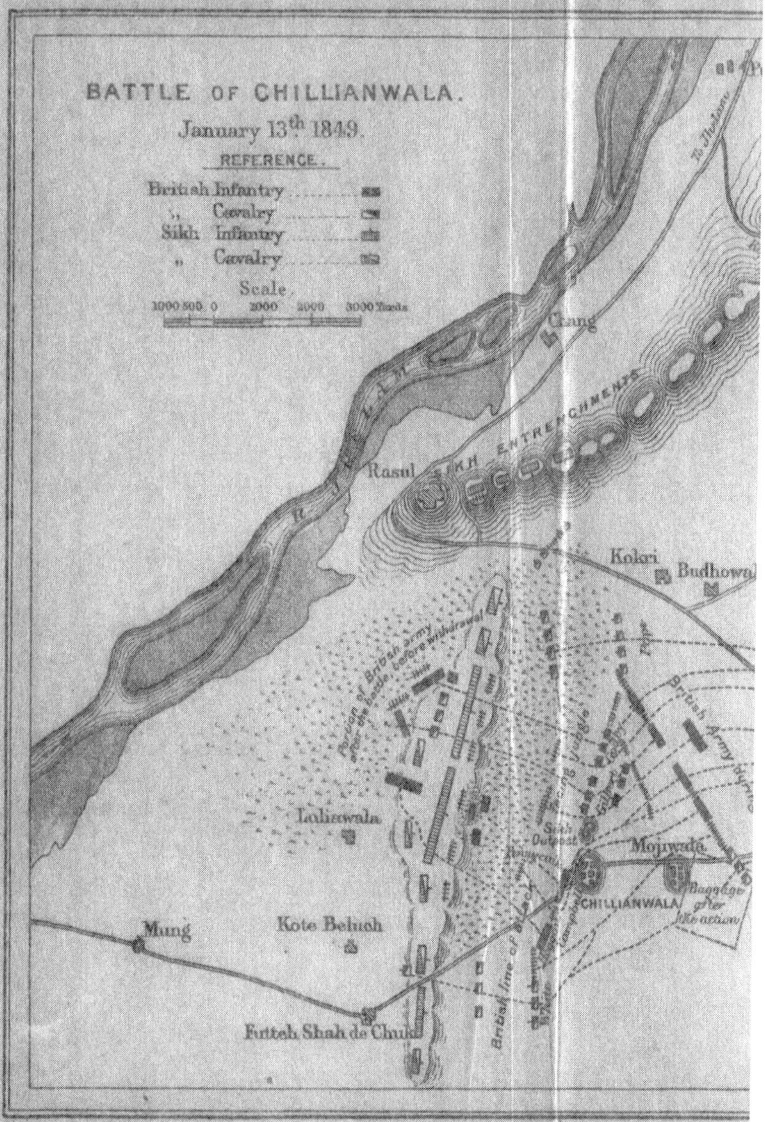
BATTLE OF CHILLIANWALA.
January 13th 1849.
REFERENCE.
British Infantry
,, Cavalry
Sikh Infantry
,, Cavalry
Scale.
Chang
SIKH ENTRENCHMENTS
Rasul
Kokri
Lolianwala
Sikh Outpost
Mojiwala.
CHILLIANWALA
Baggage after the action
Mung
Kote Beluch
Futteh Shah de Chuk
Portion of British army after the battle, before withdrawal

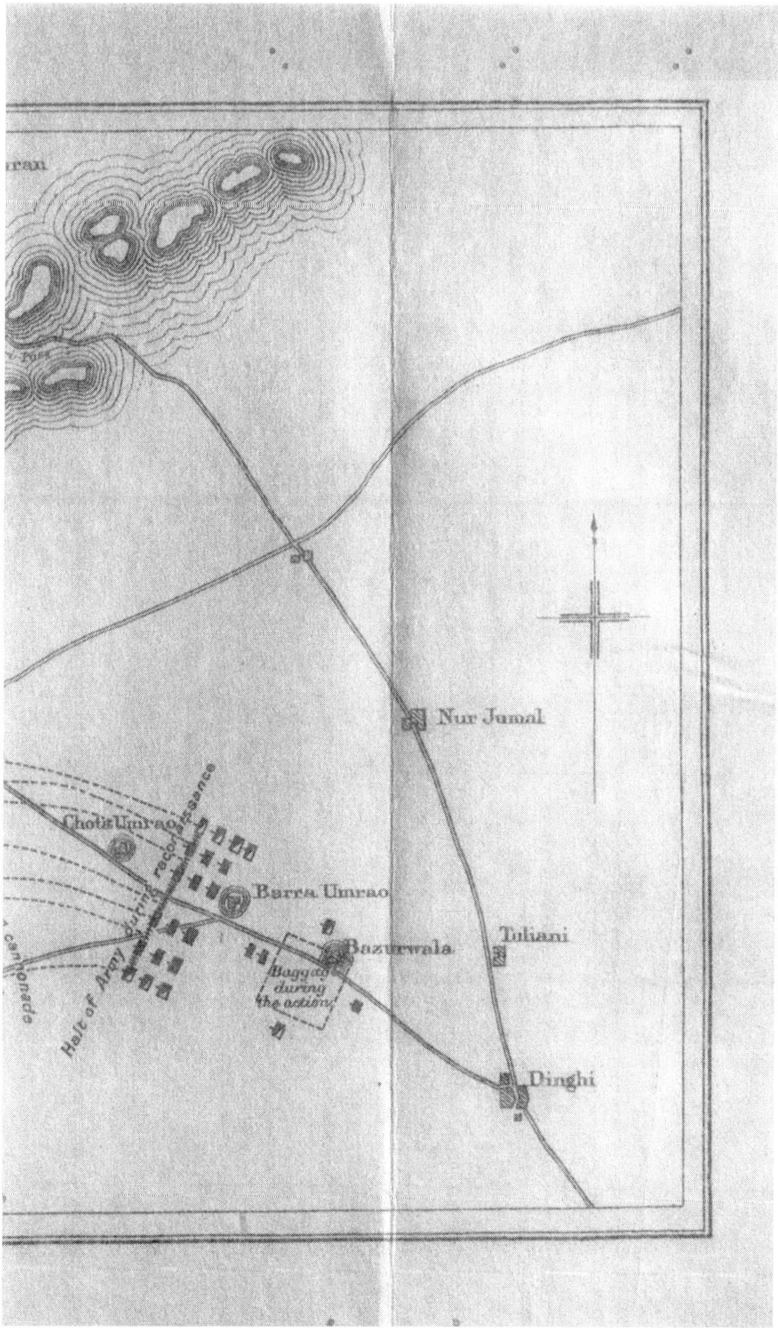
Nur Jumal
Choti Umrao
Barra Umrao
Bazurwala
Tuliani
Dinghi
during
the action

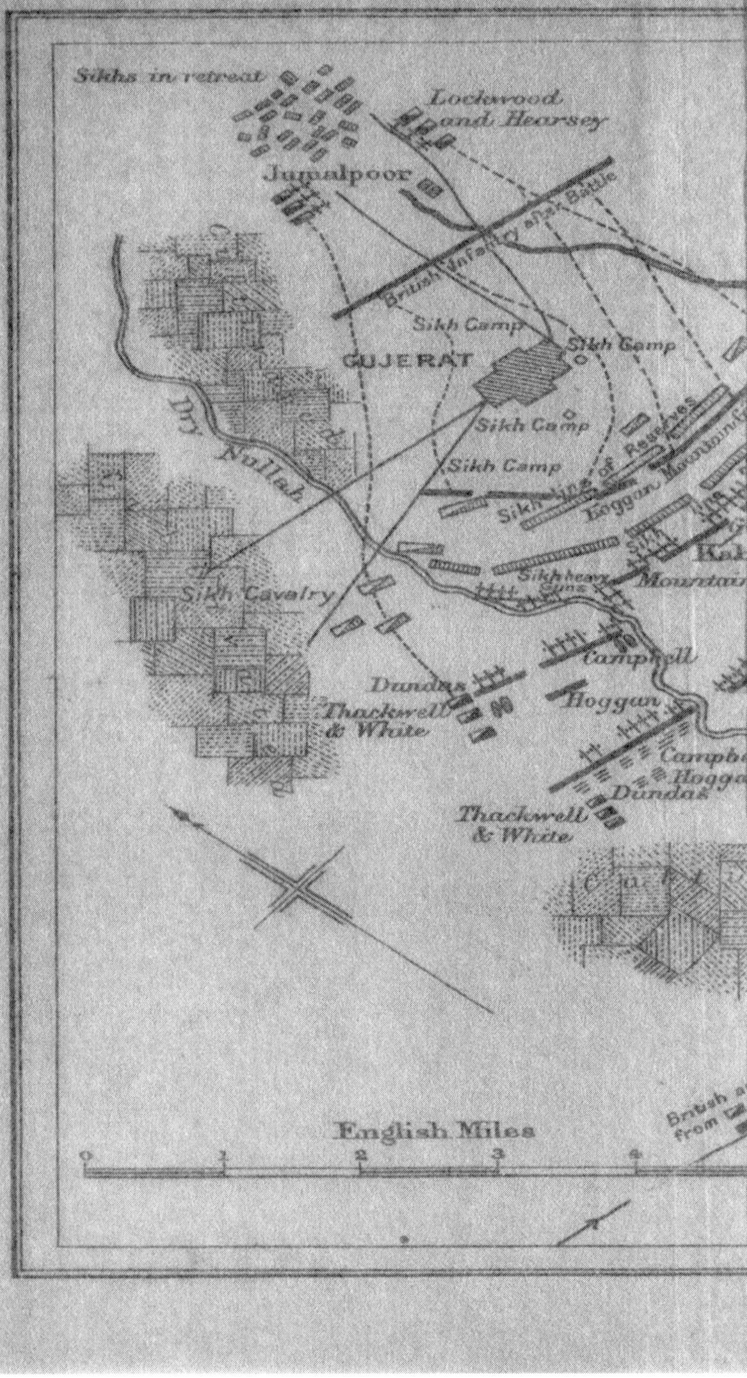
Sikhs in retreat
Lockwood and Hearsey
Jumalpoor
British Infantry after Battle
Sikh Camp
GUJERAT
Sikh Camp
Sikh Camp
Sikh Camp
Dry Nullah
Sikh Line of Reserves
Hoggan
Sikh heavy Guns
Sikh Cavalry
Campbell
Dundas
Thackwell & White
Hoggan
Dundas
Thackwell & White
English Miles
0
1
2
3
4

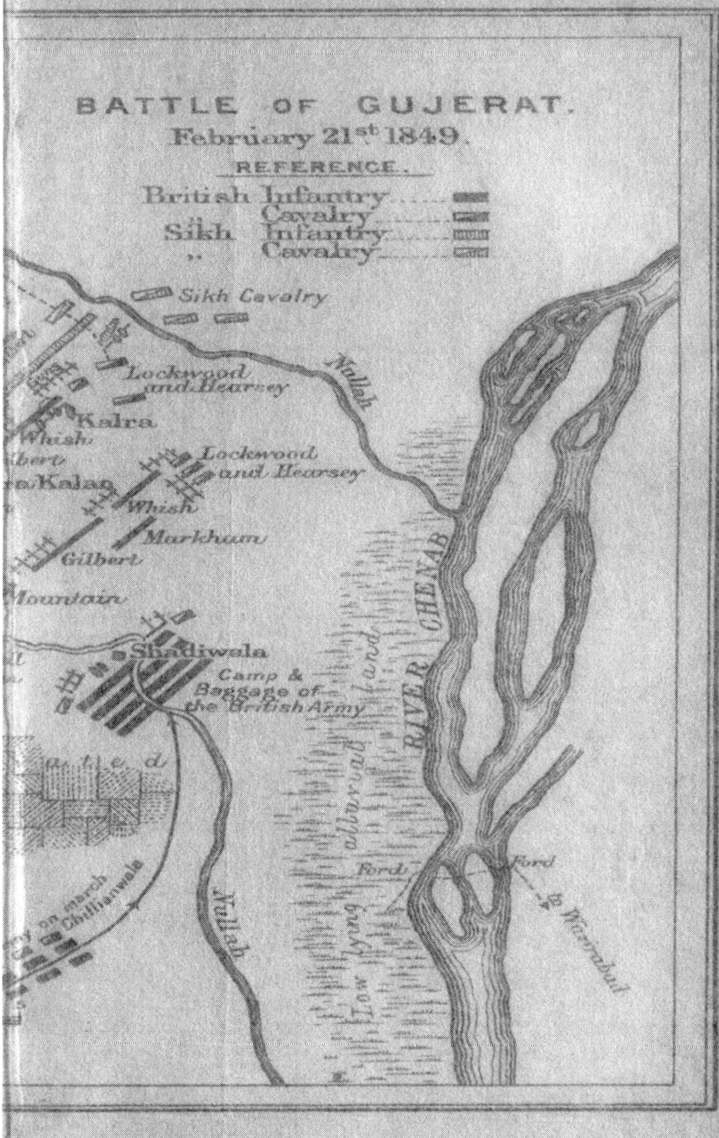
BATTLE OF GUJERAT.
February 21st 1849.
REFERENCE.
British Infantry
" Cavalry
Sikh Infantry
" Cavalry
Sikh Cavalry
Nullah
Lockwood and Hearsey
Kalra
Whish
Lockwood and Hearsey
Whish
Markham
Gilbert
Mountain
Shadiwala
Camp & Baggage of the British Army
RIVER CHENAB
alluvial Land
Low lying Land
Ford
Ford
To Wazirabad
Nullah
Chillianwala

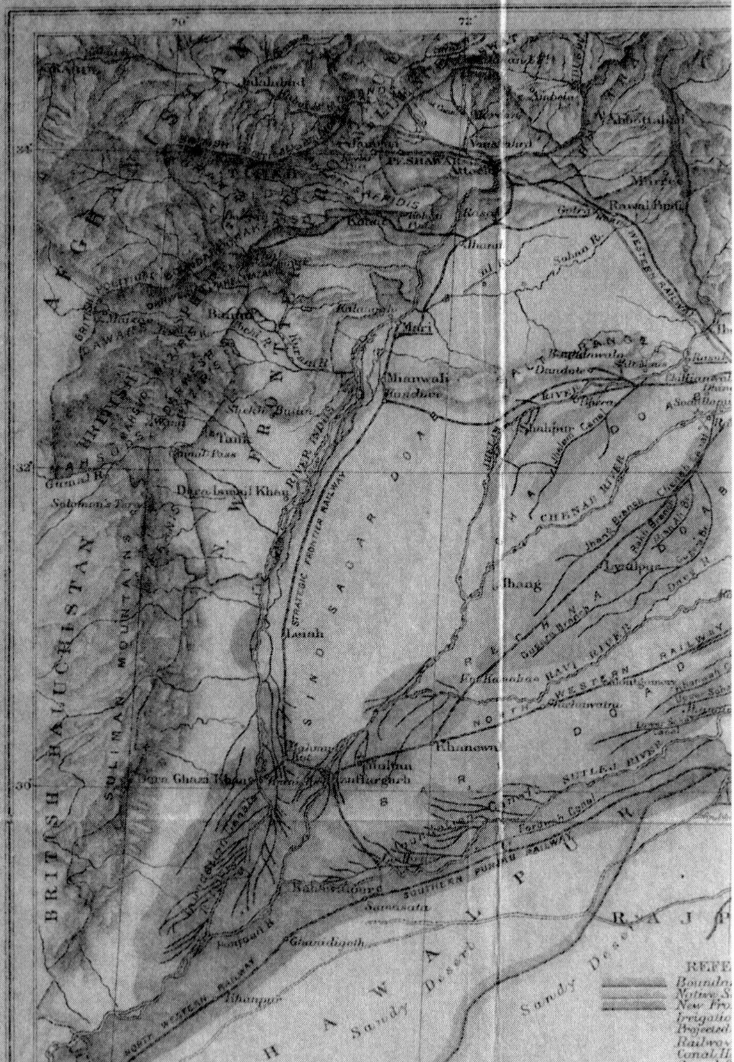

70°
72°
PESHAWAR
Attock
Rawal Pindi
Murree
Kohat
Bannu
Tank
Gumal Pass
Gumal R.
Solomon's Tomb
Dera Ismail Khan
Mianwali
Kalabagh
Leiah
Jhang
Lyallpur
Multan
Khanewal
Dera Ghazi Khan
Muzaffargarh
Khanpur
BRITISH BALUCHISTAN
SULIMAN MOUNTAINS
SIND SAGAR DOAB
RIVER INDUS
STRATEGIC FRONTIER RAILWAY
CHENAB RIVER
RAVI RIVER
SUTLEJ RIVER
NORTH WESTERN RAILWAY
SOUTHERN PUNJAB RAILWAY
Sandy Desert
AFRIDIS
REFE
70°
72°
74

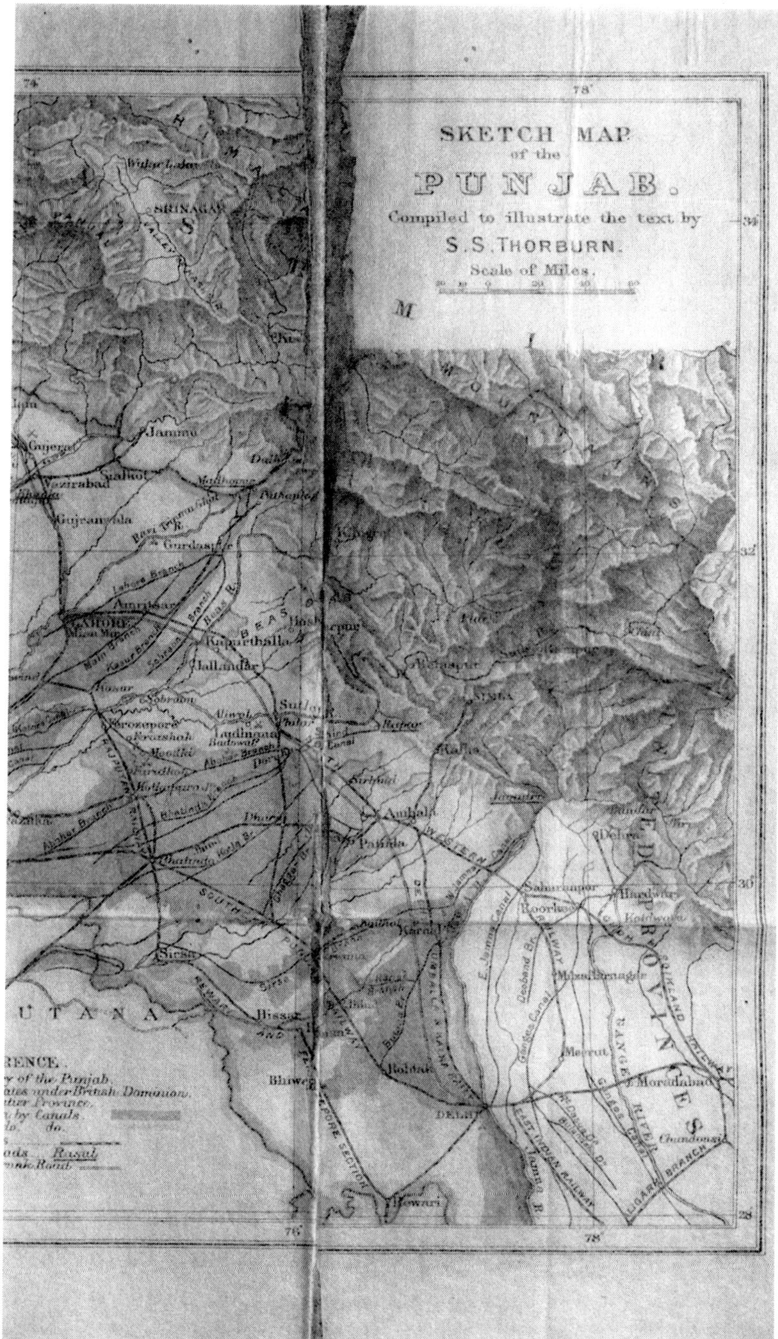
SKETCH MAP
of the
PUNJAB.
Compiled to illustrate the text by
S. S. THORBURN.
Scale of Miles.
SRINAGAR
Jammu
Sialkot
Wazirabad
Gujranwala
Gurdaspur
Amritsar
Kapurthalla
Jallandar
Ferozepore
Ludhiana
Ambala
Patiala
Saharanpur
Roorkee
Hardwar
Meerut
Moradabad
Hissar
Rohtak
Bhiwani
DELHI
Rewari
Sirsa
SIMLA
WESTERN
SOUTH
EAST INDIAN RAILWAY
GANGES RIVER
Ganges Canal

INDEX.